Analytics for the Internet of Things (IoT)

Intelligent Analytics for Your Intelligent Devices

Andrew Minteer

BIRMINGHAM - MUMBAI

Analytics for the Internet of Things (IoT)

First published: July 2017

Production reference: 1210717

Published by Packt Publishing Ltd.
Livery Place
35 Livery Street
Birmingham
B3 2PB, UK.

ISBN 978-1-78712-073-0

www.packtpub.com

Credits

Author
Andrew Minteer

Copy Editor
Yesha Gangani

Reviewer
Ruben Oliva Ramos

Project Coordinator
Judie Jose

Commissioning Editor
Kartikey Pandey

Proofreader
Safis Editing

Acquisition Editor
Namrata Patil

Indexer
Aishwarya Gangawane

Content Development Editor
Abhishek Jadhav

Graphics
Kirk D'Penha

Technical Editor
Prachi Sawant

Production Coordinator
Aparna Bhagat

About the Author

Andrew Minteer is currently the senior director, data science and research at a leading global retail company. Prior to that, he served as the director, IoT Analytics and Machine Learning at a Fortune 500 manufacturing company.

He has an MBA from Indiana University with a background in statistics, software development, database design, cloud architecture, and has led analytics teams for over 10 years.

He first taught himself to program on an Atari 800 computer at the age of 11 and fondly remembers the frustration of waiting through 20 minutes of beeps and static to load a 100-line program. He now thoroughly enjoys launching a 1 TB GPU-backed cloud instance in a few minutes and getting right to work.

Andrew is a private pilot who looks forward to spending some time in the air sometime soon. He enjoys kayaking, camping, traveling the world, and playing around with his six-year-old son and three-year-old daughter.

I would like to thank my ever-patient wife, Julie, for her constant support and tolerance of so many nights and weekends spent working on this technical book. I also thank her for credibly convincing me that this book was not actually a sleep aid, she was just tired from watching the kids. I also want to thank my energetic little princess-dress-wearing daughter, Olivia, and my intelligent Lego-wielding son, Max, for inspiring me to keep at it. Thank you to my family for your constant support and encouragement, especially my father who I suspect is more excited about this book than I am.

While I am thanking everyone, I want to give a shout-out to all the fantastic people I have worked with over the years, both bosses and colleagues. I have learned far more from them than they have from me. I have been truly lucky to work with such talented people.

Last but not least, I want to thank all my editors and reviewers for their comments and insights in developing this book.

I hope you, the reader, not only learn a lot about analytics for IoT but also enjoy the experience.

About the Reviewer

Ruben Oliva Ramos is a computer systems engineer from Tecnologico of León Institute, with a master's degree in computer and electronic systems engineering, teleinformatics, and networking specialization from the University of Salle Bajio in Leon, Guanajuato Mexico. He has more than 5 years of experience in developing web applications to control and monitor devices connected with Arduino and Raspberry Pi using web frameworks and cloud services to build applications using the Internet of Things.

He is a mechatronics teacher at the University of Salle Bajio and teaches students on the master's degree in design and engineering of mechatronics systems. He also works at Centro de Bachillerato Tecnologico Industrial 225 in Leon, Guanajuato Mexico, teaching subjects such as electronics, robotics and control, automation, and microcontrollers at Mechatronics Technician Career, consultant and developer projects in areas such as monitoring systems and datalogger data using technologies such as Android, iOS, Windows Phone, HTML5, PHP, CSS, Ajax, JavaScript, Angular, ASP .NET databases SQlite, mongoDB, MySQL, web servers Node.js, IIS, hardware programming Arduino, Raspberry pi, Ethernet Shield, GPS and GSM/GPRS, ESP8266, control, and monitor systems for data acquisition and programming.

I would like to thank my savior and lord, Jesus Christ for giving me strength and courage to pursue this project, to my dearest wife, Mayte, our two lovely sons, Ruben and Dario, To my father (Ruben), my dearest mom (Rosalia), my brother (Juan Tomas), and my sister (Rosalia) whom I love, for all their support while reviewing this book, for allowing me to pursue my dream and tolerating not being with them after my busy day job.

www.PacktPub.com

For support files and downloads related to your book, please visit www.PacktPub.com.

Did you know that Packt offers eBook versions of every book published, with PDF and ePub files available? You can upgrade to the eBook version at www.PacktPub.com and as a print book customer, you are entitled to a discount on the eBook copy. Get in touch with us at service@packtpub.com for more details.

At www.PacktPub.com, you can also read a collection of free technical articles, sign up for a range of free newsletters and receive exclusive discounts and offers on Packt books and eBooks.

https://www.packtpub.com/mapt

Get the most in-demand software skills with Mapt. Mapt gives you full access to all Packt books and video courses, as well as industry-leading tools to help you plan your personal development and advance your career.

why subscribe

- Fully searchable across every book published by Packt
- Copy and paste, print, and bookmark content
- On demand and accessible via a web browser

Customer Feedback

Thanks for purchasing this Packt book. At Packt, quality is at the heart of our editorial process. To help us improve, please leave us an honest review on this book's Amazon page at `https://www.amazon.com/dp/1787120732`.

If you'd like to join our team of regular reviewers, you can e-mail us at `customerreviews@packtpub.com`. We award our regular reviewers with free eBooks and videos in exchange for their valuable feedback. Help us be relentless in improving our products!

Table of Contents

Preface

How do you make sense of the huge amount of data generated by IoT devices? And after that, how do you find ways to make money from it? None of this will happen on its own, but it is absolutely possible to do it. This book shows how to start with a pool of messy, hard-to-understand data and turn it into a fertile analytics powerhouse.

We start with the perplexing undertaking of what to do with the data. IoT data flows through a convoluted route before it even becomes available for analysis. The resulting data is often messy, missing, and mysterious. However, insights can and do emerge through visualization and statistical modeling techniques. Throughout the book, you will learn to extract value from IoT big data using multiple analytic techniques.

Next, we review how IoT devices generate data and how the information travels over networks. We cover the major IoT communication protocols. Cloud resources are a great match for IoT analytics due to the ease of changing capacity and the availability of dozens of cloud services that you can pull into your analytics processing. Amazon Web Services, Microsoft Azure, and PTC ThingWorx are reviewed in detail. You will learn how to create a secure cloud environment where you can store data, leverage big data tools, and apply data science techniques.

You will also get to know strategies to collect and store data in a way that optimizes its potential. The book also covers strategies to handle data quality concerns. The book shows how to use Tableau to quickly visualize and learn about IoT data.

Combining IoT data with external datasets such as demographic, economic, and locational sources rockets your ability to find value in the data. We cover several useful sources for this data and how each can be used to enhance your IoT analytics capability.

Just as important as finding value in the data is communicating the analytics effectively to others. You will learn how to create effective dashboards and visuals using Tableau. This book also covers ways to quickly implement alerts in order to get day-to-day operational value.

Geospatial analytics is introduced as a way to leverage location information. Examples of geospatial processing using Python code are covered. Combining IoT data with environmental data enhances predictive capability.

We cover key concepts in data science and how they apply to IoT analytics. You will learn how to implement some examples using the R statistical programming language. We will also review the economics of IoT analytics and discover ways to optimize business value.

By the end of the book, you will know how to handle scale for both data storage and analytics, how Apache Spark can be leveraged to handle scalability, and how R and Python can be used for analytic modeling.

What this book covers

Chapter 1, *Defining IoT Analytics and Challenges*, defines, for the purposes of this book, what constitutes the Internet of Things. It will also define what is meant by the term Analytics when used in the book. The chapter will discuss special challenges that come with IoT data from the volume of data to issues with time and space that are not normally a concern with internal company data sets. The reader will have a good grasp of the scope of the book and the challenges that he or she will learn to overcome in the later chapters.

Chapter 2, *IoT Devices and Networking Protocols*, reviews in more depth the variety of IoT devices and networking protocols. The reader will learn the scope of device and example use cases, which will be discussed in easy-to-understand categories. The variety of networking protocols will be discussed along with the business need they are trying to solve. By the end of the chapter, the reader will understand the what and the why of the major categories of devices and networking protocol strategies. The reader will also start to learn how to identify characteristics of the device and network protocol from the resulting data.

Chapter 3, *IoT Analytics for the Cloud*, speaks about the advantages to cloud-based infrastructure for handling and analyzing IoT data. The reader will be introduced to cloud services, including AWS, Azure, and Thingworx. He or she will learn how to implement analytics elastically to enable a wide variety of capabilities.

Chapter 4, *Creating an AWS Cloud Analytics Environment*, provides a step-by-step walkthrough on creating an AWS environment. The environment is specifically geared towards analytics. Along with screenshots and instructions on setting it up, there will be explanation on what is being done and why.

Chapter 5, *Collecting All That Data - Strategies and Techniques*, speaks about strategies to collect IoT data in order to enable analytics. The reader will learn about tradeoffs between streaming and batch processing. He or she will also learn how to build in flexibility to allow future analytics to be integrated with data processing.

Chapter 6, *Getting to Know Your Data - Exploring IoT Data,* focuses on exploratory data analysis for IoT data. The reader will learn how to ask and answer questions of the data. Tableau and R examples will be covered. He or she will learn strategies for quickly understanding what the data represents and where to find likely value.

Chapter 7, *Decorating Your Data - Adding External Datasets to Innovate,* speaks about dramatically enhancing value by adding in additional datasets to IoT data. The datasets will be from internal and external sources. The reader will learn how to look for valuable datasets and combine them to enhance future analytics.

Chapter 8, *Communicating with Others - Visualization and Dashboarding,* talks about designing effective visualizations and dashboards for IoT data. The reader will learn how to take what they have learned about the data and convey it in an easy-to-understand way. The chapter covers both internal and customer-facing dashboards.

Chapter 9, *Applying Geospatial Analytics to IoT Data,* focuses on applying geospatial analytics to IoT data. IoT devices typically have a diverse geographic location when deployed and sometimes even move. This creates an opportunity to extract value by applying geospatial analytics. The reader will learn how to implement this for their IoT analytics.

Chapter 10, *Data Science for IoT Analytics,* describes data science techniques such as machine learning, deep learning, and forecasting using ARIMA on IoT data. The reader will learn the core concepts for each. They will understand how to implement machine learning methods and ARIMA forecasting on IoT data using R. Deep learning will be described along with a way to get started experimenting with it on AWS.

Chapter 11, *Strategies to Organize Data for Analytics,* focuses on organizing data to make it much easier for data scientists to extract value. It introduces the concept of Linked Analytical Datasets. The reader will learn how to balance maintainability with data scientist productivity.

Chapter 12, *The Economics of IoT Analytics,* talks about creating a business case for IoT analytics projects. It discusses ways to optimize the return on investment by minimizing costs and increasing opportunity for revenue streams. The reader will learn how to apply analytics to maximize value in the example case of predictive maintenance.

Chapter 13, *Bringing It All Together,* wraps up the book and reviews what the reader has learned. It includes some parting advice on how to get the most value out of Analytics for the Internet of Things.

What you need for this book

This book will guide you to know how to get the most value out of Analytics for the Internet of Things explained with the examples. You will need to install R and Rstudio, Tableau, and Python to effectively run the code samples present in this book.

Who this book is for

This book is for professionals that are either currently struggling with how to create value with IoT data or are thinking about building this capability in the near future. This includes developers, analytics practitioners, data scientists, and general IoT enthusiasts.

This book is also intended to be useful for business executives, managers, and entrepreneurs who are investigating the opportunity of IoT. This book is for anyone who wants to understand the technical needs and general strategies required to extract value from the flood of data.

A reader of this book wants to understand the components of the IoT data flow. This includes a basic understanding of the devices and sensors, the network protocols, and the data collection technology. They also want an overview of data storage and processing options and strategies. Beyond that, the reader is looking for an in-depth discussion of analytic techniques that can be used to extract value from IoT big data.

Finally, they are looking for clear strategies to build a strong analytics capability. The goal is to maximize business value using IoT big datasets. The reader wants to understand how to best utilize all levels of analytics from simple visualizations to machine learning predictive models.

Prior knowledge of IoT would be helpful but not necessary. Some prior programming experience would be useful.

Conventions

In this book, you will find a number of styles of text that distinguish between different kinds of information. Here are some examples of these styles, and an explanation of their meaning.

Code words in text, database table names, folder names, filenames, file extensions, pathnames, dummy URLs, user input, and Twitter handles are shown as follows: `SRTM.py` on GitHub is an example.

A block of code is set as follows:

```
IF SUM([Amount of Precipitation (inches)]) >= 0.2 THEN
 "Yes"
ELSE
 "No"
END
```

Any command-line input or output is written as follows:

```
hdfs dfs -put lots_o_data.csv /user/hadoop/datafolder/lots_o_data.csv
```

New terms and important words are shown in bold. Words that you see on the screen, in menus or dialog boxes for example, appear in the text like this: "In the **Parameters** section on the same page."

Warnings or important notes appear like this

Tips and tricks appear like this.

Readers feedback

Feedback from our readers is always welcome. Let us know what you think about this book-what you liked or disliked. Reader feedback is important for us as it helps us develop titles that you will really get the most out of.

To send us general feedback, simply email `feedback@packtpub.com`, and mention the book's title in the subject of your message.

If there is a topic that you have expertise in and you are interested in either writing or contributing to a book, see our author guide at `www.packtpub.com/authors`.

Customer support

Now that you are the proud owner of a Packt book, we have a number of things to help you to get the most from your purchase.

Downloading the example code

You can download the example code files for this book from your account at http://www.p acktpub.com. If you purchased this book elsewhere, you can visit http://www.packtpub.c om/support and register to have the files emailed directly to you.

You can download the code files by following these steps:

1. Log in or register to our website using your email address and password.
2. Hover the mouse pointer on the **SUPPORT** tab at the top.
3. Click on **Code Downloads & Errata**.
4. Enter the name of the book in the **Search** box.
5. Select the book for which you're looking to download the code files.
6. Choose from the drop-down menu where you purchased this book from.
7. Click on **Code Download**.

You can also download the code files by clicking on the **Code Files** button on the book's webpage at the Packt Publishing website. This page can be accessed by entering the book's name in the **Search** box. Please note that you need to be logged in to your Packt account.

Once the file is downloaded, please make sure that you unzip or extract the folder using the latest version of:

- WinRAR / 7-Zip for Windows
- Zipeg / iZip / UnRarX for Mac
- 7-Zip / PeaZip for Linux

The code bundle for the book is also hosted on GitHub at https://github.com/prachiss /Analytics-for-the-Internet-of-Things-IoT. We also have other code bundles from our rich catalog of books and videos available at https://github.com/PacktPublishing/. Check them out!

Downloading the color images of this book

We also provide you with a PDF file that has color images of the screenshots/diagrams used in this book. The color images will help you better understand the changes in the output. You can download this file from `https://www.packtpub.com/sites/default/files/downloads/AnalyticsfortheInternetofThings(IoT)_ColorImages.pdf`.

Errata

Although we have taken every care to ensure the accuracy of our content, mistakes do happen. If you find a mistake in one of our books-maybe a mistake in the text or the code-we would be grateful if you could report this to us. By doing so, you can save other readers from frustration and help us improve subsequent versions of this book. If you find any errata, please report them by visiting `http://www.packtpub.com/submit-errata`, selecting your book, clicking on the **Errata Submission Form** link, and entering the details of your errata. Once your errata are verified, your submission will be accepted and the errata will be uploaded to our website or added to any list of existing errata under the Errata section of that title.

To view the previously submitted errata, go to `https://www.packtpub.com/books/content/support` and enter the name of the book in the search field. The required information will appear under the **Errata** section.

Piracy

Piracy of copyrighted material on the Internet is an ongoing problem across all media. At Packt, we take the protection of our copyright and licenses very seriously. If you come across any illegal copies of our works in any form on the Internet, please provide us with the location address or website name immediately so that we can pursue a remedy.

Please contact us at `copyright@packtpub.com` with a link to the suspected pirated material.

We appreciate your help in protecting our authors and our ability to bring you valuable content.

Questions

If you have a problem with any aspect of this book, you can contact us at `questions@packtpub.com`, and we will do our best to address the problem.

1
Defining IoT Analytics and Challenges

In this chapter, we will discuss some concepts and challenges associated with analytics on **Internet of Things** (**IoT**) data. We will cover the following topics:

- The analytics maturity model
- Defining the IoT
- What is different about IoT data?
    - Data volume
    - Problems with time
    - Problems with space
    - Data quality
    - Analytics challenges
- Concerns with finding business value

The situation

The tense white-yellow of the fluorescent ceiling lights press down on you while you sit in your cubicle and stare at the monitors on your desk. You sense it is now night outside but can't see over the fabric walls to know for sure. You stare at the long list of filenames on one screen and the plain text rows of opaque sensor data on the other screen.

Your boss had just left to angrily brood somewhere in the office, and you are not sure where. He had been glowering over your shoulder.

"We spent $20 million in telecommunication and consulting fees last year just to get this data! The hardware costs $20 per unit. We've been getting data, and it has been piling up costing us $10,000 a month. There are 20 TB of files - that's big data, isn't it? And we can't seem to do anything with it?"he had said.

"This is ridiculous!," he continued, "It was supposed to generate $100 million in new revenue. Where is our first dollar? Why can't you do anything with it? I have five consultants a week calling me to tell me they can handle it- they'll even automate it. Maybe we should just pick one and hope they aren't selling us snake oil."

You know he does not really blame you. You were a whiz with Excel and knew how to query databases. A lot of analytics requests went to you. When the CEO decided the company needed a big data guy, they hired a VP out of Silicon Valley. But the new VP ended up taking a position with a *different* Silicon Valley company the day before he was supposed to start at your company.

You were hastily moved into the new analytics group. A group of one - you. It was to be a temporary shift until another VP was found. That was six months ago. The company is freezing funds for outside training and revenues are looking tight. So, no training for you.

Although many know the terms, no one in the company actually understands what Hadoop is or how to even start using this thing called machine learning. But others more and more seem to expect you to not only know it but already be doing it.

Executives have been reading articles in HBR and Forbes about the huge potential of the IoT combined with Artificial Intelligence or AI. They feel like the company will be left behind, and soon, if it does not have its own IoT big data solution incorporating AI. Your boss is feeling the pressure. Executives have several ideas for him where AI can be used. They seem to think that getting the idea is the hard part, implementation should be easy. Your boss is worried about his job and it rolls downhill to you.

Your screen on the left looks like this:

```
39.984702,116.318417,0,492,39744.1201851852,2008-10-23,02:53:04
39.984683,116.31845,0,492,39744.1202546296,2008-10-23,02:53:10
39.984686,116.318417,0,492,39744.1203125,2008-10-23,02:53:15
39.984688,116.318385,0,492,39744.1203703704,2008-10-23,02:53:20
39.984655,116.318263,0,492,39744.1204282407,2008-10-23,02:53:25
39.984611,116.318026,0,493,39744.1204861111,2008-10-23,02:53:30
39.984608,116.317761,0,493,39744.1205439815,2008-10-23,02:53:35
39.984563,116.317517,0,496,39744.1206018519,2008-10-23,02:53:40
39.984539,116.317294,0,500,39744.1206597222,2008-10-23,02:53:45
39.984606,116.317065,0,505,39744.1207175926,2008-10-23,02:53:50
39.984568,116.316911,0,510,39744.120775463,2008-10-23,02:53:55
39.984586,116.316716,0,515,39744.1208333333,2008-10-23,02:54:00
39.984561,116.316527,0,520,39744.1208912037,2008-10-23,02:54:05
39.984536,116.316354,0,525,39744.1209490741,2008-10-23,02:54:10
39.984523,116.316188,0,531,39744.1210069444,2008-10-23,02:54:15
39.984516,116.315963,0,536,39744.1210648148,2008-10-23,02:54:20
39.984523,116.315823,0,541,39744.1211226852,2008-10-23,02:54:25
39.984574,116.315611,0,546,39744.1211805556,2008-10-23,02:54:30
39.984568,116.315407,0,551,39744.1212384259,2008-10-23,02:54:35
39.984538,116.315148,0,556,39744.1212962963,2008-10-23,02:54:40
39.984501,116.314907,0,560,39744.1213541667,2008-10-23,02:54:45
39.984532,116.314808,0,564,39744.121412037,2008-10-23,02:54:50
39.984504,116.314625,0,569,39744.1214699074,2008-10-23,02:54:55
39.984485,116.314426,0,574,39744.1215277778,2008-10-23,02:55:00
39.984427,116.31424,0,579,39744.1215856481,2008-10-23,02:55:05
39.984485,116.314042,0,584,39744.1216435185,2008-10-23,02:55:10
39.98448,116.313818,0,589,39744.1217013889,2008-10-23,02:55:15
39.984501,116.313659,0,595,39744.1217592593,2008-10-23,02:55:20
39.984618,116.314323,0,113,39744.1218171296,2008-10-23,02:55:25
39.984649,116.314107,0,117,39744.121875,2008-10-23,02:55:30
39.984621,116.313941,0,121,39744.1219328704,2008-10-23,02:55:35
39.984655,116.313724,0,126,39744.1219907407,2008-10-23,02:55:40
39.984681,116.313521,0,129,39744.1220486111,2008-10-23,02:55:45
39.984708,116.313311,0,133,39744.1221064815,2008-10-23,02:55:50
39.984708,116.313099,0,137,39744.1221643519,2008-10-23,02:55:55
39.984696,116.312921,0,144,39744.1222222222,2008-10-23,02:56:00
39.984677,116.312746,0,153,39744.1222800926,2008-10-23,02:56:05
39.984682,116.312525,0,155,39744.122337963,2008-10-23,02:56:10
39.984649,116.312332,0,158,39744.1223958333,2008-10-23,02:56:15
39.984641,116.312123,0,164,39744.1224537037,2008-10-23,02:56:20
39.984647,116.311917,0,170,39744.1225115741,2008-10-23,02:56:25
39.984654,116.31172,0,178,39744.1225694444,2008-10-23,02:56:30
39.984631,116.311569,0,180,39744.1226273148,2008-10-23,02:56:35
39.984647,116.31138,0,184,39744.1226851852,2008-10-23,02:56:40
39.984653,116.311189,0,194,39744.1227430556,2008-10-23,02:56:45
39.984628,116.311026,0,206,39744.1228009259,2008-10-23,02:56:50
39.984652,116.310854,0,214,39744.1228587963,2008-10-23,02:56:55
```

The list goes on and on for several pages. You have been able to combine several files and do some pivot tables and charting in Excel. But it takes a lot of your time, and you can only realistically handle a month or two worth of data. The questions are coming in faster than your ability to answer them. You and your boss have been talking about bringing in temps to do the work–they don't really need to understand it, just follow the steps that you outline for them.

Your screen on the right looks like this:

Name	Type	Compressed size	Password ...	Size	Ratio
20081023055305.plt	PLT File	13 KB	No	61 KB	80%
20081023234104.plt	PLT File	27 KB	No	135 KB	80%
20081024234405.plt	PLT File	83 KB	No	449 KB	82%
20081025231428.plt	PLT File	43 KB	No	231 KB	82%
20081026081229.plt	PLT File	37 KB	No	204 KB	83%
20081027111634.plt	PLT File	12 KB	No	53 KB	79%
20081027233029.plt	PLT File	8 KB	No	32 KB	78%
20081027235802.plt	PLT File	2 KB	No	7 KB	77%
20081028102805.plt	PLT File	10 KB	No	41 KB	78%
20081028233053.plt	PLT File	6 KB	No	22 KB	77%
20081028235048.plt	PLT File	4 KB	No	17 KB	77%
20081029110529.plt	PLT File	11 KB	No	47 KB	79%
20081029234123.plt	PLT File	26 KB	No	126 KB	80%
20081030233959.plt	PLT File	21 KB	No	94 KB	79%
20081101004235.plt	PLT File	44 KB	No	234 KB	82%
20081102030834.plt	PLT File	24 KB	No	122 KB	81%
20081102233452.plt	PLT File	8 KB	No	34 KB	78%
20081103133204.plt	PLT File	7 KB	No	31 KB	78%
20081103233729.plt	PLT File	10 KB	No	42 KB	78%
20081104054859.plt	PLT File	24 KB	No	120 KB	80%
20081104234436.plt	PLT File	11 KB	No	48 KB	79%
20081105110052.plt	PLT File	58 KB	No	360 KB	85%
20081106051423.plt	PLT File	4 KB	No	17 KB	78%
20081106133604.plt	PLT File	8 KB	No	35 KB	78%
20081106233404.plt	PLT File	37 KB	No	184 KB	81%
20081108034358.plt	PLT File	46 KB	No	240 KB	81%

Your IT department has been consolidating lots of little files into several very large ones. The filesystem was being overloaded by the number of files, so the solution was to consolidate. Unfortunately, for you, many files are now too large to open in Excel, which limits what you can do with them. You end up doing more analytics on recent data simply because it is much easier (the files are still small).

Looking at the data rows, it is not obvious what you can do with it beyond sums and averages. The files are too big to do a VLOOKUP in Excel against something like your production records - which is stored in files often too big to even open in Excel.

At this point, you can't begin to think how you would apply Machine Learning to this data. You are not quite sure what it even means. You know the data is difficult to manipulate for anything beyond recent datasets. Surely, long periods of time would be needed to extract value out of it.

You hear a cough from behind you. Your boss is back.

He says quietly and stiffly, "I'm sorry. We're going to have to hire a consultant to take this over. I know how hard you've been working. You've done some amazing things considering the limitations, and nobody appreciates that enough. But I have to show results. It will probably take a month or two to fully bring someone on board. In the meantime, just keep at it–maybe we can make a breakthrough before then."

Your heart sinks. You are convinced there is huge value in the connected device data. You feel like you could make a career out of IoT analytics if you could just figure out how to get there. But you are not a quitter.

You decide you will not go down without a fight, you will find a way.

Defining IoT analytics

In order to understand IoT analytics, it is helpful to separate it out and define both analytics and the IoT. This will help frame the discussion for the rest of the book.

Defining analytics

If you ask a hundred people to define analytics, you are likely to get a hundred different answers. Each person tends to have his or her own definition in mind that can range from static reports to advanced deep learning expert systems. All tend to call efforts in the wide ranging territory analytics without much further explanation.

We will take a fairly broad definition in this book as we are covering quite a bit of territory. In their best selling book *Competing on Analytics*, Tom Davenport and Jeanne Harris created a scale, which they called **Analytics Maturity**. Companies progress to higher levels in the scale as their use of analytics matures, and they begin to compete with other companies by leveraging it.

When we use the word analytics, we will mean using techniques that fall in the range from query/drill down to optimization as shown in the following chart from Competing on Analytics:

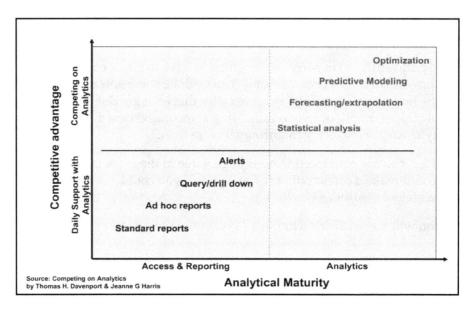

We will also take a slightly different philosophy. Unlike the notion of a company progressing through each level to get to the peak of maturity at the upper right with optimization, we will strive to reach success at all levels in parallel.

The idea of a company not being analytically mature unless it is actively employing optimization models at every turn can be dangerous. This puts pressure on a company to focus time and resources where there may not be a **return on investment** (**ROI**) for them. Since resources are always limited, this could also cause them to under-invest in projects in other areas that have a higher ROI.

The reason for the lack of ROI is often that a company simply does not have the right data to take full advantage of the more advanced techniques. This could be no fault of their own as the signal in the noise may be just too weak to tease out. This could stem from the state of technology, not yet at the point where the key predictive data can even be monitored. Or even if this is possible, it may be far too expensive to justify capturing it. We will talk about the limitations of available data quite a bit in this book. The goal will always be to maximize ROI at all levels of the maturity model.

We will also take the view that analytics maturity is about having the capability and knowing how to enable the full scale. It is not about what you are doing. It is about what you are capable of doing in order to maximize your sum total ROI across the full scale. Each level can be exploited if an opportunity is spotted. And we want there to be fertile ground for opportunities across the full scale. More about this will be covered throughout the book.

Defining the Internet of Things

Sensors have been tracking data for decades at manufacturing plants, retail stores, and remote oil and gas equipment. Why all of sudden is there this IoT hype all over the media?

The dramatic decrease in sensor costs, bandwidth costs, the spread of cellular coverage, and the rise of cloud computing all combine to create fertile conditions to easily connect devices over the internet. For example, as shown in the following graph, Goldman Sachs predicts an average sensor cost in 2020 of under $0.40 USD, 30% of what it was in 2004. Whether all these devices should be connected or not is hotly debated:

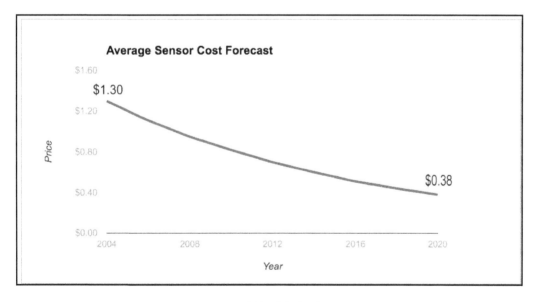

Data source: Goldman Sachs, BI estimates

The definitions of IoT seem to vary quite a bit; some include machine sensors only, others include RFID tags and smartphones.

We will use this definition from Forrest Stroud on Webopedia:

> *The IoT refers to the ever-growing network of physical objects that feature an IP address for the internet connectivity and the communication that occurs between these objects and other internet-enabled devices and systems.*

Or to get even more basic: stuff that talks to other stuff over the internet without requiring you to do anything. This clears it up, right?

Even the number of things projected to be connected by 2020 varies widely. Some sources project 20.8 billion devices, others project up to 50 billion - over twice the amount.

For our purposes, we are more concerned with how to analyze the data generated than we are about the scope of devices that should be considered part of the IoT. If something sends data remotely by way of the internet, it is fair game for us, especially if it is machine-generated on one end and machine-consumed on the other.

We are more concerned with how to extract value from the data and adapt to circumstances inherent to it. IoT is not really new, as elements of it have been developing for decades. Remote detection of oil well spills was happening in the 1970s. GPS-based vehicle telematics has been around for 20 years. IoT is also not a separate market; it blends into current products and processes. Although much of the media reports on it as if it is a different animal (perhaps even the author of this book - guilty as charged?), you should not think of it this way.

The concept of constrained

The term **constrained** is an important concept in understanding IoT devices, data, and impacts on analytics. It refers to the limited battery power, bandwidth, and hardware capability that has to be considered in the design of IoT devices. For many IoT use cases, one or more of these has to be balanced with the need to record useful data.

IoT analytics challenges

There are some special challenges that come along with IoT data. The data was created by devices operating remotely, sometimes in widely varying environmental conditions that can change from day to day. The devices are often distributed widely geographically.

The data is communicated over long distances, often across different networking technologies. It is very common for data to first transmit across a wireless network, then through a type of gateway device to be sent over the public internet–which itself includes multiple different types of networking technology working together.

The data volume

A company can easily have thousands to millions of IoT devices with several sensors on each unit, each sensor reporting values on a regular basis. The inflow of data can grow quite large very quickly. Since IoT devices send data on an ongoing basis, the volume of data in total can increase much faster than many companies are used to.

To demonstrate how this can happen, imagine a company that manufactures small monitoring devices. It produces 12,000 devices a year, starting in 2010 when the product was launched. Each one is tested at the end of assembly and the values reported by the sensors on the device are kept for analysis for five years. The data growth looks like the following image:

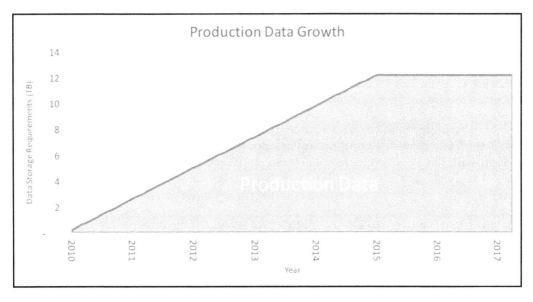

A chart showing data storage needs for production snapshot of 200 KB and 1,000 units per month. Five years of production data is kept

Now, imagine the device also had internet connectivity to track sensor values, and each one remains connected for two years. Since the data inflow continues well after the devices are built, data growth is exponential until it stabilizes when older devices stop reporting values. This looks more like the blue area in the following chart:

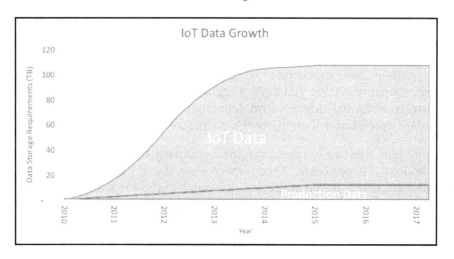

Chart shows the addition of IoT data at 0.5 KB per message, 10 messages per day. Devices are connected for two years from production

In order to illustrate how large this can get, consider the following example. If you capture 10 messages per day and the message size is half of a full production snapshot, by 2017, data storage requirements would be over 1,500 times higher than production-only data.

For many companies, this introduces some problems. The database software, storage infrastructure, and available computing horsepower is not typically intended to handle this kind of growth. The licensing agreements with software vendors tends to be tied to the number of servers and CPU cores. Storage is handled by standard backup planning and retention policies.

The data volume rapidly leads to computing and storage requirements well beyond what can be held by a single server. It gets cost prohibitive very quickly under traditional architectures to distribute it across hundreds or thousands of servers. To do the best analytics, you need lots of historical data, and since you are unlikely to know ahead of time which data is most predictive, you have to keep as much as you can on hand.

With large-scale data, computing horsepower requirements for analytics are not very predictable and change dramatically depending on the question being asked. Analytic needs are very elastic. Traditional server planning ratchets up on premise resources with the anticipated number of servers needed to meet peak needs determined in advance. Doubling compute power in a short amount of time, if even possible, is very expensive.

IoT data volumes and computing resource requirements can quickly outpace all the other company data needs combined.

Problems with time

The only reason for time is so that everything doesn't happen at once.

– Albert Einstein

Time is very tightly tied to geographical position and the date on the calendar. The international standard way of tracking a common time is using **Coordinated Universal Time** (**UTC**). UTC is geographically tied to 0^0 longitude, which passes through Greenwich, England, in the UK. Although it is tied to the location, it is actually not the same as **Greenwich Mean Time** (**GMT**). GMT is a time zone, while UTC is a time standard. UTC does not observe **Daylight Savings Time** (DST):

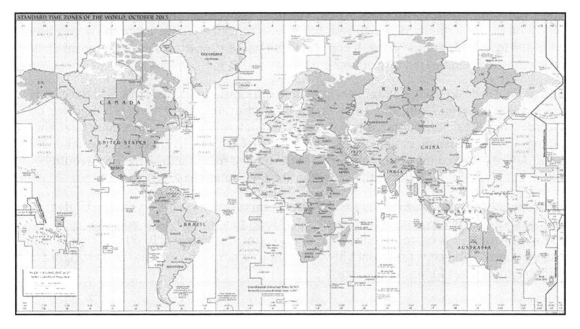

Standard time zones of the World. Source: CIA Factbook

When data used for analytics is recorded at headquarters or a manufacturing plant, everything happens at the same place and time zone. IoT devices are spread out across the globe. Events that happen at the absolute same time do not happen at the same local time. How time is recorded affects the integrity of the resulting analytics.

When IoT devices communicate sensor data, time may be captured using the local time. It can dramatically affect analytics results if it is not clear whether local time or UTC was recorded. For example, consider an analyst working at a company that makes parking spot occupancy detection sensors. She is tasked with creating predictive models to estimate future parking lot fill rates. The time of day is likely to be a very predictive data point. It makes a big difference to her on how this time is recorded. Even determining if it is night or day at the sensor location will be difficult.

This may not be apparent to the engineer creating the device. His task is to design a device that determines if the spot is open or not. He may not appreciate the importance of writing code that captures a time value that can be aggregated across multiple time zones and locations.

There can also be issues with clock synchronization. Devices set their internal clock to be in sync with the time standard being used. If it is local time, it could be using the wrong time zone due to a configuration error. It could also get out of sync due to a communication problem with the time standard source.

If local time is being used, daylight savings time can cause problems. How will the events that happen between 1 a.m. and 2 a.m. on the day autumn daylight savings is adjusted be recorded since that hour happens twice? Laws that determine which days mark daylight savings time can change, as they did in Turkey when DST was scrapped in September 2016. If the device is locked into a set date range at the time of manufacture, the time would be incorrect for several days out of the year after the DST dates change.

How daylight savings time changes is different from country to country. In the United States, daylight savings time is changed at 02:00 local time in each time zone. In the European Union, it is coordinated so that all EU countries change at 01:00 GMT for all time zones at once. This keeps time zones always an hour apart at the expense of it changing at different local times for each time zone.

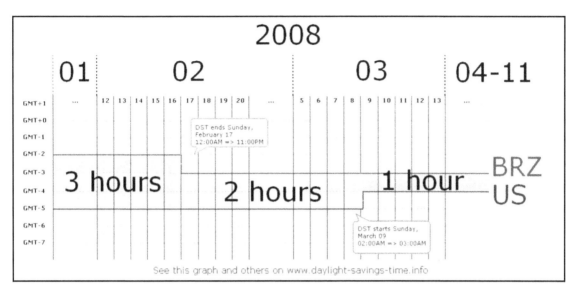

In early 2008, Central Brazil was one, two, or three hours ahead of eastern U.S., depending on the date

Source: Wikipedia commons

When time is recorded for an event, such as a parking spot being vacated, it is essential for analytics that the time is as close to the actual occurrence as possible. In practice, though, the time available for analytics can be the time the event occurred, the time the IoT device sent the data, the time the data was received, or the time the data was added to your data warehouse.

Problems with space

IoT devices are located in multiple geographic locations. Different areas of the world have different environmental conditions. Temperature variations can affect sensor accuracy. You could have less accurate readings in Calgary, Canada than in Cancun, Mexico, if cold impacts your device.

Elevation can affect equipment such as diesel engines. If location and elevation is not taken into consideration, you may falsely conclude from IoT sensor readings that a Denver-based fleet of delivery trucks is poorly managing fuel economy compared to a fleet in Indiana. Lots of mountain roads can burn up some fuel!

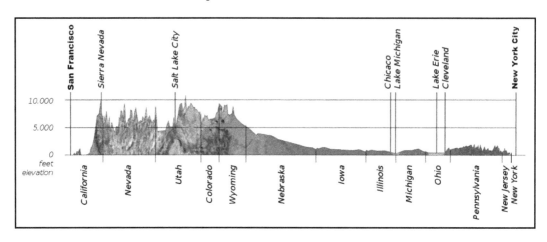

US elevation profile from LA to NYC. Source: reddit.com

Remote locations may have weaker network access. The higher data loss could cause data values for those locations to be underrepresented in the resulting analytics.

Many IoT devices are solar powered. The available battery charge can affect the frequency of data reporting. A device in Portland, Oregon, where it is often cloudy and rainy will be more impacted than the same device in Phoenix, Arizona, where it is mostly sunny.

There are also political considerations related to the location of the IoT device. Privacy laws in Europe affect how the data from devices can be stored and what type of analytics is acceptable. You may be required to anonymize the data from certain countries, which can affect what you can do with analytics.

Data quality

Constrained devices means lossy networks. For analytics, it often results in either missing or inconsistent data. The missing data is often not random. As mentioned previously, it can be impacted by the location. Devices run on a software, called firmware, which may not be consistent across locations. This could mean differences in reporting frequency or formatting of values. It can result in lost or mangled data.

Data messages from IoT devices often require the destination to know how to interpret the message being sent. Software bugs can lead to garbled messages and data records.

Messages lost in translation or never sent due to dead batteries result in missing values. The conservation of power often means not all values available on the device are sent at the same time. The resulting datasets often have missing values, as the device sends some values consistently every time it reports and sends some other values less frequently.

Analytics challenges

Analytics often requires deciding on whether to fill in or ignore the missing values. Either choice may lead to a dataset that is not a representative of reality.

As an example of how this can affect results, consider the case of inaccurate political poll results in recent years. Many experts believe it is now in near crisis due to the shift of much of the world to mobile numbers as their only phone number. For pollsters, it is cheaper and easier to reach people on landline numbers. This can lead to the over representation of people with landlines. These people tend to be both older and wealthier than mobile-only respondents.

The response rate has also dropped from near 80% in the 1970s to about 8% (if you are lucky) today. This makes it more difficult (and expensive) to obtain a representative sample leading to many embarrassingly wrong poll predictions.

There can also be outside influences, such as environment conditions, that are not captured in the data. Winter storms can lead to power failures affecting devices that are able to report back data. You may end up drawing conclusions based on a non-representative sample of data without realizing it. This can affect the results of IoT analytics – and it will not be clear why.

Since connectivity is a new thing for many devices, there is also often a lack of historical data to base predictive models on. This can limit the type of analytics that can be done with the data.

It can also lead to a recency bias in datasets, as newer products are over represented in the data simply because a higher percentage are now a part of the IoT.

This leads us to the author's number one rule in IoT analytics:

Never trust data you don't know.

Treat it like a stranger offering you candy.

Business value concerns

Many companies are struggling to find value with IoT data. The costs to store, process, and analyze IoT data can grow quickly. With future financial returns uncertain, some companies are questioning if it is worth the investment.

According to McKinsey & Company, a consulting agency, most IoT data is not used. From their research, less than 1% of data generated by an oil platform was used for decision-making purposes.

Finding value with IoT analytics is often like finding a diamond in a mountain of rubble. We can accept that 1% of the data has value, but which 1% is it? This can vary depending on the question. One man's worthless granite is another man's priceless diamond.

The business value challenge is how to keep costs low while increasing the ability to create superior financial returns. Analytics is a great way to get there.

Summary

In this chapter, we defined, for the purposes of this book, what constitutes the IoT. We also defined what is meant by the term analytics when we use it here. We discussed special challenges that come with IoT data from volume of data to issues with time and space that are not normally a concern with internal company datasets. You should have a good idea of the scope of the book and the challenges that you will learn to overcome in the later chapters.

2
IoT Devices and Networking Protocols

You have started your analysis and found that your IoT data is not always complete. You also suspect it is not always accurate. But you have no idea why that would be the case. You get several hundred records a day on average from each device.

The IoT devices your company makes are attached to freight trailers and track location, and sometimes even temperature. The temperature is monitored when the trailer is a refrigerated unit, called a *reefer* in the industry. The inside temperature of a reefer must be kept in a certain range depending on what is being transported.

Your device is located on the outside of the trailer with a lead line into the trailer to read temperature if the option is enabled. The trailer is pulled around by big rig trucks over roads all over the country.

You have been so focused on finding value in the data, you never thought about how it was captured and communicated to your company's servers. Now that you are thinking about it, you wonder about the problems you see in the data. You had assumed it was occurring randomly, but if this is not the case. A little tingle of fear creeps down your spine. It would affect much of the analysis you have already done, the analysis that the company is using to make business decisions.

This chapter will provide an overview of the variety of IoT devices and networking protocols. We will also cover the business need they are trying to solve. By the end of the chapter, you will understand the what and the why of the major categories of devices and networking protocol strategies.

This chapter covers the following topics:

- The range of IoT devices along with some example use cases
- Common IoT networking protocols
- Common IoT data messaging protocols
- The advantages/disadvantages of different device and network protocol strategies
- How to analyze the data to infer protocol and device characteristics

IoT devices

There is a wide variety of IoT devices in use today. The range of designs and ingenuity in function is expanding at a furious pace. The scope of what is being measured, monitored, and tracked would be an entire book in itself. And it is, as you can find several through the publisher of this book.

The wild world of IoT devices

For analytics purposes, it is helpful to understand the variety of devices and how they are being used. Ideas from one industry can cross-pollinate into another and create unexpected value. The combination of devices and use cases can also present very different analytics opportunities and challenges.

Healthcare

Patients in acute care are having their vital signs monitored by low-power wireless sensors where the data can be analyzed remotely. There are several startups, such as Proteus Digital Health, that are developing pill-sized ingestible sensors. Proteus makes a digestible sensor pill that, in combination with a sensor patch worn on skin, monitors when and how often patients are taking their pills.

Manufacturing

Tracking and analyzing data from monitoring sensors in manufacturing plants has a long history. There is a whole subset of media dedicated to this realm, commonly referred to as the **Industrial Internet of Things (IIoT)** or **Industry 4.0**. A wide variety of manufacturing industries are implementing IoT devices and sensors.

Ergon Refining has a facility in Mississippi that connects multiple sensor units such as vibration, acoustic, and position sensors to a central system that monitors and analyzes the data.

Emerson Process Management makes wirelessly-monitored Enardo 2000 emergency pressure relief vents (EPRVs). There are hundreds of steam trap monitoring and pressuring relief vents in many process plants. Monitoring them with inexpensive sensing capabilities can provide value by avoiding unplanned downtime due to faulty equipment.

Transportation and logistics

Geotab builds GPS tracking devices that logistics providers can attach to their vehicles to monitor and analyze routes, fuel economy, and detect accidents. These devices are referred to in the industry as **telematics** devices. Customers can create geofences on a map to receive notifications when a vehicle enters or exits the area.

Devices can monitor driver behavior and send reports of speeding or harsh braking to the home office. They also read any fault codes reported by the vehicle and transmit the information instantly to fleet managers, so problems can be addressed before a major breakdown occurs. The following image shows an example of a telematics device, the GO7:

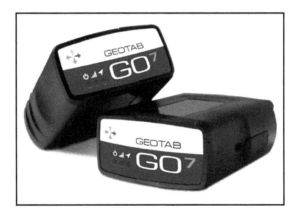

Geotab GO7 telematics device. Source: Geotab

Retail

Using its cell network and beacons in specific stores, Turkcell in Turkey along with its partners, provides customers in its loyalty program with in-store promotions when they are near certain retailers.

Many retail chains use **Radio Frequency Identification** (**RFID**) tags and sensors to optimize stocking and monitor movements inside warehouses.

Extreme Networks is partnering with the New England Patriots and their home stadium to monitor visitor traffic patterns. The stadium uses the data to understand where customers gather and price advertisements and product placements appropriately using traffic heat maps generated from the IoT sensor data.

Oil and gas

One of the earliest pioneers in what is now called the IoT is the oil and gas industry. With advances in the IoT technology, oil wells can more easily connect sensors located throughout the well. Data readings can also be sampled more frequently, every 30 seconds as an example.

In combination with **edge analytics** on sensor data, companies can do things such as optimize the oil well plunger lift cycle. As reported in an Intel industry article, this can increase the production up to 30 percent. Edge analytics refers to applied analytics that operate either on the device itself or at a nearby device that supports a hub of units. The analytic processing occurs at multiple locations at the boundary of the network or the *edge*, versus occurring at a centralized location.

The same information is used by companies to optimize their asset portfolio management. They can reuse the data to rank wells by production efficiency.

Home automation or monitoring

Ecobee Smart Wi-Fi thermostats connect with battery operated wireless sensors placed in different rooms throughout a home. It tracks not only Heating Ventilation and Air Conditioning (HVAC) but temperatures reported by each sensor. It can not only balance temperatures in the rooms, but it can also notify you when the furnace is not behaving properly.

Wearables

It can be argued that we walk around with an IoT device all day long. You may know it as a cell phone, mobile, or *ein Handy* (for our readers in Germany). It can and does communicate with remote servers without any human interaction. Google compiles signal data and generates alerts using the phone as the remote sensor. Foursquare checks you in and out of geofenced locations. Cell networks monitor connections along with time and position and then translate it into real-time traffic data.

Along with cell phones, there is a plethora of devices such as the Fitbit step tracking wristband, Garmin heart rate monitoring chest band, and Nike smart shoes. No kidding, there is even an IoT-enabled umbrella that sends weather alerts to your phone (assuming your eyes and ability to detect wetness need some additional confirmation).

Sensor types

Sensors may report real numbers or conditional states (such as on/off or raining/not raining). Even if it is reporting conditional states, in many cases, the signal is continuous and some logic determines if it has crossed a threshold that is interpreted as a change in state.

Sensors vary in accuracy, and there is usually a cost trade off in order to increase measurement accuracy.

External conditions may also affect accuracy. For example, extremes in cold can affect the accuracy of some motion sensors. This is important to know for analytics, as it can affect the results of prediction from machine-learning models. This external influencer can be what is referred to as a **confounding variable**. It has an effect on two or more measured variables but is not itself directly measured.

You may need to adjust for it when processing the data for analytics on the backend. In the case of the temperature example, you can apply a formula to adjust the reading based on external weather data you will have mashed in on the backend.

There is also some level of noise in sensor readings that sometimes has to be filtered or transformed to smooth out the reported values. This often happens on the device itself through various algorithms. The algorithms employed on the device to infer measurements may be implemented incorrectly resulting in some misreading of values.

Most of these issues will be caught and corrected by the product validation processes. However, it is important to know if there are any product limitations or adjustments needed when it is near the edges of its operating ranges.

Networking basics

Here is an oversimplified view of the networking protocol stack. There is much more going on here than we will cover in this chapter, but to help in understanding the discussion, it is useful to reduce it to a simple diagram:

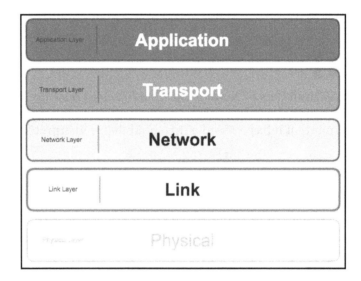

Network communications operates in layers with the bottom layers not needing to know about the layers above it. It can get confusing talking about all the options available at each layer of the stack. The diagram shows the key layers that we are concerned with for IoT analytics, but know that there is more to the story.

The diagram is based on the simplified **OSI model**, which divides communication into five fundamental layers. There is a Physical layer at bottom that has more to do with device electrical engineering. We will leave that out to simplify things since we are focusing on analytics.

Connectivity will refer to options primarily in the Link layer of the stack. Data communication or messaging will be referring mainly to the Application layer. The Network layer is (usually) the **Internet Protocol** (**IP**) that we all know and love. It is a great consolidator that enables so much flexibility in the networking stack for internet communications.

Transport is either TCP or UDP for most networking schemes that transmit data over long distances. TCP has more delivery guarantees but more overhead; UDP has less overhead but less guarantees on delivery.

There is a wide variety of networking protocols for both connectivity from the internet to the IoT device and for the communication of the data the device generates. They solve two main problems:

- **How do I establish communication, so I can send data packets?**
  - Let's use snail mail as an analogy. If you have limited funds, you prefer sending brief postcards even it takes longer to arrive to the recipient. It costs less, and it does not take much effort to write. If money is not a problem, you would hire some professional authors and send prose approaching poetry. You would use airmail so it arrives quickly. In this analogy, battery power is like money and CPU/memory is like writing effort.
- **How are the data packets delivered so that my needs are met?**
  - Do you and I agree to get each other's address and send letters direct? Or do you always give them to Tom, in the cubicle down the hall, and he sends it out to whoever needs it? Do you send it certified mail because you have to be certain it was delivered? Or do you send it third-class post because it is much cheaper and not the end of the world if it gets lost?

The network protocol used depends on the type of device and the environment in which it is located. It can also depend on the business priorities for which the data will be used.

For example, in the case of monitoring aircraft engines in flight, it is more important to get the most recent data than to get all of the data. You need problems identified as soon as possible more than you need a complete recording of all in flight data, which is mostly the same. So if you have to make a choice between waiting but getting everything or never waiting but losing some data packets from time to time, you choose the latter.

This is different from the logistics provider that has a sensor, which detects tractor trailers entering and leaving a distribution hub. In this case, you want a complete record of traffic, and you would be willing to wait a minute or two to have it.

Another important component to understand for IoT is that of a **gateway**. A gateway is a network node that connects two separate networks that use different protocols. The gateway handles the translation between them. A gateway is common in many IoT networks of constrained devices. It translates from the protocol optimized for the constrained devices to (usually) the protocol used by the wider internet (IP).

There are multiple standards spread across several organizations such as the Industrial Internet Consortium, the IPSO Alliance, and the IEEE P2413. It is continuously evolving with many companies and alliances aligned along different connectivity protocols. It may be another five to 10 ten years before the options coalesce into a smaller group of consistently used standards.

We will review the top ones you are likely to run across with an eye on the problems they are trying to solve.

IoT networking connectivity protocols

Connectivity is all about solving the main problem - establishing a method to communicate. The strategies used are affected by the constraints on the network devices. Power availability often is the most significant one.

Connectivity protocols (when the available power is limited)

The following protocols are specifically designed to address low power constraints. They are usually associated with lower complexity and bit transfer rates in the supported IoT devices.

Bluetooth Low Energy (also called Bluetooth Smart)

Named after a tenth-century Danish king who unified several fractious tribes, Bluetooth is a familiar technology to most consumers. The specification is maintained by an organization called the **Bluetooth Special Interest Group** (**SIG**) made up of 25,000 companies. **Bluetooth Low Energy** (**BLE**) is a newer implementation that is not directly compatible with Bluetooth classic (of mobile phone headset fame). It was designed for low power needs and a less frequent data exchange rate. The following chart represents the network protocol stack for BLE:

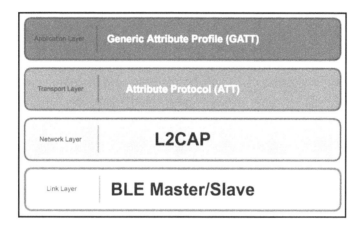

A BLE device is either a master or a slave in the network. A master acts as an advertiser in the connection while the slave acts as receiver. A master can have several slaves connected to it while a slave can link to only one master. The network group involving the slaves connected to a master is called a **piconet**.

To make data available for analytics, the master device passes it over the internet using one of the data messaging protocols that will be discussed later in this chapter. There is typically a gateway device that is both part of the bluetooth network and also linked to the internet. It translates data reported from BLE nodes into the appropriate format for data messaging over the internet. It is commonly an unconstrained device that does not need to worry much about power.

Bluetooth 5.0 specification released mid-2016 promises to double the speed, quadruple the range, and bring an eight-fold increase in the capability for data broadcasting for low-power scenarios.

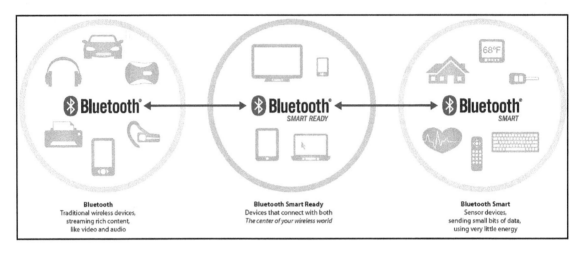

Source: Bluetooth SIG

6LoWPAN

IPv6 over Low-Power Wireless Personal Area Networks (6LoWPANs) works as an adaptation layer in the data link portion of the protocol stack. It adapts wireless standard IEEE 802.15.4 devices to communicate using IPv6. This makes communication over the internet much easier since IP is the *lingua franca*.

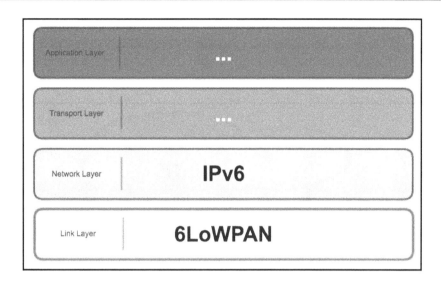

6LoWPAN optimizes the IPv6 datagram transmission over low-power and lossy networks. One of the ways it does this is through header compression. This reduces the addressing information in the data packet down to a few bytes.

Security can be implemented with **Advanced Encryption Standard** (**AES**)-128 encryption at the link layer. **Transport Layer Security** (**TLS**) encryption can also be used at the transport layer.

Mesh style networks are supported. Devices inside the network use stateless auto configuration where they generate their own IPv6 addresses.

The 6LoWPAN mesh network is connected to the IPv6 internet through an edge router. The edger router has three jobs:

- Local data exchanges between devices in the 6LoWPAN
- Data exchange between the internet and 6LoWPAN devices
- The creation and maintenance of the 6LoWPAN wireless network

6LoWPAN networks are connected to other networks using common IP-based routers. This connectivity can be through any type of linkage such as Wi-Fi, Ethernet, or cellular. This makes it simpler to connect to the wider internet than other connectivity options, which require *stateful* gateway devices in order to communicate to IP networks. Stateful gateway devices are more complicated as they need to remember the communication state and status for each IoT device.

There are two types of device inside a 6LoWPAN network, **hosts** and **routers**. Routers can forward datagrams to other devices. Hosts are simply endpoints. They can operate in sleepy states, periodically waking up and checking in with their parent device (router) for new data.

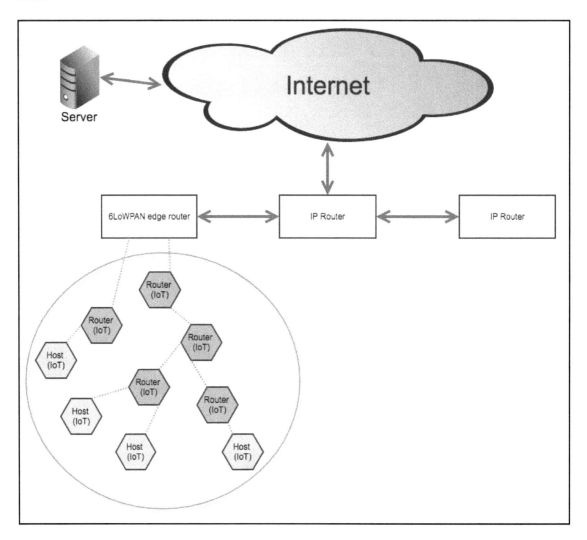

Example of a 6LoWPAN network

ZigBee

ZigBee is a little different animal than what we have talked about so far. It covers multiple layers of the protocol stack. It is the network protocol, the transport layer, and an application framework that is the underpinnings of a customer developed application layer.

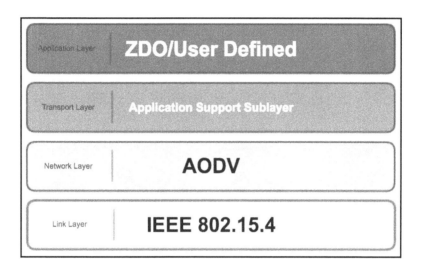

It has security builtin as a requirement and works using small, low power digital radios. It is a self-organizing wireless mesh-style network. The name comes from the waggle dance honey bees often do on returning to the hive.

The range is short, up to 100 meters line of sight, but it can travel long distances by passing data through a mesh network of other ZigBee devices.

The ZigBee alliance is a consortium of companies that maintain and publish Zigbee standards. ZigBee was first released as a standard in 2003. It is intended to be simpler and cheaper than other wireless protocols. Development code can be as little as 2% of equivalent code on Bluetooth.

Data rates are low and devices tend to be simple. ZigBee standards require at least a two-year battery life for a device to qualify. The data transmission is periodic and intermittent. There are different categories of ZigBee device. A fully functioning device can act as a network coordinator and operates in both star and mesh topologies. A reduced functionality device can only communicate with a network coordinator and works in a star topology.

These devices form a **Personal Area Network** (**PAN**). Network interaction times can be very fast. A device can join a network in 30 ms and change from sleeping to active in 15 ms.

There are three types of ZigBee devices in a network:

- A **coordinator device** that initiates network formation. There is one and only of these for each network. It may also act as a router once the network is formed. It serves as the trust center and is the repository for security keys.
- A **router device** is optional. It can join with a coordinator or another router device and acts as a multi-hop intermediary in routing of messages.
- An **end device** has just enough functionality to communicate with its coordinator. It is optional and cannot participate in the routing of messages.

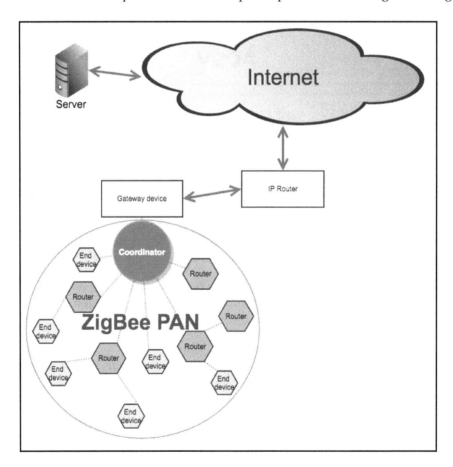

Example of ZigBee network

The ZigBee networking routing protocol is reactive. It establishes a route path on demand instead of proactively such as IP. The network protocol used is **Ad hoc On-Demand Distant Vector** (**AODV**) which finds a destination by broadcasting to all its neighbors, which then send a requests to all their neighbors, until the destination is found.

The network is silent between connections. Networks are self-healing. ZigBee networks are secured by 128 bit AES encryption. There is often a gateway device that is part of the ZigBee network and also linked to the internet. It translates data into the appropriate format for messaging over the internet. It can also convert ZigBee network routing protocol into IP routing protocol. The gateway is commonly an unconstrained device that does not need to worry much about power.

Advantages of ZigBee

There are several advantages to ZigBee networks:

- **Reliable and robust**: Networks are self-forming and self-healing.
- **Low power requirements**: Devices can operate for years without needing a new battery. Solar power could last even longer.
- **Global**: The wireless protocol it is built on is available globally.
- **Security**: Encryption is part of the standard instead of an optional add on.

Disadvantages of ZigBee

There are also some disadvantages:

- **Not free**: It costs $3,500 USD at the time of writing to license the standard
- **Low data rates**: It is not designed to support higher data rates
- **Star network is limited**: The coordinator device supports up to 65,000 devices

Common use cases

ZigBee is commonly used in the following applications:

- Home automation
- Utilities monitoring and control
- Smart lighting
- Building automation
- Security systems
- Medical data collection

NFC

Near Field Communication (**NFC**) allows two devices to communicate when brought within very short distances of each other - about 4 cm. It is a set of communication protocols that offer low speeds and simple setup. There is a variety of NFC protocol stacks depending on the type and use case.

NFC logo

NFC uses electromagnetic induction between two loop style antennas when devices exchange information. Data rates are around 100-400 kbit/s. It operates over radio frequency band 13.56 MHz, which is unlicensed and globally available.

There is usually a full NFC device, such as a smartphone, and an NFC tag, such as a chip reader. All full NFC devices can operate in three modes:

- **NFC peer-to-peer**: Devices exchange information on the fly.
- **NFC card emulation**: Smartphones can act like smart cards in this mode, allowing mobile payments or ticketing.
- **NFC reader/writer**: Full NFC devices can read information stored in inexpensive NFC tags, such as the type used on posters or pamphlets. You have probably used this at a conference to scan your attendee badge.

NFC tags are usually read-only, but it is possible for them to be writeable. There is an initiator device and a target device in NFC communications. The initiator device creates an RF field that can power a target device. This means NFC tags do not need batteries in what is called passive mode. Unpowered NFC tag devices are very inexpensive, just a few pennies.

There is also an active mode where each device can communicate with the other by alternatively generating its own field to read data, then turning it off to receive data. This mode typically requires both the devices to have a power supply.

For data records that eventually end up in an analytics dataset, the full NFC device would act as a gateway, translate the message, and then communicate over a different network protocol stack. In the case of a smartphone, it would take the NFC tag data and create its own data message to send over 4G/LTE for a destination on the internet.

Common use cases

NFC is commonly used in the following applications:

- Smartphone payments:
    - Apple pay
    - **Host Card Emulation (HCE)** - Android supported
- Smart posters
- Identification cards
- Event logging
- Triggering a programmable action

Sigfox

Sigfox is a company based in France that has developed a cellular style, ultra low power, long-range networking technology. It is intended for small messages that are sent infrequently. Data rates are very low at 100 bits per second (tops). The signals used can travel up to 25 miles, and a base station can handle up to a million nodes. Similar to cellular, it is not intended to be for private networks, as it requires coverage in the area to use it.

sigfox logo

Sigfox devices can be very low cost due to low complexity and power requirements. Power requirements could be as low as one thousandth of equivalent cellular communications. It has been used in inexpensive, but crucial, things such as smoke detectors and a fitness tracking collar for dogs (seriously).

The current coverage includes the entirety of France and Spain, several other pockets in Europe, and some metropolitan areas in North America.

Connectivity protocols (when power is not a problem)

These protocols are more about speed and high bit rates. Power constraints are less of a concern. They usually require more complexity in the supported IoT devices.

Wi-Fi

Wi-Fi is any wireless network that follows IEEE 802.11 specifications. It is ubiquitous and global. Provided you have not been hiding in a cave for the last decade, you know it well. Many IoT devices use it to connect to the internet, so it is useful to review how it works.

WiFi logo

To connect to a **Wi-Fi Local Area Network (WLAN)**, a device needs a network interface controller. This may be a separate controller card or simply integrated as part of the chipset inside the device. Communication uses Ethernet-style data packets over pre-identified radio communication bands. Packet delivery is not guaranteed and uses best effort delivery mechanism. Network protocol layers higher up in the stack, such as TCP or UDP, can offer guarantees of data delivery on top of the Wi-Fi standards.

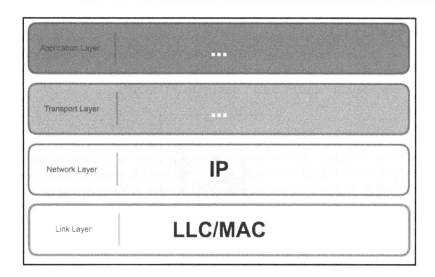

IoT devices connect to a Wi-Fi access point that itself is (usually) connected to a wired Ethernet network that has internet access.

Wi-Fi offers very fast data rates but requires more power to support the constant back and forth communications. The universality of it makes it attractive for IoT devices. New standards such as 802.11ah are designed for low power scenarios. You should expect Wi-Fi to continue to be a heavily used connectivity option for IoT.

Common use cases

Wi-Fi is commonly used in the following applications:

- Home automation
- Amazon dash button
- Home security
- Manufacturing plant machine monitoring

Cellular (4G/LTE)

Cellular data operates over radio waves. The fourth generation networking technology, 4G, is an IP-based networking architecture handling both voice and data. **Long Term Evolution** (**LTE**) is a 4G technology. It handles data rates up to 300 Mbit/s.

4G LTE logo

LTE can handle fast moving mobile devices (such as mobile phones or telematics units). It can handle devices moving out of range of one network and into another without disruption. Due to higher power needs, it usually requires either constant power or frequent battery charges. LTE supports different categories of services.

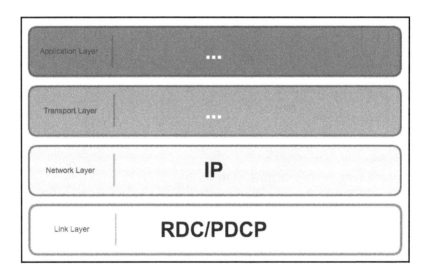

A newer category, **LTE Category 0** (**LTE Cat 0**), is designed for IoT requirements. It has lower data rates, capped at 1 Mbit/s maximum. LTE Cat 0 also reduces bandwidth ranges, which allows for significant complexity reduction. It is still able to operate on all existing LTE networks and supports low power constrained IoT devices.

Cellular coverage is not available in all areas, though. There are still some places where you will not find a signal. For analytics, this means that if your IoT device moves around, it could venture into an area without a signal. Data could be lost in this case, unless it is buffered until the signal is recovered.

Common use cases

Cellular is commonly used in the follow applications:

- Freight tracking
- Vehicle connectivity (telematics)
- Smartphones (obviously)
- Remote equipment monitoring

IoT networking data messaging protocols

There are many strategies that IoT networked devices use to transfer data messages. Although connectivity and data messaging can sometimes blend together, we will discuss them separately for simplicity.

Not that it is really all that simple, but we will cover the most commonly used protocols. We will spend more time with the more frequently used ones.

Message Queue Telemetry Transport (MQTT)

MQTT is the most common data messaging protocol associated with IoT. It is supported by all the major cloud infrastructure providers (AWS, Microsoft, and Google). And it is most likely the protocol that is being used to deliver your data. It was designed for minimal power loss and minimal bandwidth requirements. It originated to support remote oil and gas use cases over satellite communication networks. It translated well into the broader IoT world as it developed in recent years.

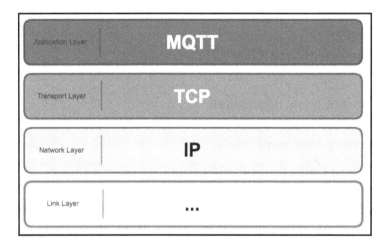

At its heart, it is similar in concept to a messaging queue architecture but, despite the name, not a traditional queue. This means that new data comes into an intermediary **broker** as a message, and then it is delivered to the end server. The IoT device is called the **publisher** and the ending server is called the **subscriber**. Both connect to the broker but never to each other.

MQTT follows the publish/subscribe architecture pattern or pub/sub, but it is implemented differently than a traditional message queue. It is a queue of one, in that the message for the topic is replaced with the latest data instead of being added to an expanding line of messages, as with a traditional message queue.

The message on the broker exists regardless of if the publisher or the subscriber is online and willing to interact with it. This makes it robust against intermittent connections (intentional or unintentional). The subscriber does not have to wait until the publisher is awake and willing to chat. The publisher can send a message without caring about the details of who is willing and able to receive it.

The broker has no knowledge of, nor does it care, what is inside the message. The message is published by the device to an address on the broker known as a topic. Topics are a key concept in MQTT and will be discussed in detail later on.

Differences between MQTT queue (topics) and traditional message queues are as follows:

- **Topics do not have to be created ahead of time**: They are flexible and can be created on the fly. Traditional message queues have to be created and named explicitly before they can receive messages.
- **Topics do not keep all messages until they are consumed**: Traditional queues keep everything until it has been consumed by a subscriber. Topics just replace old messages with new ones.
- **Topics can have multiple subscribers receiving the same message**: Traditional message queues are designed for a message to be consumed by one client.
- **Messages do not require a subscriber**: Traditional message queues require someone to consume them. Otherwise, it will eventually fill up and be unable to accept more items.

MQTT is intended to be very light overhead. A device can switch on periodically, connect to the broker, send a message, then go back to sleep without worrying about if the subscriber is able to receive it right away.

However, most implementations keep a persistent connection. Communication tends to be near real time in practice.

Topics

Topics are hierarchical and are similar to a filing system. For example, `vehicleID/engine/oil/temperature` and `vehicleID/engine/oil/pressure`. An IoT device linked to a vehicle might publish a message that holds the value of 122.2 to the address called `vehicleID/engine/oil/temperature` (where `vehicleID` would be the unique identifier of that specific vehicle) on the broker. A subscriber to this topic would then get a message that includes the value 122.2 when it establishes a connection to the broker. If a constant connection to the broker is held, the subscriber will receive the message in near real time.

The concept of topic matching is supported for subscribers. This allows wildcard characters, + or #, to be used when subscribing to topics. This is not allowed for publishers.

A + is a wildcard character for a single level. It works like a search pattern where all non + levels must match. A # is a wildcard character for multiple levels and must be used at the end of the string. It will return the entire hierarchy specified. Similar to copying a folder in your filesystem, it will subscribe to all subdirectories and files included for the level specified.

The wildcard allows simpler subscription management to topics. You could subscribe to `vehicleID/engine/+/temperature` to get all the temperature values in the engine topic. You could also subscribe to `+/engine/oil/temperature` to get engine oil temperature values for all devices publishing to that broker. You could subscribe to `vehicleID/engine/#` to get all values in that hierarchy no matter how deep the levels go.

It is important that the topic tree is designed with flexibility in mind. It should be extensible so that new branches can be added without requiring a redesign of the tree. From an analytical point of view, this means that adding more information from the devices is relatively inexpensive if designed well. If designed poorly, it requires a redesign of the topic tree, which makes it more expensive and therefore unlikely to happen. In the constantly adapting world of analytics where you learn new things and exploit them, you want flexibility at all levels.

Advantages to MQTT

- **Packet agnostic**: Any type of data can be transported in the payload carried by the packet. The data could be text or binary. It does not matter as long as the receiving party knows how to interpret it.
- **Reliability**: There are some **Quality of Service** (**QoS**) options that can be used to guarantee delivery.
- **Scalability**: The publish/subscribe model scales well in a power-efficient way.
- **Decoupled design**: There are several elements to the design that decouple the device and the subscribing server, which result in a more robust communication strategy.

- **Time**: A device can publish its data regardless of the state of the subscribing server. The subscribing server can then connect and receive the data when it is able. This decouples the two ends of the communication on a time basis. Think of it like the ability to text someone on your phone. He can reply whenever he gets the chance. If you called him, he would have to be available to talk at the same time as you are. If you both are busy in meetings all day, you end up trading voicemails and the communication slows. This allows the devices to remain in sleepy states without having to worry about if the subscriber is able to receive the data at the time the device wakes up to communicate.

- **Space** (delivery details): The publisher needs to know the broker IP address and how to communicate with it, but it does not need to know anything about the subscribers. Subscribers do not need to know the network connection details of the publisher. This keeps the communication overhead low on the device side (usually much more constrained in terms of power availability). It also allows both ends to operate independently. The subscriber can be changed or upgraded and additional subscribers added with no change needed on the publishing device end.

- **Synchronizing**: Neither side has to pause what they are doing to communicate or receive a message. The process is asynchronous. There is no need to interrupt work in progress to publish a message.

- **Security**: This is in both the advantage and disadvantage lists. You can have security with MQTT, which is why it is on the advantage list. Since MQTT operations over TCP, you can and absolutely should use the TLS/SSL encryption in the communication. But MQTT is natively unencrypted, which is why it is also in the disadvantage list - more about this will be explained later.

- **Bidirectional**: A device can be both a publisher and a subscriber. In this way, it can receive commands by subscribing to a topic on the broker. It could also receive data from other devices that could be an input into the data it publishes. In practice, a hub and spoke model is typically the case.

- **Maturity**: MQTT was invented by IBM with the first draft of the protocol in 1999 based on its MQSeries product (this is where the message queue part of the name comes from). It was released royalty free in 2010 and has since been donated as an open source project to the Eclipse foundation. It is in use by millions of connected products.

Disadvantages to MQTT

- **It operates over TCP**: TCP was designed for devices that had more memory and processing power than many of the lightweight, power constrained IoT devices have available to them. TCP requires more handshaking to set up communication links before any messages can be exchanged. This increases wake-up and communication times, which affects the long-term battery consumption. TCP connected devices tend to keep sockets open for each other with a persistent session. This adds to power and memory requirements.

- **Centralized broker can limit scale**: The broker can affect scalability as there is additional overhead for each device connected to it. The network can only grow as large as the local broker hub can support it. This puts a limit on expansion for each hub and spoke group.

- **Broker single point of failure**: It can also be a single point of failure in the network. A common situation is a broker device that is plugged into a wall socket with several publishing devices that are battery powered. In the event of a power failure, the publishing devices would keep operating but the broker would be offline. The network would be useless until the power is resumed.

- **Security**: MQTT is unencrypted by default. This makes it natively unsecured and requires you to take additional steps and absorb some overhead to make sure TLS/SSL is implemented. If not, any communication over MQTT, including username and password, is open to hackers.

QoS levels

There is a trade-off inherent to QoS levels. QoS is the MQTT terminology for message delivery reliability requirements. It is a common term in networking, and we will review how it is implemented specifically for MQTT.

The trade-off is between bandwidth used and reliability of message delivery. More back and forth messaging is required to ensure higher reliability, which increases bandwidth requirements for the same message packet. MQTT gives you some options to choose between.

 QoS is set separately for both the ends of the communication. There is a QoS that is set for the publisher to broker messaging connection and a separate QoS that is set for the broker to subscriber connection. Often, QoS is the same for both, but not always.

QoS 0

Fire and forget - sir, yes, sir!

QoS 0 is the minimal QoS level, often referred to as fire and forget. Messages are sent to the broker without confirmation that it has been sent on by the broker to subscribers. It still has all the guarantees of the TCP protocol, as do all forms of standard MQTT.

As can be seen in the following diagram, there is minimal communication overhead, which translates into minimal power requirements. Once sent to the broker, the message is deleted on the device (publisher). The broker immediately sends on to subscribers that have an open connection. Unlike the other QoS levels, the message is not stored for offline subscribers when QoS is set to zero.

QoS 0 is often used when there is a stable connection and disruption is unlikely, like in the case of a wired connection. It is also used when power constraints are more important than message delivery. In this case, either the resulting data is acceptable even with some messages lost, or the frequency of messages is high enough that if one is lost, then no big deal, another will be on the way shortly.

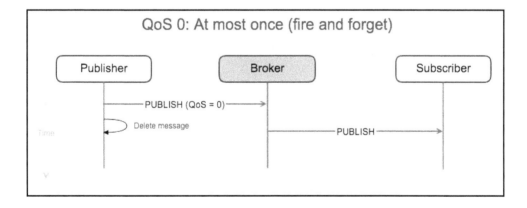

QoS 1

Deliver once - I don't care if you send it 10 times, just make sure they get it.

QoS 1 is the most commonly used level. It guarantees the message is delivered at least once. Duplicate messages need to be handled either on the subscriber side or in some post processing. There is a higher communication overhead than QoS 0 but only half as much back and forth as QoS 2.

QoS 1 is used when delivery needs to be guaranteed and the use case can handle duplicate messages.

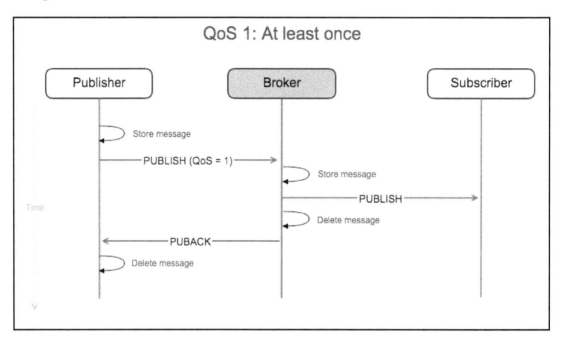

QoS 2

Deliver exactly once - Make sure they get it, but make sure they only get it once - they get confused.

QoS 2 guarantees the message is delivered and delivered only once. As can be seen in the diagram, there are multiple back and forth communications to orchestrate this guarantee. The state of the communication needs to be stored by both the sides until full confirmation of delivery is communicated back to the publisher. This requires both a higher level of power on the device and a larger memory footprint in order to store the more complex state. It also takes a bit longer to complete QoS 2 communications.

QoS 2 is used when delivery needs to be guaranteed and the end application or subscribing client is unable to handle duplicate messages.

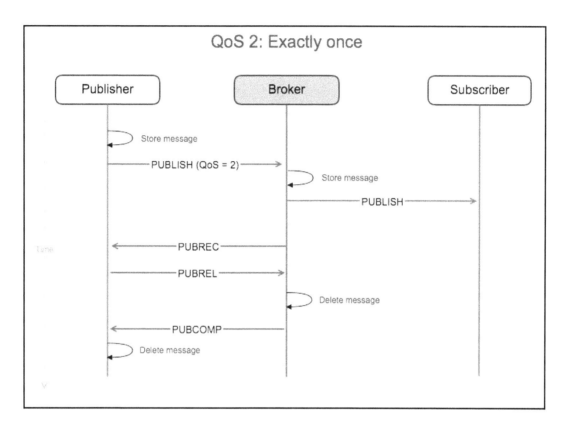

Last Will and Testament (LWT)

This creatively named feature helps MQTT deal with lossy networks and enhances scalability. It is a message that can be stored on the broker in case the publisher drops off the network unexpectedly.

It stores state and purpose including the commands it published and its subscriptions. When it drops out, the broker notifies all subscribers of the LWT. When it returns, the broker sends it back to its prior state.

Tips for analytics

Make sure the time the device records the data is tracked along with the time the data is received. You can monitor delivery times to diagnose issues and keep a close eye on information lag times. For example, if you notice the delivery time steadily increases just before you get a data loss, it is probably something in the networking and not the device that is causing the issue.

Since MQTT enables subscribers and publishers to be offline if necessary, the time the message is received could be very different from when it was originated. This can affect the predictive modeling accuracy if the time received becomes significantly distant from when the event being analyzed actually occurred. If connections are persistent, this should be a non issue.

Common use cases

MQTT protocol is commonly used in the following applications:

- Casino gambling devices
- Home healthcare
- Automotive telematics
- Oil and gas remote monitoring
- Inventory tracking
- Cargo trailer tracking
- Monitoring of energy usage

Hyper-Text Transport Protocol (HTTP)

Web pages use HTTP protocol to exchange data. HTTP is a character-based protocol. It operates at the application layer and conforms to RESTful principles. You are intimately familiar with it but may not realize that it can be used with IoT devices even when there is no web page present.

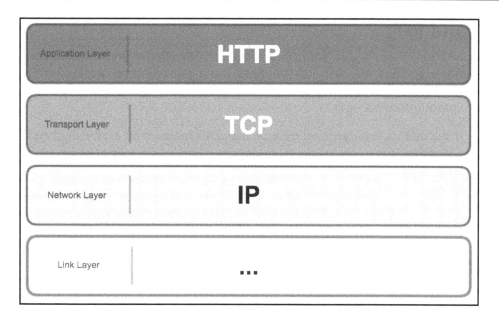

Representational State Transfer (REST) principles

REST allows internet-enabled devices to inter-operate with each other using a uniform **Application Programming Interface** (**API**). A device or server that complies to this is called RESTful. It assumes interactions are client/server-based and are stateless. The following table shows the key commands supported by the HTTP REST API Interface:

HTTP REST API
HTTP POST: Adds a new resource
HTTP PUT: Updates a specific resource by replacing it with an updated version
HTTP GET: Reads a specified resource
HTTP PATCH: Partially updates a resource in a collection
HTTP DELETE: Deletes a resource

HTTP and IoT

In many cases, HTTP is not ideal for IoT applications. The latency is not predictable, and it often depends on polling to detect state changes. It is a text-based protocol, which means message size tends to be large. This adds power needs and complexity overhead, for IoT devices to communicate using it.

However, it is a mature standard and in wide use. This makes it an established and well supported interface.

Connections are established from a client device to a server device and remain open until the communication is completed. Delivery is guaranteed and data message receipts are acknowledged at every step of the process. It operates on top of TCP and is reliable.

Advantages to HTTP

There are several advantages to HTTP as an IoT protocol:

- **Reliability**: Message delivery is guaranteed and acknowledged.
- **Ubiquity**: HTTP is used all over the place and is very easy to implement.
- **Ease of implementation**: If you can connect to the internet, you can use HTTP anywhere in the world. No special hardware or software is required.

Disadvantages to HTTP

There are some disadvantages to HTTP as an IoT protocol:

- **Higher power needs**: Communications have frequent back and forth interactions, connections need to be sustained, and plain text results in larger message sizes. All of this requires more power to support.
- **The IoT device complexity**: The device needs enough memory and CPU power to support the TCP protocol and high level HTTP RESTful APIs.

Constrained Application Protocol (CoAP)

CoAP is point-to-point communication over **User Datagram Protocol** (UDP). It has low overhead requirements and was specifically developed for low-power devices operating over the internet. It was designed to work on microcontrollers with as low as 10 KiB of RAM and needs only 100 KiB for the operating codes.

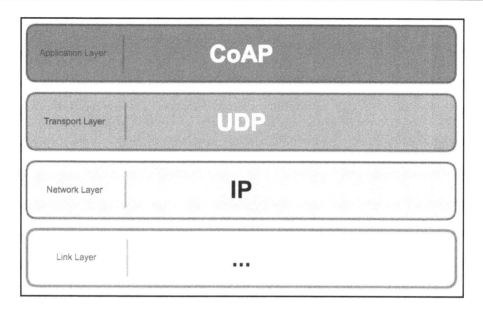

CoAP was created by the **Internet Engineering Task Force** (**IETF**) to address the needs of power constrained IoT devices. It is also supported by the Eclipse foundation as an open standard.

CoAP follows a client/server architecture and is a one-to-one communication convention. It does allow for some multicast capabilities, which are early in development at the time of this writing.

CoAP is similar to HTTP in that it is a document transfer protocol and interoperates with the RESTful web. It is different from HTTP, in that it was designed for applications where networks are low-powered and often lossy.

CoAP operates on UDP protocol where data packets are much smaller than HTTP, which uses larger TCP packets. Clients and servers communicate without established connections. Information is transferred using self-contained datagrams. Datagrams are the core of the UDP protocol and each datagram contains all necessary information for routing without any reliance on previous exchanges between client and server.

It may help to think of a datagram like communicating with someone over mail (old school snail mail). The envelope has a delivery address and a return address and the payload would be the letter inside, but this is hidden from the mail man. You send regular letters to your cousin in Poland. She sends regular letters to you.

You have no guarantee that all your letters will be delivered or delivered in the same order that you sent them. It is your responsibility, once letters are received, to open them up, put them in the right order, and figure out if there are any missing. If you find one to be missing, you would handle mailing your cousin to request a resend of it.

CoAP works in the same manner where the sending and receiving applications play the role of you and your cousin. Applications need to be programmed appropriately to handle the required level of delivery reliability.

Advantages to CoAP

There are some advantages to CoAP:

- **Reduced power requirements**: It operates over UDP, which requires minimal overhead for communications. It also allows faster wake up times and extended sleepy states. Taken together, this means batteries last longer for IoT devices.
- **Smaller packet size**: Another advantage of UDP is small packet sizes. This leads to faster communication cycles. Again, this allows batteries to last longer.
- **Security**: Like MQTT, this is on both the advantage and disadvantage lists. When **Datagram Transport Layer Security** (**DTLS**) is employed over UDP, communication is encrypted and secure. Even though there is some additional overhead required to implement this, you can and should use it.
- **Asynchronous communication option**: Clients can request to observe a device by setting a flag. The server (IoT device) can then stream state changes to the client as they happen. Either side can cancel the observe request.
- **IPv6 based**: It was designed from the beginning to support IPv6. This also allows for a multicasting option.
- **Resource discovery**: Servers can provide a list of resources and media types. The client can then review and discover what is available.

Disadvantages to CoAP

There are also some disadvantages to CoAP:

- **Message unreliability**: UDP does not guarantee the delivery of datagrams. CoAP adds a method to request a confirmation acknowledgement to confirm the message was received. This does not verify that it was received in its entirety and decoded properly.
- **Standards are still maturing**: CoAP is still evolving, although there is a lot of market momentum behind it. It is likely to mature quickly as use becomes more widespread.
- **NAT issues**: **Network Address Translation (NAT)** devices are commonly used in enterprise networks and cloud environments. CoAP can have problems communicating with devices behind a NAT since the IP can be dynamic over time.
- **Security**: Like MQTT, CoAP is unencrypted by default. This makes it natively unsecure and you need to take additional steps to make sure communication is not open to hackers.

Message reliability

This equates to MQTT QoS. With CoAP, there is an option to mark the request and response datagrams as confirmable. In this case, the receiver responds with an **Acknowledgement (ACK)** message.

If this flag is not marked, datagrams are fire and forget. This is the equivalent of MQTT QoS 0.

Common use cases

CoAP protocol is commonly used in the following applications:

- Utility field area networks
- Remote weather station sensors
- Sealed battery-operated sensor devices

Data Distribution Service (DDS)

DDS is a type of networking middleware. Its standards are managed by the **Object Management Group** (**OMG**). It is a bus-style architecture; a centralized node is not required. Communication is peer-to-peer and not centrally controlled.

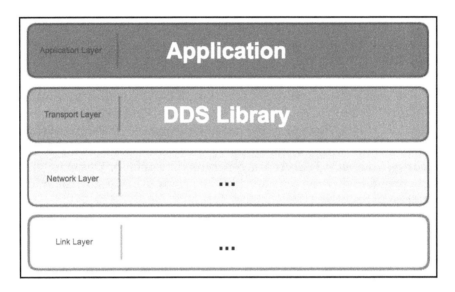

Endpoints for communication are automatically discovered by DDS through a process called dynamic discovery. DDS uses a variant of the publish/subscribe model, where nodes on the bus announce what data they are publishing and what data they want to subscribe to.

DDS participants could be on the same machine or at the same factory or even spread over a wide area. It could be all of those combined when individual DDS domains are linked together. It is a very scalable architecture.

Data exchange is real time and dependable with high transfer rates. DDS handles the details of the transfer work for you such as message addressing, delivery, flow control, retries, and data marshaling/demarshaling. Any node could be a publisher, a subscriber, or both at the same time.

To an application on a device using DDS, the data looks like native memory that is accessed through an API. This is through the local data store maintained by DDS called the Global Data Space. It is an illusion to the application; only data that is needed is kept locally and only as long as it is needed.

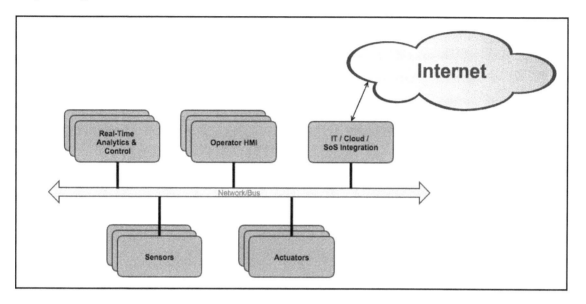

Example of DDS network architecture

Common use cases

DDS is commonly used in the following applications:

- In-hospital patient monitoring
- Automotive driver safety systems
- Defense control systems
- Aircraft jet engine monitoring
- Financial trading
- Wind turbine monitoring/control
- High-performance computing
- Remote surgical devices

Analyzing data to infer protocol and device characteristics

Back to the number-one rule in IoT analytics: *Never trust data you don't know.*

You need to get to know your data. Just like that new guy you just met, you Google him, ask around about him, and do a criminal background check (we know you do) before agreeing to go to dinner with him.

Here is a step-by-step strategy to start to understand the source of the data:

1. **Draw a picture of the device**: Sketch it out or use blueprints if you have them. This is where you make friends with the design engineer and ask her some questions. Draw the key sensors in the place they are located and note the sensor type and any limitations. Ask about any environmental conditions that affect accuracy and note it.
2. **Find out how the device connects to a network**: Note the connectivity type on your sketch.
3. **Determine what data messaging protocol the device uses to communicate**: Note this on your sketch. A simple example follows:

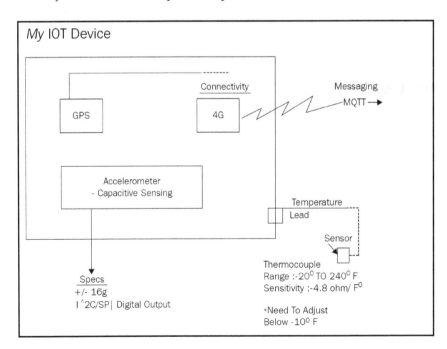

4. **If you can visit an actual site where the device is in use, do so**: Take pictures. If not, have someone that travels in the field take some for you. Try to get a few different locations. The idea is to capture real-world conditions for later reference.

5. **Combine the real-world pictures and the sketch into a reference document**: Pin it to your cubicle wall for reference; you will probably need it.

6. **Analyze your data to infer some things about it**:
    1. Take a few months worth of complete data. Keep it small enough to easily work with but large enough that you have some history.
    2. Calculate the frequency between records by subtracting the time of the previous record on the same individual device from the time of the current record. This will get an interval number for each message.
    3. Randomly select at least 30 individual devices and set aside all the records for them.
    4. For each device, visually review the records. If the interval number is consistent for the most part, you now know it has a regular frequency of reporting and the length of time between reports. If it is not consistent, there is probably not a set interval and data is communicated when the device gets in range of a network (it moves) or an irregular event triggers the communication. Either way, note this on your reference document.

5. Look for irregular increases in the interval numbers. If this happens frequently, the devices are likely in a lossy network situation. Note this on your reference document.

6. If the interval is large, several hours or days and the message size (number of columns) is low, then your IoT device is probably constrained and dependent on a long-term battery. It is more likely to be in a lossy network situation.

7. If the interval is small, every few seconds, or minutes, then it probably has easy access to power. It is less likely to be in a lossy network situation.

8. Calculate the average interval by date for each device. Plot them on the same chart, each one having its own line. If the changes in the average interval happen on the exact same dates for all the devices, you have a network or data processing problem with the centralized data collection process.

Summary

This chapter reviewed in more depth the variety of IoT devices and networking protocols. You learned the scope of devices and some example use cases. The variety of networking protocols were discussed along with the business need they are trying to solve.

We reviewed how to understand the what and the why of the major categories of devices and networking protocol strategies. We also discussed some techniques to identify the characteristics of the device and the network protocol by analyzing the data.

3
IoT Analytics for the Cloud

Now that you know how your data is transmitted back to the corporate servers, you feel you have a better understanding of it. You also have a reference frame in your head of how it is operating out in the real world.

Your boss stops by again.

"Is that rolling average job done running yet?" he asks impatiently.

It used to run fine and finished in an hour three months ago. It has steadily taken longer and longer and now sometimes does not even finish. Today, it has been going on six hours, and you are crossing your fingers. Yesterday, it crashed twice with what looked like out-of-memory errors.

You have talked to your IT group and finance group about getting a faster server with more memory. The cost would be significant and will probably take months to complete the process of going through purchasing, putting it on order, and having it installed. Your friend in finance is hesitant to approve it. The money was not budgeted for this fiscal year. You feel bad, especially since this is the only analytic job causing you problems. It just runs once a month but produces key data.

Not knowing what else to say, you give your boss a hopeful, strained smile, and show him your crossed fingers.

"It's still running...that's good, right?"

This chapter is about the advantages to cloud-based infrastructure for handling and analyzing IoT data. We will discuss cloud services including **Amazon Web Services** (AWS), **Azure**, and **ThingWorx**. You will learn how to implement analytics elastically to enable a wide variety of capabilities.

This chapter will cover the following:

- Building elastic analytics
- Designing for scale
- Cloud security and analytics
- Key cloud providers:
    - Amazon AWS
    - Microsoft Azure
- PTC ThingWorx

Building elastic analytics

IoT data volumes increase quickly. Analytics for IoT is particularly compute intensive at times that are difficult to predict. Business value is uncertain and requires a lot of experimentation to find the right implementation.

Combine all this together and you need something that scales quickly, is dynamic and responsive to resource needs, and has virtually unlimited capacity at just the right time. And all of this needs to be implemented quickly with a low cost and low maintenance needs.

Enter the cloud. IoT analytics and cloud infrastructure fit together like a hand in a glove.

What is cloud infrastructure?

The National Institute of Standards and Technology defines five essential characteristics:

- **On-demand self-service**: You can provision things such as servers and storage as needed and without interacting with someone.
- **Broad network access**: Your cloud resources are accessible over the internet (if enabled) by various methods, such as web browser or mobile phone.
- **Resource pooling**: Cloud providers pool their servers and storage capacity across many customers using a multi-tenant model. Resources, both physical and virtual, are dynamically assigned and reassigned as needed. The specific location of resources is unknown and generally unimportant.

- **Rapid elasticity**: Your resources can be elastically created and destroyed. This can happen automatically as needed to meet demand. You can scale out rapidly. You can also contract rapidly. The supply of resources is effectively unlimited from your viewpoint.
- **Measured service**: The resource usage is monitored, controlled, and reported by the cloud provider. You have access to the same information, providing transparency to your utilization. Cloud systems continuously optimize resources automatically.

There is a notion of private clouds that exist on the premises or that arecustom built by a third party for a specific organization. For our concerns, we will be discussing public clouds only. By and large, most analytics will be done on public clouds, so we will concentrate our efforts there.

The capacity available at your fingertips on the public clouds is staggering. AWS, in June 2016, had an estimated 1.3 million servers online. These servers were thought to be three times more efficient than enterprise systems.

Cloud providers own the hardware and maintain the network and systems required for the available services. You just have to provision what you need to use, typically through a web application.

Providers offer different levels of abstraction. They offer lower-level servers and storage where you have fine-grained control. They also offer managed services that handle the provisioning of servers, networking, and storage for you. These are used in conjunction with each other without much distinction between the two.

Hardware failures are handled automatically. Resources are transferred to new hardware and brought back online. The physical components become unimportant when you design for the cloud, it is abstracted away, and you can focus on resource needs.

The advantages of using the cloud are:

- **Speed**: You can bring cloud resources online in minutes.
- **Agility**: The ability to quickly create and destroy resources leads to ease of experimentation. This increases the agility of analytics organizations.
- **Variety of services**: Cloud providers have many services available to support analytics workflows that can be deployed within minutes. These services manage hardware and storage needs for you.

- **Global reach**: You can extend the reach of analytics to the other side of the world with a few clicks.
- **Cost control**: You only pay for the resources you need at the time you need them. You can do more for less.

To get an idea of the power that is at your fingertips, here is an architectural diagram of something NASA built on AWS as part of an outreach program to school children:

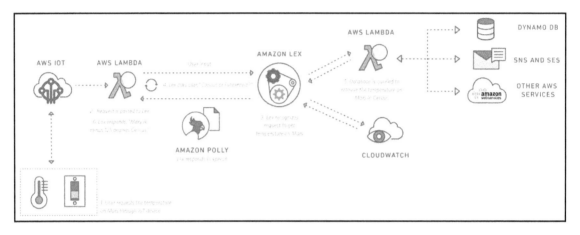

Source: Amazon Web Services, https://aws.amazon.com/lex/

When given voice commands, it will communicate with a Mars rover replica to retrieve IoT data, such as temperature readings. The process includes voice recognition, natural speech generation from text, data storage and processing, interaction with an IoT device, networking, security, and the ability to send text messages. This was not a years' worth of development effort, it was built by tying together cloud-based services already in place.

And it is not just for well funded government agencies such as NASA. All of these services and many more are available to you today if your analytics runs in the cloud.

Elastic analytics concepts

What do we mean by **elastic analytics**? Let's define it as designing your analytics processes so that scale is not a concern. You want your focus to be on the analytics and not on the underlying technology. You want to avoid constraining your analytics capability so it will fit within some set hardware limitations. Focus instead on the potential value of your analytics versus the limit of what can be done with existing hardware.

You also want your analytics to be able to scale. It should go from supporting 100 IoT devices to 1 million IoT devices without requiring any fundamental changes. All that should happen is that the costs increase as demand increases.

This reduces complexity and increases maintainability. This translates into lower costs, which enables you to do more analytics. More analytics increases the probability of finding value. Finding more value enables even more analytics. Virtuous circle!

Some core elastic analytics concepts:

- **Separate compute from storage**: We are used to thinking about resources as we think about laptop specifications. You buy one device that has 16 GB memory and 500 GB hard drive because you think that will meet 90% of your needs, and it is the top of your budget. Cloud infrastructure abstracts this away. Doing analytics in the cloud is like renting a magic laptop where you can change 4 GB memory into 16 GB by snapping your fingers. Your rental bill increases for only the time you have it at 16 GB. You snap your fingers again and drop it back down to 4 GB to save some money. Your hard drive can grow and shrink independently of the memory specification. You are not stuck having to choose a good balance between them. You can match compute needs with requirements.
- **Build for scale from the start**: Use software, services, and programming code that can scale from 1 to 1 million without changes. Each analytic process you put in production has continuing maintenance efforts that will build up over time as you add more and more processes. Make it easy on yourself later on. You do not want to have to stop what you are doing to re-architect a process you built a year ago because it hit the limits of scale.
- **Make your bottleneck wetware not hardware**: By wetware, we mean brain power. *My laptop doesn't have enough memory to run the job* should never be the problem. It should always be *I haven't figured it out yet, but I have several possibilities in test as we speak*.
- **Manage to a spend budget, not to available hardware**: Use as many cloud resources as you need as long as it fits within your spend budget. There is no need to limit analytics to fit within a set number of servers when you run analytics in the cloud. The traditional enterprise architecture purchases hardware ahead of time, which incurs a capital expense. Your finance guy does not (usually) like capital expense. You should not like it either, as it means a ceiling has just been set on what you can do (at least in the near term). Managing to spend means keeping an eye on costs, not on resource limitations. Expand when needed and make sure to contract quickly to keep costs down.

- **Experiment, experiment, and experiment**: Create resources, try things out, and kill them off if they do not work. Then, try something else. Iterate to the right answer. Scale out resources to run experiments. Stretch when you need to. Bring it back down when you are done.

If elastic analytics is done correctly, you will find your biggest limitations are time and wetware, not hardware and capital.

Design with the endgame in mind

Consider how the analytics you develop in the cloud would end up, if successful. Would it turn into a regularly updated dashboard? Would it be something deployed to run under certain conditions to predict customer behavior? Would it periodically run against a new set of data and send an alert if an anomaly is detected?

When you list the likely outcomes, think about how easy it would be to transition from the analytics in development to the production version that will be embedded in your standard processes. Choose tools and analytics that make the transition quick and easy.

Designing for scale

Following some key concepts will help keep changes to your analytics processes to a minimum, as your needs scale.

Decouple key components

Decoupling means separating functional groups into components so they are not dependent upon each other to operate. This allows functionality to change or new functionality to be added with minimal impact on other components.

Encapsulate analytics

Encapsulate means grouping together similar functions and activities into distinct units. It is a core principle of object-oriented programming, and you should employ it in analytics as well. The goal is to reduce complexity and simplify future changes.

As your analytics develop, you will have a list of actions that is either transforming the data, running it through a model or algorithm, or reacting to the result. It can get complicated quickly. By encapsulating the analytics, it is easier to know where to make changes when needed down the road. You will also be able reconfigure parts of the process without affecting the other components.

The encapsulation process follows these steps:

1. Make a list of the steps.
2. Organize them into groups.
3. Think which groups are likely to change together.
4. Separate the groups that are independent into their own processes.

It is a good idea to have the data transformation steps separate from the analytical steps if possible. Sometimes, the analysis is tightly tied to the data transformation, and it does not make sense to separate, but in most cases, it can be separated. The action steps based on the results of the analysis should almost always be separate.

Each group of steps will also have its own resource needs. By encapsulating them and separating the processes, you can assign resources independently and scale more efficiently where you need it. You can do more with less.

Decoupling with message queues

Decoupling encapsulated analytics processes with message queues has several advantages. It allows for change in any process without requiring the other ones to adjust. This is because there is no direct link between them.

It also builds in some robustness in case one process has a failure. The queue can continue to expand without losing data while the down process restarts, and nothing will be lost after things get going again.

What is a message queue?

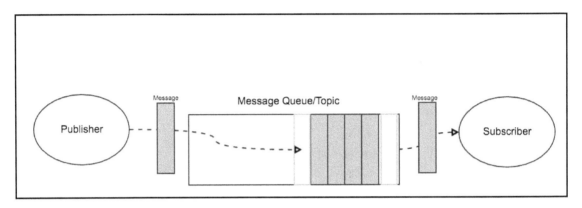

Simple diagram of a message queue

New data comes into a queue as a message, it goes into line for delivery, and then it is delivered to the end server when it gets its turn. The process adding a message is called the **publisher**, and the process receiving the message is called the **subscriber**.

The message queue exists regardless of whether the publisher or subscriber is connected and online. This makes it robust against intermittent connections (intentional or unintentional). The subscriber does not have to wait until the publisher is willing to chat and vice versa.

The size of the queue can also grow and shrink as needed. If the subscriber gets behind, the queue just grows to compensate until it can catch up. This can be useful if there is a sudden burst in messages by the publisher. The queue will act as a buffer and expand to capture the messages while the subscriber is working through the sudden influx.

There is a limit, of course. If the queue reaches some set threshold, it will reject (and you will most likely lose) any incoming messages until the queue gets back under control.

Here is a contrived but real-world example of how this can happen:

Joe Cut-rate (the developer): *Hey, when do you want this doo-hickey device to wake up and report?*

Jim Unawares (the engineer): *Every 4 hours*

Joe Cut-rate: *No sweat. I'll program it to start at 12 a.m. UTC, then every 4 hours after. How many of these you gonna sell again?*

Jim Unawares: *About 20 million.*

Joe Cut-rate: *Um….friggin awesome! I better hardcode that 12 a.m. UTC then, huh?*

4 months later

Jim Unawares: *We're only getting data from 10% of the devices. And it is never the same 10%. What the heck?*

Angela the analyst: *Every device in the world reports at exactly the same time. That's the first thing I checked. The message queues are filling up since our subscribers can't process that fast and new messages are dropped. If you hard coded the report time, we're going to have to get the checkbook out to buy a ton of bandwidth for the queues. And we need to do it now, since we are losing 90% of the data every 4 hours. You guys didn't do that, did you?*

Although queues in practice typically operate with little lag, make sure the origination time of the data is tracked and not just the time the data was pulled off the queue. It can be tempting to just capture the time the message was processed to save space, but this can cause problems for your analytics.

Why is this important for analytics? If you only have the date and time the message was received by the subscribing server, it may not be as close as you think to the time the message was generated at the originating device. If there are recurring problems with message queues, the spread in time difference would ebb and flow without you being aware of it.

You will be using time values extensively in predictive modeling. If the time values are sometimes accurate and sometimes off, the models will have a harder time finding predictive value in your data.

Your potential revenue from re-purposing the data can also be affected. Customers are unlikely to pay for a service tracking event times for them if it is not always accurate. There is a simple solution. Make sure the time the device sends the data is tracked along with the time the data is received. You can monitor delivery times to diagnose issues and keep a close eye on information lag times. For example, if you notice the delivery time steadily increases just before you get a data loss, it is probably the message queue filling up. If there is no change in delivery time before a loss, it is unlikely to be the queue.

Another benefit of using the cloud is (virtually) unlimited queue sizes when using a managed queue service. This makes the situation described much less likely to occur.

Distributed computing

Also called cluster computing, distributed computing refers to spreading processes across multiple servers using frameworks that abstract the coordination of each individual server. The frameworks make it appear as if you are using one unified system. Under the covers, it could be a few servers (called nodes) to thousands. The framework handles the orchestration for you.

Avoid containing analytics to one server

The advantage to this for IoT analytics is in scale. You can add resources by adding nodes to the cluster; no change to the analytics code is required. The most common framework in use today is Hadoop, which we will talk about in `Chapter 4`, *Creating an AWS Cloud Analytics Environment*.

Try and avoid containing analytics to one server (with a few exceptions). This puts a ceiling on scale.

When to use distributed and when to use one server

There is a complexity cost to distributed computing though. It is not as simple as single server analytics. Even though the frameworks handle a lot of the complexity for you, you still have to think and design your analytics to work across multiple nodes.

Here are some guidelines on when to keep it simple and on one server:

- **There is not much need for scale**: Your analytics process needs little change even if the number of IoT devices and data explodes. For example, the analytics process runs a forecast on data already summarized by month. The volume of devices makes little difference in that case.
- **Small data instead of big data**: The analytics run on a small subset of data without much impact from data size. Analytics on random samples is an example.
- **Resource needs are minimal**: Even at orders of magnitude more data, you are unlikely to need more than what is available with a standard server. In this case, keep it simple.

Assuming that change is constant

The world of IoT analytics moves quickly. The analytics you create today will change many times over as you get feedback on results and adapt to the changing business conditions. Your analytics processes will need to change. Assume this will happen continuously and design for change. This brings us to the concept of **continuous delivery**.

Continuous delivery is a concept from software development. It automates the release of code into production. The idea is to make change a regular process. Bring this concept into your analytics by keeping a set of simultaneous copies that you use to progress through three stages:

1. **Development**: Keep a copy of your analytics for improving and trying out new things.
2. **Test**: When ready, merge your improvements into this copy where the functionality stays the same, but it is repeatedly tested. The testing ensures it is working as intended. Keeping a separate copy for test allows development to continue on other functionality.
3. **Master**: This is the copy that goes into production. When you merge things from test to the master copy, it is the same as putting it into live use. Cloud providers often have a continuous delivery service that can make this process simpler.

For any software developer readers out there, this is a simplification of the **git flow** method, which is a little outside the scope of this book. If the author can drop a suggestion, it is worth some additional research to learn git flow and apply it to your analytics development in the cloud.

Leverage managed services

Cloud infrastructure providers, such as AWS and Microsoft Azure, offer services for things such as message queues, big data storage, and machine learning processing. The services handle the underlying resource needs such as server, storage provisioning, and also network requirements. You do not have to worry about how this happens under the hood, and it scales as big as you need it.

Cloud providers also manage global distribution of services to ensure low latency. The following image shows the AWS regional data center locations combined with underwater internet cabling:

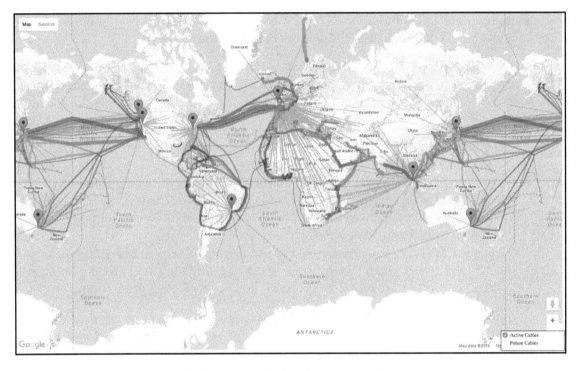

AWS regional data center locations and underwater internet cables.

Source: http://turnkeylinux.github.io/aws-datacenters/

This reduces the amount of things you have to worry about for analytics. It allows you to focus more on the business application and less on the technology. This is a good thing and you should take advantage of it.

An example of a managed service is Amazon **Simple Queue Service** (**SQS**). SQS is a message queue where the underlying server, storage, and compute needs are managed automatically by AWS systems. You only need to set it up and configure it, which takes just a few minutes.

Use Application Programming Interfaces (API)

APIs are a way for other processes, software, or services to access analytics code that you have created. It allows you to easily reuse your code in other applications. You can also allow your customers to directly access this functionality through web-based APIs.

An API builds on of encapsulation principle. It is a defined list of supported actions and information that another system can call and retrieve. The calling system does not need to know how the action is performed or the information created and retrieved. The complexity is hidden.

The API defines how to interact with an encapsulated set of analytic processes. It abstracts away the details. It also supports low friction change as the analytics processes can be improved without requiring other systems to alter what they are doing. As long as the API definition is held constant, the other systems will not know the difference.

APIs are a great way to create building blocks for more complex analytics. You can use multiple APIs to build rich, fully-functional analytic applications in a short period of time. It is also far easier to adapt to changing business conditions by reconfiguring the assembled applications to use a different mix of APIs.

A Web API uses the internet to handle the communication between systems. Cloud providers offer this as a managed service. It can help a great deal in handling security and scale. Using this service, you can quickly implement new analytics functionality securely and at scale. The API can be either public or private. Private is only accessible to your internal applications. Public opens it up to systems outside your company.

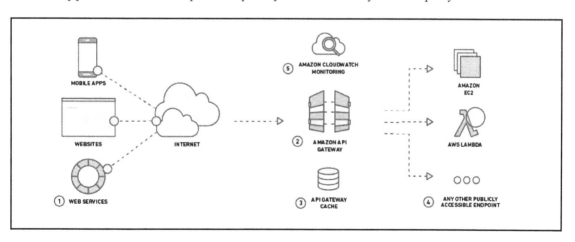

Example architecture using Web API gateway. Source: Amazon Web Services

Cloud providers can even handle usage tracking and billing if you decide to offer the functionality behind your API as a paid service to your customers.

Cloud security and analytics

You can build security into analytics using several methods supported by major cloud infrastructure providers.

Public/private keys

Cloud providers use asymmetric cryptography throughout their services. The public and private keys are generated. You keep the private key, so the service does not have a copy. The service holds the public key. Communication using public/private key is secure and has never been broken.

The cloud provider could publish the public key in tomorrow's newspaper and it would not matter; the encryption cannot be broken with just the public key. It may seem counterintuitive that a public key is used to encrypt data but cannot be used to decrypt it. But it works.

Every time you visit a website starting with HTTPS:, a public/private key encryption is being used. It is the basis of SSL and TLS encryption, which is employed for HTTPS communications.

You will use the public/private keys often for IoT analytics when you build secure processes. Think of it like a username and password for your analytics, but better. Cryptography is a fascinating subject (for some of us at least); read up on it for more details. Otherwise, take it on faith that it is all good - it is!

Public versus private subnets

When you set up a cloud environment for analytics, you are creating your own networking environment. You, or hopefully a skilled network guru, will need to define the networking structure. A basic component of this is the concept of subnets.

Subnets are logical subdivisions of the overall network in your cloud environment. You launch resources into a subnet where it will follow the internet addressing rules defining for the subnet. A public subnet has resources that can be addressable from the outside internet. This does not mean that all resources in the subnet can be found from the outside; you would need to assign a public IP address to it first.

A private subnet is not addressable from the outside internet. There are methods to allow internet communication through a gateway device, usually a **Network Address Translation (NAT)** device, but an outside object cannot initiate communication directly with something in a private subnet.

Most analytic processing should happen in a private subnet for security reasons, which adds some complexity in connecting with resources. This is why we are discussing it here. However, it is more than worth it to secure it from mischief. Know which of your subnets are private and make sure to spin up new resources there.

Access restrictions

Restrict access to your analytic resources to named users only. Avoid the trap of keeping a single user ID and password that everyone uses. For resources accessed by public/private keys, make sure to keep the private key in a safe, secure place.

For networking security, only allow network traffic through to your resources that are needed. Block all others. Lock everything down from the start and then open things up only when needed.

In a distributed computing environment, such as you will use for IoT analytics, networking is a key element in both security and problem solving. You will run into situations where your analytic jobs will not run correctly and find that the source was a network or security related setting. It is best to understand this and use best practices from the start of your analytics projects.

Securing customer data

Keep your IoT data secure, use access controls, and encrypt data files. IoT data can be used to infer things about your customers, so take special care with it. You are the guardian of their information. You could be unintentionally exposing your company to legal risk by not properly securing customer data.

Encryption can be enabled in two ways, in transit and at rest. In transit refers to network transmission such as SSL or TLS. Most cloud services require their use. Make sure all the network communication in support of your analytic processes is encrypted in transit.

Encryption at rest refers to data storage. This could be data files on a server or data inside a database. Cloud providers can encrypt your data and make it transparent to you if you are using public/private key pairs to secure it.

Use this when data could be accessed by a wide set of users, such as all employees of your company. If the data is only accessible by a few people due to tight access controls and it is in a private subnet, you can be a little less strict - it is unlikely to get out. In general, if encryption is seamless, use it. If your data is accessible through the public internet, definitely use it.

Cloud providers were born operating inside the public internet. Security is built in at every level. Take advantage of it and use public/private keys, private subnets, access control, and encryption to secure your valuable data.

The AWS overview

In the land of cloud infrastructure, AWS is the king. It was the first of its kind, launched in 2005, and is the largest by a wide margin. It is ranked number one in every segment of Gartner magic quadrants on cloud infrastructure providers.

As reported by Computerworld in 2016, it has ten times the compute capacity of its 14 closest rivals combined. Entire companies, such as Netflix and AirBnB, run their operations on it. As can be seen in the following chart, AWS has over 30% of the market share, with the next closest competitor at 9%.

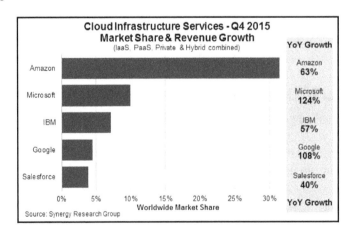

AWS offers a wide range of services from networking to compute to IoT. The following is a listing of the services from AWS management console. The management console is where you launch new services, monitor existing ones, and review billing:

AWS services list. Source: AWS management console

You can reduce these into three categories of services that you need to have configured properly to support your analytics: networking, compute, and storage.

Networking includes security and handles communication routing. Your services need to be able to talk to each other.

Compute handles processing, calculations, and running applications. This is where the fun stuff happens - your analytics will operate here.

Storage handles where you keep the input data and output results of your IoT analytics. This needs to match the requirements of your analytics.

Managed services preconfigure a combination of the three categories so that much of the detail is handled automatically for you. The launching and configuring of underlying services is abstracted away and is handled under the covers. This enables you to add functionality quickly while reducing overall complexity. The penalty is that you are locking yourself into the AWS ecosystem. But the benefit typically outweighs the cost. There is enormous analytical power at your fingertips.

AWS key concepts

Now, we will discuss some key concepts in the AWS cloud design. These include Regions, Availability Zones, subnets, and security groups.

Regions

Regions are the major division in AWS and correspond to general data center geographic location areas. Singapore, Tokyo, and US East are some example Regions. Your environment exists within a Region. Environments in one Region are unaware and unable to communicate with environments in other Regions without setting up special pathways (outside the scope of this book). You can easily extend your global presence by duplicating your environment into another Region.

Availability Zones

Within Regions, there are multiple Availability Zones (AZ). The number depends on the Region. These are physically separate locations but are closely linked to each other. Communication between Availability Zones is simple to configure. Your environment will likely cross multiple Availability Zones for availability reasons. If one AZ goes down, the other is unlikely to do so and the functionality can automatically be shifted.

Subnet

Subnets are divisions of your network, represented by IP ranges. Subnets are created within an Availability Zone. Resources are launched into a subnet and can talk to other resources in the same subnet. Communication outside subnets needs to be defined.

Security groups

These define what network traffic is allowed in and also out. They wrap around the compute (and some other) resources that you launch. One or more resources can belong to a group. Server instances, databases, and cluster nodes all require them. They block everything by default, so you must specify what traffic to allow. This is an important safety net. For example, even if you launch a new Linux server and make it totally open and vulnerable to the world (but do not do that) as long as the security group is locked down, no malicious traffic can get to it. Cloud environments are very much a *trust no-one* world.

AWS key core services

Now that we have covered some key concepts, we can hit the services of interest to IoT analytics. We will start with some core services.

Virtual Private Cloud (VPC)

A VPC is your own logically isolated part of the AWS cloud. This is where you create and configure your own network as you define it. Think of it as your self-contained environment where your analytics will exist. You have complete control here, you create and can configure your own IP address range, subnets, network gateways, and route tables. Although it was not originally the case, there is now no escaping VPCs. Even if you do not create a custom VPC, AWS will create one for you (called a default VPC). You are not limited to one VPC; you could have several of your own little analytical worlds to lord over.

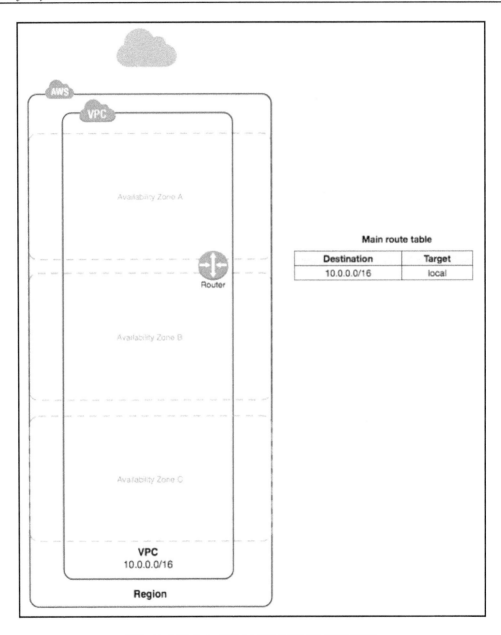

VPC and Availability Zone architecture example. Source: Amazon Web Services

Identity and Access Management (IAM)

This is where users are defined (IAM user), access key pairs created, and security roles defined (IAM role). IAM roles are a key concept, as they allow a simple and secure way for your instances and other AWS services to communicate. You will assign these on creation of a resource, and it will then natively have permissions to the services defined in the role. This happens without storing any access keys on the server instance. This means that even if the server is compromised, the villains will not have the keys to the kingdom.

Elastic Compute (EC2)

EC2 allows you to create virtual servers (called instances). You define the virtual hardware configuration (think CPU/RAM mix) and the amount of storage. Then, a few minutes later, it is up and running and ready for you to use. At the time of this writing, there are 55 different EC2 virtual hardware configuration options. Many operating systems are supported, including Windows and several versions of Linux. We will refer to a virtual server as an EC2 instance for the rest of this section.

M4

M4 instances are the latest generation of General Purpose Instances. This family provides a balance of compute, memory, and network resources, and it is a good choice for many applications.

Features:

- 2.3 GHz Intel Xeon® E5-2686 v4 (Broadwell) processors or 2.4 GHz Intel Xeon® E5-2676 v3 (Haswell) processors
- EBS-optimized by default at no additional cost
- Support for Enhanced Networking
- Balance of compute, memory, and network resources

Model	vCPU	Mem (GiB)	SSD Storage (GB)	Dedicated EBS Bandwidth (Mbps)
m4.large	2	8	EBS-only	450
m4.xlarge	4	16	EBS-only	750
m4.2xlarge	8	32	EBS-only	1,000
m4.4xlarge	16	64	EBS-only	2,000
m4.10xlarge	40	160	EBS-only	4,000
m4.16xlarge	64	256	EBS-only	10,000

AWS memory optimized EC2 instances. Source: Amazon Web Services

The EC2 instance is created from an **Amazon Machine Image** (**AMI**) and there are thousands of different types, when the community AMIs are included. Think of an AMI as an image of your hard drive after you get your favorite software and settings installed. With an EC2, you can effectively pause it, define a new hardware configuration, and restart it. Storage can also be dynamically added to it as needed. You can also stop the instance, pay only for storage, then restart it later when needed. This can save quite a bit of money using these for analytic jobs that run only periodically.

Simple Storage Service (S3)

S3 is an object-based storage service. It automatically handles scaling and redundancy. The multiple copies of files are made across multiple devices and locations automatically. Durability is extremely high at 99.999999999% over a given year. A single file can be from 0 bytes to 5 terabytes. Overage storage size is limited only by your bank account.

Objects are the base entity stored in Amazon S3, but you can think of it simply as a file that can be of (almost) any size or type. Everything is contained in what is called a **bucket**. Buckets are the highest level S3 namespace and are linked to the AWS account that owns it. S3 buckets are like internet domain names. Objects have a unique key value and are retrieved using a HTTP URL address.

Taken all together for analytics purposes, this means you can stuff tons of data there and not worry about backups, hard drive failures, or running out of space. It can be accessed easily using a URL-like format (assuming you have the correct security keys/permissions).

AWS key services for IoT analytics

There are far too many AWS services to cover in one section. We will cover the ones of interest for IoT analytics but know that there are many more with new services being added all the time (such as speech recognition and deep learning image recognition services).

Amazon Simple Queue Service (SQS)

This is the AWS managed message queue service. It handles the underlying compute and storage resources, you just need to create it. You pay only for the API calls to it for message processing.

Amazon Elastic Map Reduce (EMR)

EMR is a fully managed Hadoop framework that can be launched in minutes. It handles the tasks of node provisioning, cluster setup, configuration, and cluster tuning for you. It operates using EC2 instances and can scale from one node to thousands.

You can increase or decrease the number of instances manually or use auto scaling to do it dynamically, even while the cluster is running. The EMR service monitors your cluster; it can handle retries for failed tasks and will replace poor performing instances automatically.

Even though it is managed, you have complete control over the cluster, including root access. You can install additional applications. EMR has the option to choose from several Hadoop distributions and applications such as Apache Spark, Presto, and HBase.

Data storage can be linked to S3 using the **EMR File System** (**EMRFS**). You can store your data in Amazon S3 and use multiple EMR clusters to process the same dataset. This allows you to configure the cluster to the requirements for the task at hand without forcing a best compromise between all tasks. It aligns with the goal of separating compute and storage.

You can also programmatically create an EMR cluster, run a job, then automatically shut it down when complete. This makes it very useful for large-scale batch processing or analytical jobs.

AWS machine learning

This service has wizards and visualization tools that guide you through the process of creating machine learning models. You can deploy the trained models to make predictions on new data without having to set up a separate system. You pay as you go, there are no upfront costs. It is highly scalable and can handle billions of predictions in a day.

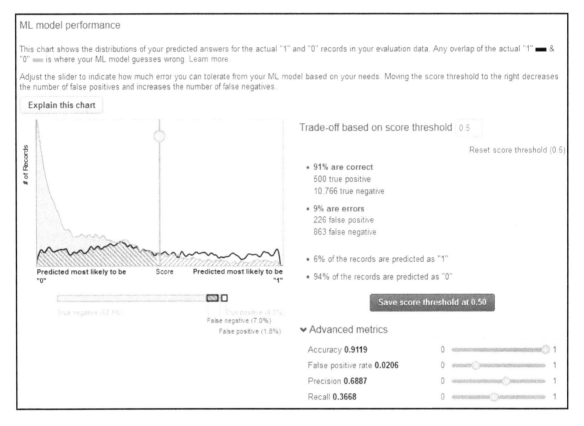

Amazon machine learning evaluation screenshot example. Source: Amazon Web Services

Amazon Relational Database Service (RDS)

RDS is a set of managed relational databases and includes database engines such as Oracle, Microsoft SQL Server, PostgreSQL, MySQL, and MariaDB. You have full control over the database but do not have any access to the underlying server it is hosted on. RDS handles this part and also provides monitoring on the health of the database management system. You can connect to and manage databases on RDS using the same tools that you would use on a non-RDS Oracle or SQL Server database, for example.

This is great for most standard relational database needs but can be limited for custom or complicated implementations. For analytics, this is rarely a problem.

Amazon Redshift

Redshift is a fully managed, SQL-compliant data warehouse service. You can store up to a petabyte in a Redshift cluster. It has its own JDBC and ODBC drivers but also supports standard PostgreSQL drivers. This means most **Business Intelligence** (**BI**) tools can connect directly to it. Redshift is useful for commonly queried data and is a common place to put processed and summarized IoT data for wider enterprise consumption.

Microsoft Azure overview

Microsoft offers a cloud infrastructure service called Azure that competes directly with AWS. It is generally ranked as number two in the industry in size and capabilities, although it has been closing that gap recently.

The range of services is similar to AWS but with a Microsoft flavor. Microsoft markets the services as easier to integrate with corporate on-premise networks. Integration leans more toward Microsoft technology, such as the Windows operating system, the .NET programming language, and the SQL Server database.

We will review some of the services of interest for IoT analytics.

Azure Data Lake Store

Azure Data Lake Store is compatible with **Hadoop Distributed File System** (**HDFS**), which we will be discussing in Chapter 4, *Creating an AWS Cloud Analytics Environment*. It also has a REST interface for applications that is WebHDFS-compatible.

Data stored in Data Lake Store can be analyzed using analytic frameworks within the Hadoop ecosystem, such as MapReduce and Hive. Microsoft Azure HDInsight clusters can be provisioned and configured to directly access data stored in Data Lake Store.

You can store a variety of data types for analytics and storage size is effectively unlimited. Individual files sizes can be from kilobytes to petabytes. Storage is durable as multiple copies are created and managed automatically.

Azure Analysis Services

Azure Analysis Services is built on Microsoft **SQL Server Analysis Services** (**SSAS**) and is compatible with SQL Server 2016 Analysis Services Enterprise Edition. It supports tabular models. Functionality includes DirectQuery, partitions, row-level security, bidirectional relationships, and translations.

You can use the same tools you use for SSAS to create data models for Azure Analysis Services. You can create and deploy tabular data models using **SQL Server Data Tools** (**SSDT**) or using some Azure templates in **SQL Server Management Studio** (**SSMS**). If you are a Microsoft shop, this will all feel familiar to you.

You can connect to data sources in the Azure cloud and also to on-premise data in your organization. Connecting to cloud data sources is fairly seamless as it is essentially in the same local network from the perspective of the cloud server. Connecting to on-premises data sources is supported by an on-premises data gateway, which enables secure connections to your Analysis Services server in the cloud.

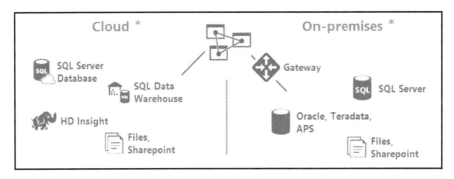

* Some data sources are not yet supported in preview as of Microsoft December 2016. Image source: Microsoft Azure

You can connect to data from Microsoft tools such as Power BI Desktop and Excel. You can also use connectors to link custom applications and some browser-based tools.

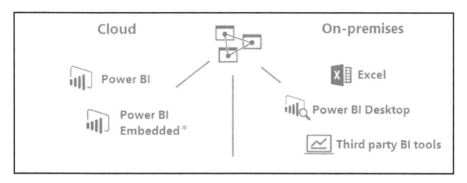

* Power BI Embedded is not yet supported in preview as of Microsoft December 2016. Image source: Microsoft Azure

HDInsight

Azure HDInsight uses the Hadoop components from the **Hortonworks Data Platform (HDP)** distribution. It deploys managed clusters in the cloud with a focus on high reliability and availability. Microsoft Active Directory is used for security and governance.

HDInsight includes the implementations of Hadoop ecosystem tools, such as Apache Spark, HBase, Kafka, Storm, Pig, Hive, Interactive Hive, Sqoop, Oozie, and Ambari. It also integrates with **Business Intelligence (BI)** tools, such as Power BI, Excel, SQL Server Analysis Services, and SQL Server Reporting Services.

Default storage for the HDFS used by HDInsight clusters can be either an Azure storage account or a Azure Data Lake store.

The R server option

In 2015, Microsoft bought a company called revolution analytics, which maintained a managed version of the open source R distribution. Since then, Microsoft has been integrating R into several of its software products and Azure has been no exception.

HDInsight includes an option to integrate an R Server into your HDInsight cluster when the cluster is created. This allows R scripts to use Hadoop to run distributed computations. Microsoft includes a big data analytics R package called ScaleR.

You can connect to your cluster and run R scripts on an edge node. You have the option of running parallelized distributed functions across the cores of the edge node server using ScaleR. You can also run them across the nodes of the cluster by using the ScaleR Hadoop MapReduce or Spark compute contexts.

The ThingWorx overview

The company PTC, which has a long history in creating software for the world of machines talking to machines, developed ThingWorx. It is an application development environment for building IoT solutions. It is a software platform that abstracts IoT devices and related components and services into model-based development objects. You install the software on your own hardware (or using cloud providers virtual instances).

The platform makes it easy to model your devices, the data, and has the ability to quickly create dashboards through a web-based application. No code is required. ThingWorx is also extensible to third-party components through its marketplace. This makes it easy to add in a third-party functionality without special configuration. It can also integrate with both AWS and Azure IoT hub services.

There are multiple components of ThingWorx. ThingWorx Foundation is the center of the platform. It is divided into three areas, as shown in the following image:

- ThingWorx Core
- ThingWorx Connection Services
- ThingWorx Edge

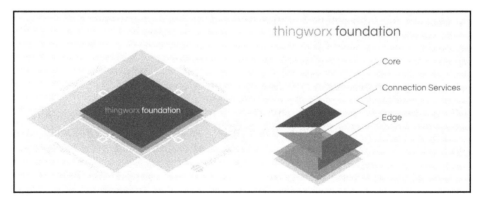

ThingWorx Foundation. Source: thingworx.com

ThingWorx Core

ThingWorx Core is a software platform environment that allows you to design, run, and implement analytics for IoT applications that control and report data from remote devices. These devices could be sensors, consumer electronics, or industrial equipment.

ThingWorx uses a representational object-based design. This means that you create software objects to represent your IoT devices and other assets. The representation includes relevant properties and related data items.

You then use the objects to create applications, which can monitor and manage your IoT devices. You can create dashboards, implement response logic, and integrate third-party applications.

The ThingWorx Core is the hub of your ThingWorx environment. You logically define behavior and relationships between IoT devices or remote assets that are set up in your environment. Once the actual devices have been modeled in the software, they can register and communicate with the Core. You can then collect data and manage the physical devices.

ThingWorx Core includes two main tools for you to create IoT solutions:

- **ThingWorx Composer**: This is a modeling environment where you set up the remote assets, business logic, data storage, and security.
- **ThingWorx Mashup Builder**: This is a drag and drop tool where you can quickly create dashboards and mobile interfaces without needing to write code. This is where you can do things like show a location on a map and chart sensor value trends.

ThingWorx Connection Services

ThingWorx Connection Services handle communication and connectivity between the Core and remote assets. Components can handle connectivity over different protocols and with different device clouds. They handle message routing to and from the remote devices and also message translation when required.

Connection Services have connection adapters to link up devices that are using AWS IoT SDK or Azure IoT SDK. They link into the cloud providers and allow you to translate the data into ThingWorx.

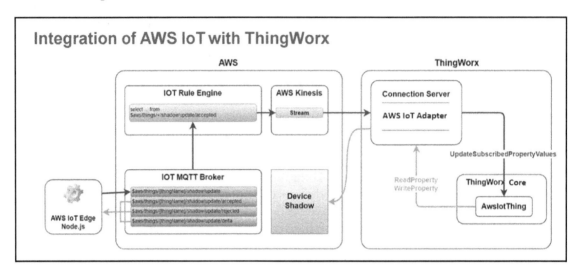

The Connector Services components have a core connection server and also an adapter. ThingWorx documentation refers to these two combined as a **Connector**. They are both packaged and installed together.

Each Connector supports a specific protocol where inbound messages are translated into ThingWorx format and sent on to the Core. The reverse occurs for outbound messages from the Core to the remote device.

ThingWorx Edge

The third component of ThingWorx Foundation consists of a couple of software products that operate out in the edge of the IoT network. The first one operates as a small server and hub for communication back to the Core component at a centralized system. It is called **ThingWorx Websocket-Based Edge MicroServer** (**WS EMS**). The second is a **Software Development Kit** (**SDK**) that your developer would install on your IoT device as part of your device software. It is called ThingWorx Edge SDK.

WS EMS is a standalone application that is installed on a remote device. It uses a ThingWorx protocol called AlwaysOn to communicate with the ThingWorx Core. The WS EMS supports several operating systems and has a small footprint. It can work with a large number of devices to provide a way to establish communication between an edge device and the ThingWorx Core.

Depending on what language your developers are using for your IoT device code, there are several versions of **ThingWorx Edge SDKs** that allow you to add connectivity to your device. There are SDKs that support C, .NET (C#), and Java languages, along with the ones for the Android and iOS platforms.

The SDK is embedded within the IoT device: one instance of it for each device. All the SDKs have common interfaces and provide secure communication channel to the Core.

ThingWorx concepts

We will discuss the main objects and concepts used on the ThingWorx core to model your environment to get a good feel for how it works.

Thing templates

A **thing template** sets up and defines the base functionality that you build multiple things from. This defines a general category with a common set of properties, services, events, and subscriptions. These will be included in any thing definition that is based upon the template. The thing will *inherit* from the thing template.

Things

A **thing** is used to represent an object. It is based on a thing template but will often include additional properties, services, or events unique to the implementation of the more generic base thing, which was defined in the template.

There are several types of thing:

- **Things**: This represents a real-world asset, device, or system.
- **Remote thing**: A remote thing is a special type of thing that represents an asset in a remote location. When using a ThingWorx Edge SDK, the edge devices where your application is running needs to be created in ThingWorx Composer using the RemoteThing template.
- **Custom things**: Extensions provide custom thing templates that you can use to create the custom things to represent your devices.

Properties

A property is a variable that represents a behavior of a thing.

Properties have either of the following:

- **Remote bindings**: Remote bindings support egress. They can be written to the edge device when it connects to ThingWorx. The edge device must know of any Properties with Remote bindings.
- **Non-remote bindings**: These are not sent to the edge device when written and are not read from the edge device when a value is requested.

Services

A service represents a function that a thing can perform. It can be defined as part of a thing, a thing template, or a thing shape.

Events

An event is triggered from a change in the state or value of a property. It sends data to an object that subscribes to it.

Thing shapes

A thing shape is an abstraction of concrete things. Typically, the thing shape is used by a thing template, which itself is used for thing definitions.

Data shapes

Data shapes define the structure of tables in ThingWorx, which represent informational data structures or the output of ThingWorx services. They are composed of field definitions.

Some types of data shapes are here:

- **Data table structures**: These are storage tables that have a primary key that can support indexing
- **Stream structures**: These can access data continuously
- **Value stream structures**: Data stored from a property bound to a thing
- **Event data**: This stores data linked to events

Entities

Entities is the general term in ThingWorx for all the types of objects that you can create. They include things, thing templates, thing shapes, and data shapes. You can also import entities into ThingWorx.

Summary

In this chapter, we reviewed what is meant by elastic analytics and learned the advantages of using cloud infrastructure for IoT analytics. Designing for scale was discussed along with distributed computing.

The two main cloud providers were introduced, AWS and Microsoft Azure. We also reviewed a purpose-built software platform, ThingWorx, made for IoT devices, communications, and analysis.

4
Creating an AWS Cloud Analytics Environment

This chapter is a step-by-step walk-through of creating an AWS cloud environment. The environment is specifically geared toward analytics and uses AWS best practices. Along with screenshots and instructions on setting things up, there will be explanations of what is being done and why. This walk-through will incur AWS usage charges. Make sure to delete all the resources after the walk-through if you do not intend on keeping the environment running as the total cost could be over $130 USD for a full month. Starting and stopping the EC2 instances as needed can reduce the cost somewhat.

This chapter will cover the following topics:

- AWS CloudFormation
- Setting a best practice virtual private cloud setup:
  - NAT gateway
  - Bastion hosts
- How to terminate and clean up the environment

The AWS CloudFormation overview

AWS CloudFormation is, putting it simply, an infrastructure as code. It is an AWS service, you do not need to install any additional software. This allows developers and system administrators to design and implement the entire network and server configurations directly from a code template file. CloudFormation handles the ordering and creation of the resources automatically when the template is implemented. When a template is launched to create resources, it is called a stack.

Think of a stack like architectural blueprints. The architect (you) hands the blueprints over to the contractor (AWS) to build it as per your specifications. The contractor knows how to order the construction jobs and what materials are needed.

You can create your own templates, use publicly available ones (such as on GitHub), or use AWS quick start templates. CloudFormation also has a visual designer to help lay out your planned infrastructure. Templates are saved as text files in either the JSON or YAML format. The following image shows an example of the CloudFormation designer. The designer is accessible through your browser:

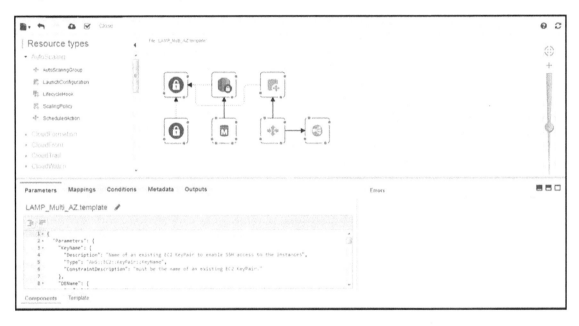

AWS CloudFormation designer. Source: AWS

You could create your own big data IoT analytics playground infrastructure as a stack, and then email the template file to your buddy on the other side of the world where he could replicate it in his own environment in minutes. You can also (and should) keep the template files in source control systems such as git in the event that you need to revert backward or recreate your infrastructure from scratch.

We will use one of the AWS quick start templates to create a secure environment to get started with IoT analytics. The quick start template incorporates AWS best practices into the design. You will have your own mini-data center up and running in a matter of minutes. The template we will be using was designed for high availability and will have room to grow if you decide to expand your use.

Your author recommends that you bring in a consulting company that specializes in creating cloud environments, if you are setting up an environment for your company to use in standard operations. This is to ensure the underlying security and the architecture is set up correctly. It is far easier to have it configured properly from the start than to try to correct it later on.

For experimentation and general analytic use, however, the environment we will create in the walk-through will work fine. It has several security and connectivity best practices in place.

The AWS Virtual Private Cloud (VPC) setup walk-through

The walk-through assumes you already have the following set up:

- **AWS account**: If you do not have an account, visit the AWS console page and follow the instructions to set up an account. The instructions are available at `https://aws.amazon.com/free/`.
- **Root accounts with Multi-Factor Authorization (MFA) active**: This is essential for security purposes. If you have not turned on MFA, do it right away. Download an app on your phone such as Google Authenticator and set up MFA on your account. The instructions are available at `https://aws.amazon.com/iam/details/mfa/`.
- **IAM users with administrative rights and MFA active**: Set up an IAM user for yourself with administrator rights to use for day-to-day operations. For security purposes, avoid using the root to log in. Also set up MFA for the IAM user.

- **Follow all other recommended steps on the IAM welcome screen to secure your account**: Your security status on the page should be all green checkmarks and look like the following screenshot:

Now, we will begin the initial steps for the walk-through:

1. Start the walk-through by logging into the AWS management console using your IAM user ID. If the login screen asks for an email address, you are at the root user login and not the IAM user login. You will need to go to the IAM user login screen. If you are having trouble getting to the page, the trick is to type in the URL in this format `https://[AccountName].signin.aws.amazon.com/console`, where you replace `[AccountName]` with your own account name. This link can also be found on the IAM start page after you log in.

2. Make sure the AWS region is set to the one where you want to create the environment. It is best to set it to the region closest to your geographic location for most use cases. You can check the region by looking in the upper right of the management console. If necessary, you can change it by the clicking the little arrow to the right of the name:

Creating a key pair for the NAT and bastion instances

You will need to create a public/private key pair to use later on in the quick start setup. The key pair will be saved as a file that you should keep in a secure place where only people that need it can access it:

1. Go to **Services** in the AWS management console at the top of the screen:

Services location on console

2. Then, click on **EC2** in the **Compute** section:

EC2 location

3. From the **EC2 Dashboard**, click on **Key Pairs**:

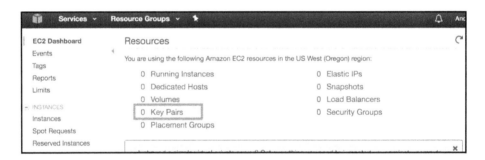

4. Click on the **Create Key Pair** button:

5. Give it a name such as `vpc_keypair` and click on **Create**. Avoid using capital letters, spaces, or non-standard characters in the name. This will make it more portable to different operating systems and file storage systems.

6. After clicking on the create button, you will get a download of the key pair file with the `.pem` extension (that is `vpc_keypair.pem`). Make sure you know where the file is saved. Now is a good time to move it to the secure location where you want to keep it. The console screen will update it, and you will see your new key pair listed:

Creating an S3 bucket to store data

You will need to create an S3 bucket to store data files. S3 bucket names need to be globally unique; no other bucket by any AWS user can have the same name. You may need to do a little trial and error to get an acceptable name:

1. Navigate to the S3 dashboard by clicking on **Services** and then **S3** (in the **Storage** section):

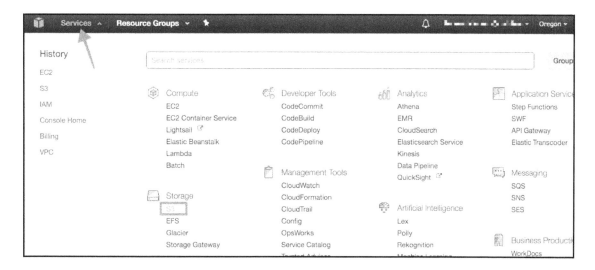

2. Click on the **Create Bucket** button in the upper-left corner of the screen:

3. Name your bucket something unlikely to already exist. Avoid uppercase letters or spaces. You can use a hyphen (-) to separate words but not an underscore (_). Choose the same region that you have been using so far in the walk-through. S3 buckets are globally accessible, but it is best practice to keep the data in the same region as the analytic work. Network performance will be better as well:

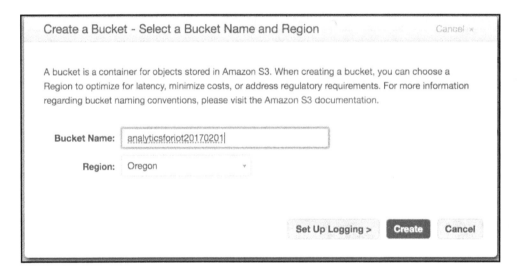

4. You should now see the new bucket in the list on your S3 dashboard:

Creating a VPC for IoT Analytics

Now, we will get into the fun part by creating a fully-fledged, highly available cloud environment. You will have a secure functioning data center at your fingertips in about 20 minutes. We will leverage CloudFormation and a quick start template to create a VPC that has some key elements:

- **Public subnets**: Resources in this subnet can be discoverable over the public internet if configured with a public IP, an attached internet gateway, and appropriate route tables. You would only want to put things such as web servers or NAT instances here.
- **Private subnets**: Resources in these subnets are hidden from public view. Anything outside your VPC cannot find what you put here even if it has a public IP address. For security reasons; put things such as Hadoop clusters, databases, and EC2 instances created for analytics processing purposes here.
- **NAT gateways**: **Network Address Translation** (**NAT**) gateways serve as an intermediary between resources in private subnets and the public internet.
- **Bastion hosts**: These are necessary to allow you to connect to your EC2 instances and Hadoop clusters in the private subnets.

What is a NAT gateway?

NAT gateways hide information about your resources while still allowing communication with the outside internet. They work by translating a private IP address into a different public IP address and remembering the translation and connection state when your internal resources request outside communication. Anything in the public internet is blocked from doing the reverse and never knows the real IP address of the resource in the private subnet.

In AWS, a NAT gateway is a managed service that automatically scales to meet internet traffic requirements. Some AWS regions and **Availability Zone** (**AZ**) do not support a NAT gateway and a NAT instance must be used. A NAT instance is an EC2 instance with software to handle NAT activities. You will need to manage and monitor a NAT instance, but it maybe a cheaper option for you when the internet traffic is low even if a NAT gateway is available in your region. We will use quick start to create the environment that automatically checks for a NAT gateway support and creates a NAT instance if it is not available.

What is a bastion host?

Bastion hosts are EC2 instances located in a public subnet on your VPC. They are accessed using SSH (if you're using Linux OS) from outside your VPC (that is, your laptop). Once you are connected remotely, it then can function as a jump server. This allows you to use SSH to connect from the bastion server to an EC2 instance or other resource in your private subnets.

A bastion host gives you a secure route to connect to your private subnet resources. A VPC is a walled garden; you have to create a path to access the delights inside. Bastion hosts provide a secure way to do this. Hosts should only allow SSH traffic and only from source locations that you trust. They are secured through the use of security groups and network ACLs.

Your VPC architecture

The following diagram shows the network structure of the VPC we will be creating through the AWS quick start template. There are two sets of public subnets, private subnets, NATs, and bastion hosts. Each set is located in a different AZ. This provides high availability. In the event that one AZ is down, you can still get work done using the other one.

The quick start will create and configure route tables and security groups for you. It will create and attach an internet gateway that allows traffic to the public internet. The following image shows the architecture for the VPC:

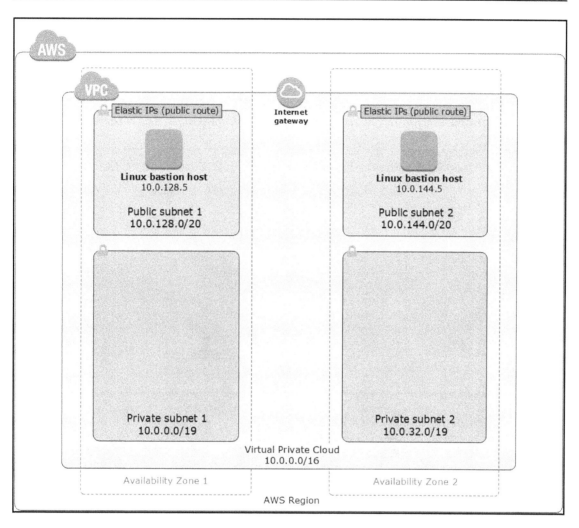

VPC architecture diagram. Source: AWS

There will also be a NAT gateway in each public subnet (although not shown in the previous diagram). The IP address range defined for the VPC allows plenty of room to grow for your future analytics projects. Each EC2 instance, database, or node in a Hadoop cluster will reserve an IP address number. The range of available IP addresses is therefore a constraint on the number of resources you can have in your VPC. The VPC we will create has over 65,000 available IP addresses.

The VPC Creation walk-through

The following walk-through shows you how to create the VPC discussed in the previous section:

1. Click on **Services** in the upper-left corner of the console page and then **CloudFormation** in the services list (in the **Management Tools** section):

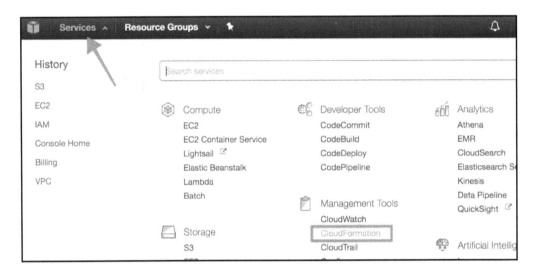

2. Click on the **Create Stack** button:

3. Under the **Choose a template** section, click on the radio button for **Specify an Amazon S3 template URL**. Then type or copy and paste the following: `https://s3.amazonaws.com/quickstart-reference/linux/bastion/latest/templates/linux-bastion-master.template`:

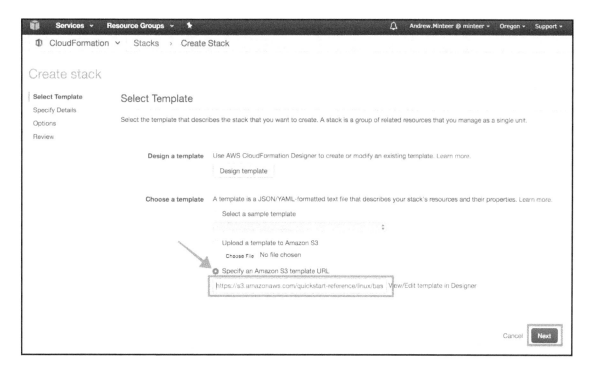

4. Click on **Next**.
5. The **Specify Details** section will come up. Give the stack you are creating a name, but do not use spaces or special characters except for hyphens (-):

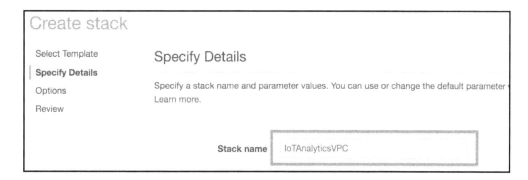

6. In the **Parameters** section on the same page, click on the text box for **Availability Zones**. A drop-down box will appear listing the available AZs in your region:

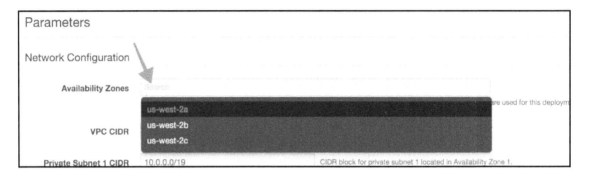

7. Click on one AZ in the list, and then choose one more by clicking on it as well. You will see both in the AZ text box, and it should look like the following, except with the AZ locations you selected:

8. Continuing down the page, use the default settings for the CIDR blocks for the public and private subnets; no need to change anything here.

9. In the **Allowed Bastion External Access CIDR** text box, type in the CIDR block that represents the IP range of your corporate network or geographic area. This defines the source locations that are allowed to even attempt to communicate with the bastion hosts. A **Classless Inter-Domain Routing** (**CIDR**) block is a notation that defines a range of IP addresses. If you are not sure what to use, consult your company's networking guru. This should only be the range from where users would acceptably be logging in from. Keep it as small and realistic as possible. A CIDR block of **0.0.0.0/0** will work but opens up traffic to everyone and everywhere. It is absolutely not recommended for a bastion.

The CIDR block highlighted is an example; you would type in a different one:

VPC CIDR	10.0.0.0/16	CIDR Block for the VPC
Private Subnet 1 CIDR	10.0.0.0/19	CIDR block for private subnet 1 located in Availability Zone 1.
Private Subnet 2 CIDR	10.0.32.0/19	CIDR block for private subnet 2 located in Availability Zone 2.
Public Subnet 1 CIDR	10.0.128.0/20	CIDR Block for the public DMZ subnet 1 located in Availability Zone 1
Public Subnet 2 CIDR	10.0.144.0/20	CIDR Block for the public DMZ subnet 2 located in Availability Zone 2
Allowed Bastion External Access CIDR	8.8.4.4/32	Allowed CIDR block for external SSH access to the bastions

10. In the **Amazon EC2 Configuration** section, click on the **Key Pair Name** text box. A drop-down box will appear. Click on the **Key Pair** you created earlier. Use the defaults already filled in for you for the other options in the section:

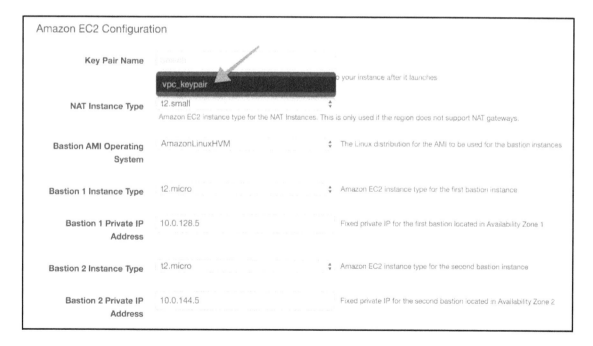

11. In the **Linux Bastion Configuration** section on the same page, change the banner option to **true**. This is useful to give your bastion login screen a different look so you can distinguish it from other Linux SSH sessions:

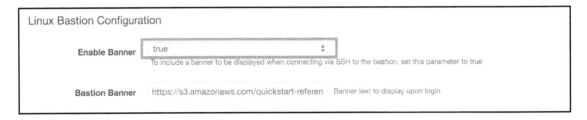

12. Use the defaults in the **AWS Quick Start Configuration** section, and click on the **Next** button to go to the **Options** screen:

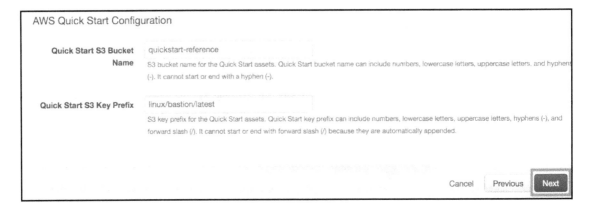

13. In the **Options** screen, you can add tags to your stack. Tags are key/value pairs that are stored as part of your stack information. They can be anything that you want and are useful for tracking things such as who created what resources and why. It is recommended that you at least create a key/value tag for a name and for the individual creating the stack. To create a tag, you click on the text box under **Key**. The Key text string should be consistent across resources (that is, always use Name with the exact same spelling whether you are creating the EC2 instance or a Hadoop cluster). Click on the text box under **Value** to complete the tag. Click on the + button to add an additional tag. When finished, click on the **Next** button to review your selections:

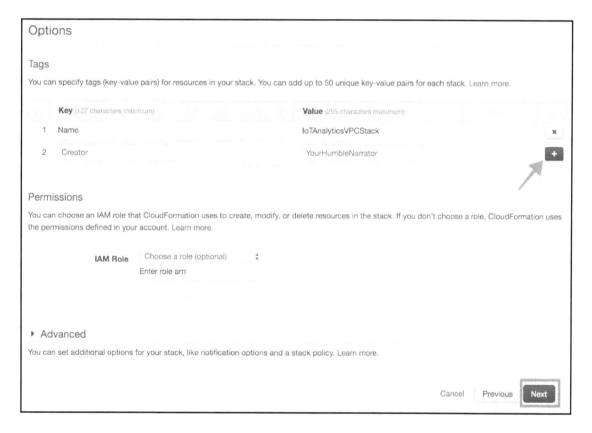

14. On the **Review** screen, scroll down to double-check the settings for the stack. At the bottom of the **Capabilities** section, check the acknowledgement box, and then click on the **Create** button to begin creating your stack:

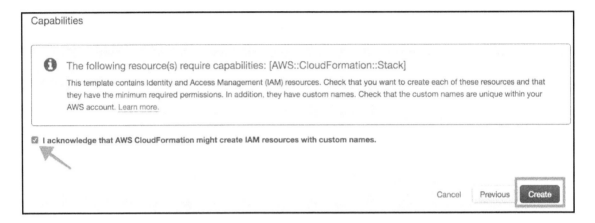

15. You will be sent back to the CloudFormation stack list screen. You will notice your stack is now in the list with the status of **CREATE_IN_PROGRESS**. The quick start template calls other stacks to create portions of the VPC. You will see additional stacks added to the list as the creation process progresses:

16. When the stack creating process is finished, the status for each stack (there will be three in total) will change to **CREATE_COMPLETE**. You can go to **Services** and VPC to check on the networking resources in your new environment:

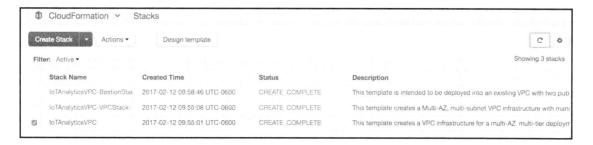

17. Go to **Services** and **EC2** to go to the **EC2 Dashboard** to check on your Linux bastion instances. They will need to finish spinning up and the status checks before you can connect to them.

18. To check on the bastion hosts, on **EC2 Dashboard**, click on **Running Instances** to view the EC2 list:

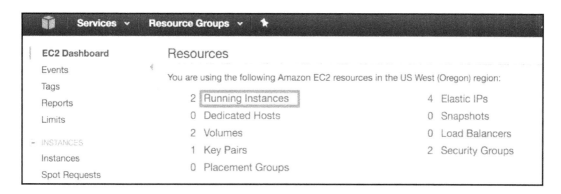

19. When both the Linux bastion hosts have an **Instance State** as running and the **Status Checks** are passed, they are ready. This will only take a few minutes:

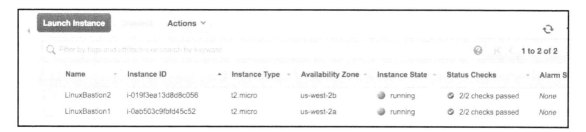

20. Connect to one of the bastion instances to verify that the setup worked correctly. You can do this by clicking the box to the left of the name of the instance to select it. Then, click on the **Connect** button at the top of the list. Follow the instructions that come up to establish the connection. If you are using a Windows computer, you will need to download and install PuTTY or similar terminal software in order to make the SSH connection. There is a link in step 1 in the instruction window that gives directions on how to do this:

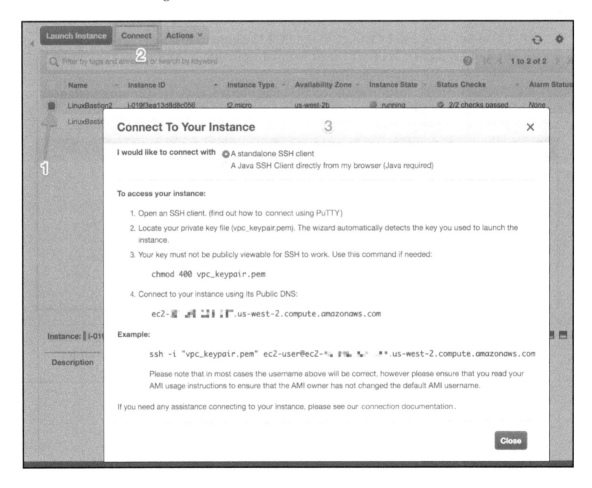

How to terminate and clean up the environment

If you do not intend on keeping the VPC environment or would like to reduce costs by eliminating it and recreating it later, follow these simple steps:

1. Go to **Services**, then CloudFormation to return to the CloudFormation stack list.
2. Delete the stacks one at a time, starting with the stack that has **BastionStack** in the name. To do this, click on the square to the left of the name to select the stack:

3. Click the **Actions** button, then select **Delete Stack**:

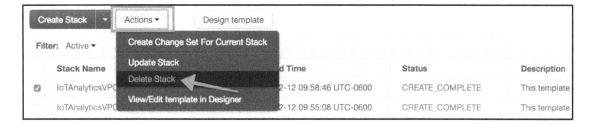

4. Confirm the delete by clicking on the **Yes, Delete** button. This will delete the bastion instances and the associated security groups:

5. The status of the stack will change to **DELETE_IN_PROGRESS**. When the deletion is complete, the stack will be removed from the list. You can click on the **refresh** button (circular arrow) in the upper-right corner after a few minutes if you do not see a change:

6. Repeat steps 2 through 5 for the stack with **VPCStack** in the name, then finally the remaining stacks with the name you gave them when creating them (**IOTAnalyticsVPC** for this walk-through).

7. The NAT gateways and the bastion hosts are the larger cost items in the environment. Verify that the NAT gateways have been deleted by going to **Services**, then **VPC**. The NAT gateway count may not be zero on the dashboard and can still show a count of two for several hours before being removed from the list. Click on **NAT Gateways** in the dashboard to go to the list of gateways:

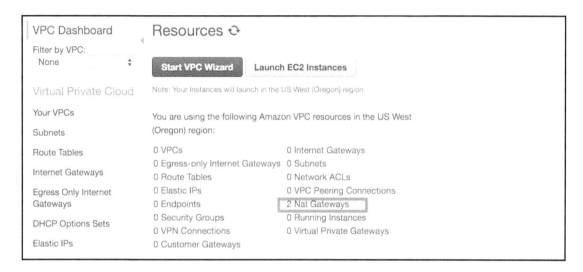

8. You should see both with a status of **Deleted**:

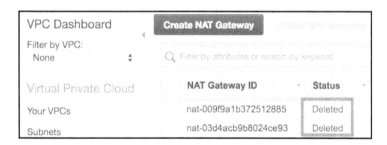

9. Verify that the bastion hosts have been deleted by going to **Services**, then **EC2**. The **EC2 Dashboard** should have a count of **0 Running Instances**. You can click on the **Running Instances** link to go to the **EC2** list. The Linux bastion instances should either have a status of terminated or not be listed at all. If you are checking shortly after deleting the stacks, the instances will most likely still be visible in the list. As long as the status is terminated, you will not be charged:

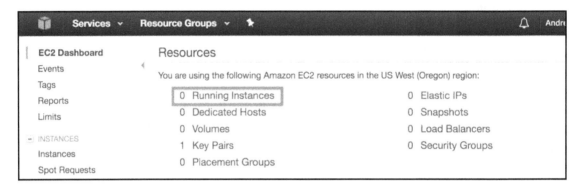

10. When recreating the environment, you will not need to recreate the key pair or the S3 bucket. Since the key pair and the S3 bucket were not part of the CloudFormation stack, it will remain in your environment after all the stacks are deleted. There is no charge for these unless you have data in the S3 bucket; even then, the costs are very low.

Summary

In this chapter, we created a secure virtual private cloud in less than half an hour that is ready to support IoT analytics. We also reviewed how to delete and clean up the environment when no longer needed. We discussed AWS CloudFormation, NAT gateways, and Linux bastion hosts. You now have a secure and flexible place to launch large-scale analytics, which we will do later on in this book.

5

Collecting All That Data - Strategies and Techniques

You stare at your drawing of the IoT device hanging on the wall of your cubicle, lost in thought on the ways you might manipulate the data to squeeze out game changing insights. You can almost hear your colleagues cheer as you accept the Executive Award for best project of the year and the huge bonus that goes with it.

"Ahem!" someone coughs behind you. You almost jump out of your chair.

Your boss has sidled up to your cubicle. He looks both cheerful and amused. You are a little concerned at the amused part.

"You did an excellent job selling them on using the cloud for analytics, and they are fully on board and want to start immediately," he says with a big grin. You perk up, as this is great news.

"You did so well," he continues with a smirk, "that they want to double the data capture rate on the next generation of devices. They figure the cost will not change much if it is routed through cloud infrastructure. And since capacity restraints won't be an issue anymore, they want the monthly reports on a weekly schedule now. And several of the executives in other departments were very excited and want their own people to be able to use the data as well. Good work!"

He walks off chuckling to himself. You are, at the same time, happy at the outcome and bewildered about how to deliver on their expectations. How do you store the data in a way others can interact with it? And you are certain there will be a much broader set of questions that will need to be answered now, especially when other departments have people looking at the data as well. Whatever you do has to be able to handle huge scale with lots of flexibility.

This chapter is about strategies to collect IoT data in order to enable analytics. There are many options to store IoT data for analytics. We will review a common technology in the field, Hadoop, along with how to use Amazon S3 as a big data store. The chapter also describes when and why to use Spark for data processing. We will discuss tradeoffs between streaming and batch processing. Building flexibility into data processing in order to allow integration of future analytics will also be reviewed.

The chapter covers the following topics:

- Designing data processing for analytics
- Applying big data technology to storage
- Apache Spark for data processing
- Handling change

Designing data processing for analytics

There are some key cloud services that are likely to be employed in your IoT data processing environment. Both AWS and Microsoft Azure have IoT-specific services that we will review. There are also services that support data processing and transformation that are worth a review to increase your familiarity with them.

Amazon Kinesis

Amazon Kinesis is a set of services for loading and analyzing streaming data. It handles all the underlying compute, storage, and messaging services for you.

The services in the Kinesis family are as follows:

- **Amazon Kinesis Firehose**: This enables loading of massive volumes of streaming data into AWS.
- **Amazon Kinesis Streams**: This service allows you to create custom applications to process and analyze streaming data in real time. There are two ends to each stream; you use the Amazon **Kinesis Producer Library** (**KPL**) to build the application that sends data into the stream. The Amazon **Kinesis Client Library** (**KCL**) is used in the application that reads data from the stream - typically a real-time dashboard or rules engine-type application. Stream data can also be directed into other AWS services, such as S3 or SQS.

- **Amazon Kinesis Analytics**: This allows you to easily analyze stream data with standard SQL. Queries can run continuously, and AWS handles the scaling needed to run them automatically.

AWS Lambda

Lambda allows you to run code without provisioning servers. Python, Node.js, C#, and Java programming languages are all currently supported. Scale is handled automatically. You only pay when your code executes. Everything runs in parallel and your code needs to either be stateless or manage state in an external database. The code is essentially event-driven since you configure when and under what conditions it executes.

Using a service such as Lambda is often referred to as **serverless computing** and opens up a whole new range of possibilities. You could create a fully-functional web application with Lambda that has no server behind it. You can create analytic code that scales to millions of device events without ever having to worry about managing a server. The following diagram gives an overview of how it works in practice:

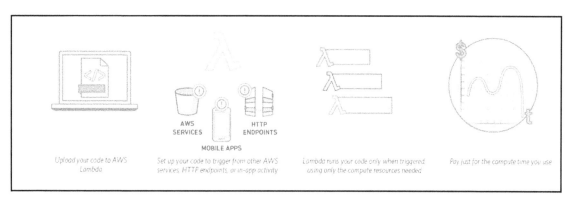

Overview on how Lambda works. Source: AWS

AWS Athena

Athena is a new service launched in late 2016 and operates over the data stored in S3. It allows you to query datasets using ANSI SQL. No data needs to be loaded into Athena; it queries directly against the raw files in it. This allows you to analyze large amounts of data without any **Extract, Transform, and Load** (ETL) to load it into a data analysis system. There are no clusters or data warehouses to manage. You pay for the amount of data scanned, which means you can compress it to lower costs.

Combine this with Lambda and you could have yourself a fairly decent low-cost big data solution. Store raw IoT files in S3 and schedule a Lambda job to periodically transform new data into an analysis-ready dataset - also in S3. Use SQL in Athena to analyze. You can do all this without worrying about servers, clusters, scaling, or managing complicated ETL.

The AWS IoT platform

The AWS IoT platform handles data messaging and security for communications between connected IoT devices and your AWS environment. It can support billions of devices and trillions of messages.

MQTT, HTTP, and WebSockets protocols are also supported. It provides authentication and encryption services for communications. All AWS services can be used to process, analyze, and make decisions on IoT data. The communication can be both ways.

Device shadows are used to store the latest state information on each IoT device. This makes it appear to applications that the device is always available, so commands can be given and values read without waiting for the device to be connected. The device shadow will sync with the IoT device when the device connects.

The AWS IoT device SDK is installed on the remote IoT device to handle communications. Registration and authentication services are handled in the AWS IoT platform. A rules engine can direct messages to other AWS services, such as Lambda, when certain conditions are met (such as [device temperature < 0 degrees Celsius]).

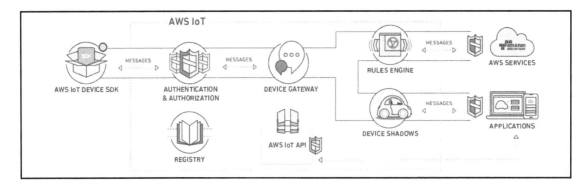

Basic overview of AWS IoT platform. Source: Amazon Web Services

AWS Greengrass is a new product in the IoT family, which was in the preview stage at the time of writing. It allows simplified edge analytics. This makes it exciting for the IoT analytic possibilities. It is software that is installed locally on a device or a nearby device hub. It can automatically handle buffering event data when the device is not connected. It also, and this is the exciting part, supports the same Lambda functions as the AWS cloud. You can build and test the functions in your AWS environment and then move them with minimal effort to operate at the edge using Greengrass.

Microsoft Azure IoT Hub

Azure IoT Hub is a managed service for bidirectional communications between the Azure backend and IoT devices. Millions of devices can operate on the IoT Hub; the service can scale as needed. Communications can be one-way messaging, file transfer, and request-reply methods. It integrates with other Azure services.

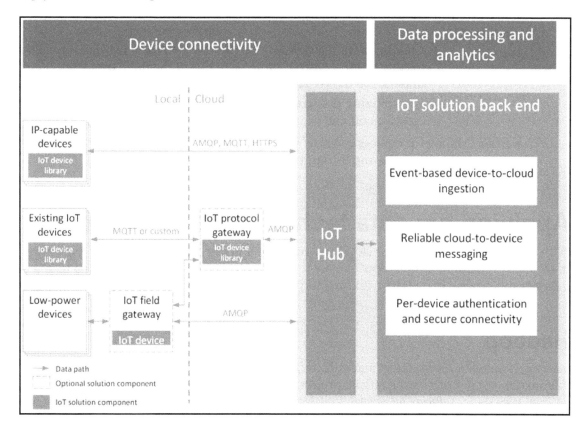

Example Azure IoT Hub solution architecture. Image source: Microsoft Azure

Azure IoT Hub has some key features, which give some insight into how it works:

- **Authentication and connectivity security**: Each device is provisioned with its own security key that allows it to connect to IoT Hub. Identities and keys are stored in the IoT Hub identity registry.
- **Device twins**: These are JSON documents that store state information such as configuration and parameter values. It is stored in the cloud and persists for each device connected to the IoT Hub. A twin allows you to store, synchronize, and query device data even if the device is offline.
- **Connectivity monitoring**: Here, you can receive detailed logs on identity management and connectivity events for your devices.
- **The IoT protocols support**: MQTT, HTTP, and AMQP protocols are supported by Azure IoT device SDKs that you would install on your IoT device. They are also supported through an exposed public protocol in the event you cannot use the SDK on your device.
- **IoT protocol extensibility**: You can support custom protocols by either of the following:
    - **Creating a field gateway**: You can use the Azure IoT gateway SDK to convert your custom protocol to one of the three protocols understood by IoT Hub.
    - **Customizing the Azure IoT protocol gateway**: This runs in the Azure cloud and is an open source component.
- **Scale**: Millions of devices can be connected at the same time with millions of events per second flowing through the hub.

Applying big data technology to storage

With IoT data flooding into your cloud environment and after processing and transforming it, the next problem to solve is how to store it. The solution should support holding large datasets and be easy to interact with for analytics.

Hadoop

Hadoop is an open source effort that falls under the umbrella of the Apache Software Foundation. As defined by the official project documentation, *The Apache Hadoop project develops open source software for reliable, scalable, distributed computing*. Hadoop is available for free in its pure open source form.

Unless you have some Hadoop experts on your team, you should opt for one of the managed Hadoop distributions. This will give you a level of troubleshooting support and implementation advice. Cloudera and Hortonworks are two main providers of managed distributions and support. Amazon AWS and Microsoft Azure both have their own Hadoop managed services, EMR and HDInsights respectively.

Hadoop is a little difficult to describe at first blush. It is commonly referred to in most media articles as if it was a new data warehouse program that you simply install and go forth to tossing in tons and tons of data. This is an oversimplified view as it is much more of an ecosystem of related projects than any one thing.

Some components rely on other components and some can operate independently. Some have the role of data storage, some of data processing, and some of resource management. Some are even debatable whether they belong in the Hadoop category or if they should have their own.

Reviewing them all in a single chapter would make your head spin, so we will focus on the key ones for IoT analytics. The following picture gives an idea of the number of projects in the ecosystem. It shows all of the Hadoop components included in the Hortonworks managed distribution (version 2.5). We will leave out most of the resource management, security, and developer-focused components, such as Zookeeper, Knox, and Pig:

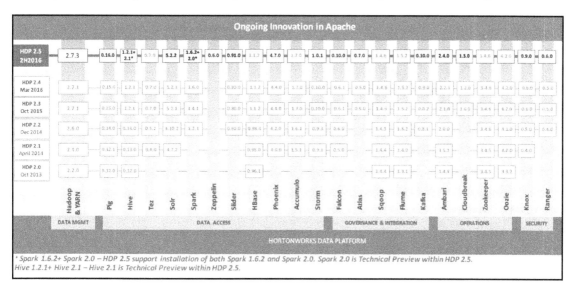

Hortonworks Data Platform (HDP) ecosystem. Source: Hortonworks

The Hadoop components are designed to operate distributed across multiple servers. One cluster could have thousands of separate servers. It is fault tolerant, server failures are expected by design, and adding or removing servers can be done while the cluster is up and operating normally.

It can be helpful, from the viewpoint of analytics, to think of the Hadoop ecosystem as four interconnected but loosely coupled services. These services communicate with each other but handle their roles for the most part completely independently. A high-level view of this is shown in the following diagram:

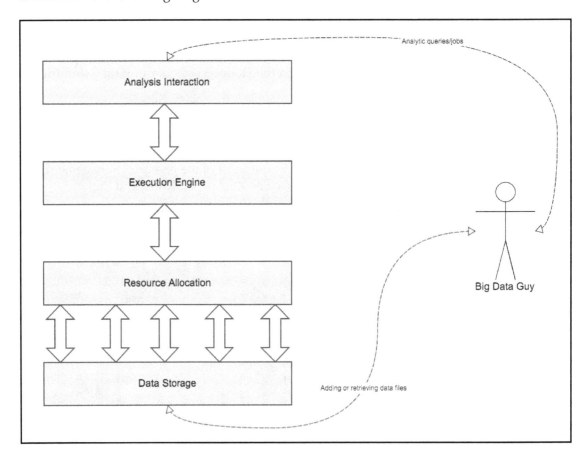

These four services in our conceptual view are as follows:

- **Analysis interactions**: This is where you will spend most of your time. It is where you write and submit code, SQL, or link up a visualization tool. Components in this area take higher-level instructions and break them up into lower-level processing steps for the execution. They abstract away a lot of the messy details for you. Hive and SparkContexts are examples.
- **Execution engines**: You should understand how components in this area work, but it is unlikely that you will directly interact with them. Apache MapReduce and Tez are examples. These services handle how and in what order the processing steps will be executed.
- **Resource allocations**: This is important to understand for optimization purposes. Here is where each node is monitored and work is allocated. YARN is the key player.
- **Data storage**: This area handles the organization and storage of data files. You will interact directly here, and it is important to understand what happens in these services and how they work. HDFS and S3 are the examples. File formatting and types are also important, as this directly impacts the flexibility and efficiency in the analysis interaction services.

Hadoop cluster architectures

Next, we will review the node types that make up a Hadoop cluster, what role they play, and how they integrate to ensure the cluster is a functioning unit. Servers in the same cluster communicate frequently with each other; they are very chatty.

Most cluster configurations keep the physical units close to each other (in networking terms) to minimize bandwidth bottlenecks. The managed cloud-based distributions of Hadoop handle this for you on the setup. But if you decide to go the route of manually creating your own cluster, you will need to keep networking considerations on top of mind when designing the architecture.

Getting to know Linux

Linux is ubiquitous in big data computing clusters. Since it is open source, licensing costs are minimal to nonexistent. It has lower system overhead than **Operating Systems** (**OS**) such as Windows. This makes it ideal for cluster computing where nodes can get into the thousands, each with its own OS. Imagine paying Windows licensing fees for a thousand servers.... yikes.

To put it simply, you *will* need to know how to interact with the Linux OS for IoT analytics. It is unavoidable and not so bad once you get used to it. You will not need to be an expert, but you will need to know how to find your way around, run programs, and do some basic scripting. Brush up on Bash! You'll get to learn what a shebang is (Google it).

What is a Node?

A node is a unit in a cluster that has control of its own amount of CPU and memory resources. It also has its own OS. In most implementations of Hadoop, this is a single server; although it is possible to have more than one node on a physical server if each node can control its assigned compute and memory resources (typically through virtualization).

Node types

A Hadoop cluster has one **MasterNode** and one to many **slave** nodes. The MasterNode operates what is called the **NameNode**. The role of the NameNode is to track which other nodes are healthy and some other key information about the cluster, such as file locations. There is also the role of the **ResourceManager**, one per cluster, which may or may not be on the same server. You will learn more about the NameNode in the HDFS section and more about the ResourceManager in the YARN section.

The rest of the machines in the cluster act as both **DataNode** and **NodeManager**. These are the workers. This is where, you guessed it, the data is distributed and where the distributed computing happens. There are several types of slave node that serve different roles for the cluster. Most of them will be referred to as data nodes. There can also be slave nodes that are primarily meant to interface with the outside network, these are called **edge nodes**.

Some other services on the cluster, such as Web App Proxy Server and MapReduce Job History server, are usually run either on dedicated nodes or on shared nodes–typically the edge nodes. The decision on where to place them depends on the load requirements of the services sharing the resources of a node.

Hadoop Distributed File System

Hadoop Distributed File System (**HDFS**) is a filesystem spread across multiple servers and is designed to run on low-cost commodity hardware. HDFS supports a write-once and read many philosophy. It was designed for large-scale batch processing work on large to enormous sized files.

Files are divided up into **blocks**. A typical block size is 128 MB. A file on HDFS is sliced up into 128 MB chunks (the blocks) and distributed across different data nodes. Files in HDFS normally range from gigabytes to terabytes.

HDFS was designed for batch processing more than low-latency interactive queries from users. HDFS is not meant for files that frequently change with data updates. New data is typically appended to files or added in new files. Many small files are detrimental to HDFS operations, so files are often combined into a single larger file for performance reasons.

The following diagram shows the general HDFS architecture. The NameNode controls file namespace and is the gatekeeper for file operations across the nodes. It tracks where file blocks are located and handles client requests for reading and update files:

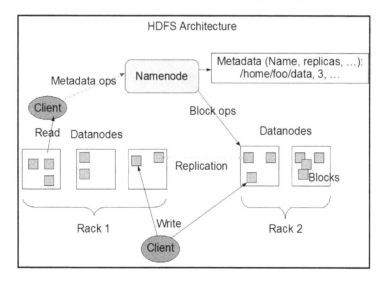

HDFS architecture. Source: Apache Software Foundation

HDFS assumes hardware will fail and files will get lost or corrupted. One of the ways it address this is by keeping multiple copies of the file distributed across nodes. No single node will have all the copies of a file. The number of copies is configurable but the default setting is three. HDFS uses some intelligence on determining location and distribution of file blocks to balance fault tolerance and performance.

If a node fails and file blocks are lost, HDFS automatically generates another copy of the blocks from the remaining copies on other nodes to replace them. These are distributed across the other normally operating nodes. The NameNode keeps track of all these operations. File blocks are also moved around for performance optimization purposes. The actual duplication of file blocks is handled by the data nodes in communication with each other.

To get an idea of how this works, we will describe the high-level process of writing a file. A client, which could be a command-line prompt on the MasterNode or some other software that connects to the cluster, requests a write or read of a file. This request goes to the NameNode, which returns the list of node identifiers where the file blocks can be retrieved or written to. When a file is written, the file blocks are written once by the client request to the nodes in the list. Then, the data nodes duplicate it the set number of times by communicating among themselves.

HDFS file commands are very similar to Linux filesystem commands. The following example instructs HDFS to take the local file called `lots_o_data.csv` and distribute it across the HDFS cluster in the name space, `/user/hadoop/datafolder`:

```
hdfs dfs -put lots_o_data.csv /user/hadoop/datafolder/lots_o_data.csv
```

The following example would copy the same file from its distributed form in HDFS to the local (non-HDFS single server) file directory:

```
hdfs dgs -get /user/hadoop/datafolder/lots_o_data.csv lots_o_data.csv
```

The NameNode abstracts the true distributed location of the pieces of the file. This allows clients to address it with the familiar file folder nomenclature as if it was stored in one file on a single drive. The namespace automatically grows to incorporate new nodes, which add more storage space.

Files can be of any type and do not have to be a standard format. You can have unstructured files, such as word documents, and also very structured files, such as relational database table extracts. HDFS is indifferent to the level of structure in the data that resides in the files.

Many of the tools that interact with HDFS for analysis purposes do rely on structure. The structure can be applied as needed just before a file is read, known as **schema-on-read**. It could also be defined within the file itself as it is written. The second is what is called **schema-on-write**.

Schema-on-write is how relational databases, such as Oracle or Microsoft SQL Server, operate. This is a key thing that differentiates HDFS from traditional database systems: HDFS can be used to apply multiple structures to the same dataset (schema-on-read). The downside is that the application reading the dataset must know and apply the structure in order to use it for analytics. There are some open source projects meant to solve this downside for datasets which need a clear structure. We will discuss the two major ones next.

Parquet

Apache Parquet is a columnar storage format for data where the structure of the data is incorporated into the file. It is available to any project in the Hadoop ecosystem and is a key format for analytics. It was designed to meet the goals of interoperability, space efficiency, and query efficiency. Parquet files can be stored in HDFS as well as non-HDFS filesystems.

Parquet logo

Columnar storage works well for analytics as the data is stored and arranged by table columns instead of rows. Analytics use cases typically select multiple columns and perform aggregation functions on the values, such as sum, average, or standard deviation. When the data is stored in columns, it is both faster and requires less disk **Input/Output (I/O)** to read in the requested data.

The data is typically stored in an ordered form making it easy to grab the needed sections and only the data for the selected columns is read. In contrast, a row-oriented format typically requires the entire row to be read in order to get to the necessary column values. Columnar is great for analytics but not all sunshine and roses; it is poor for transactional use cases.

Parquet is intended to support very efficient compression and encoding schemes. It allows different compression schemes for each column in the dataset. It was also designed to be extensible by allowing more encoding to be added as they are invented.

A Parquet file is organized into nested components. A **row group** contains all data from a division of the dataset; the column data values are guaranteed to be stored next to each other to minimize disk I/O requirements.

Each dataset of the column values is called a **column chunk**. The column chuck is further divided into **pages**. The tail end of the file and footer stores the overall metadata on the file and the column chunks. It is at the end so that the write operation that creates the file can be done in one sweep. This is necessary since the full metadata is not known until all of the data is processed into the file. The following diagram represents the divisions within the Parquet file:

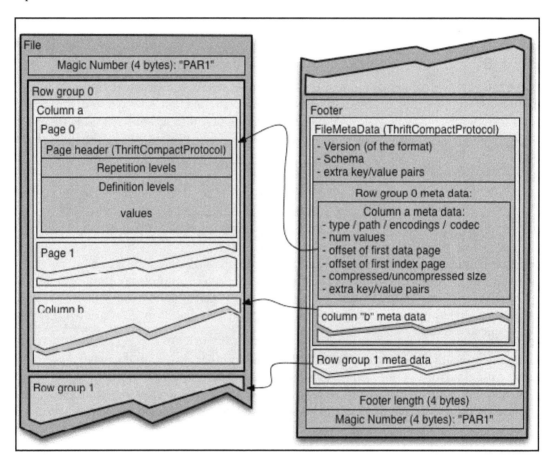

Parquet file representation. Source: Apache Parquet documentation

The file metadata holds the information necessary to locate and interpret the data properly. There are three types of metadata, which match up with the key nested components: file metadata, column (chunk) metadata, and page header metadata. The following diagram shows the logical relationships of the metadata parts:

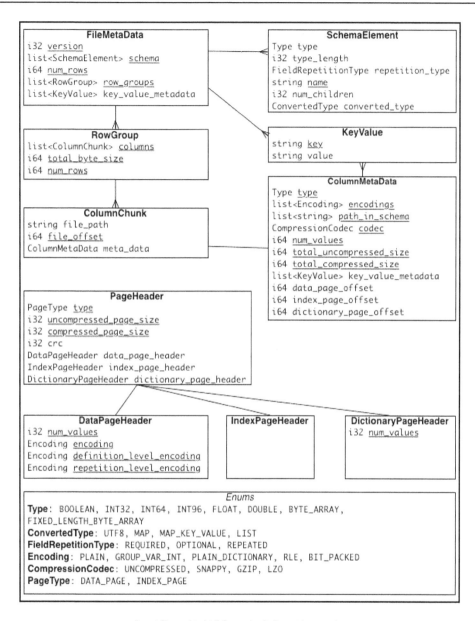

Parquet file metadata detail. Source: Apache Parquet documentation

The data types are intentionally simple to foster more options in frameworks that use it; see the enums box in the previous diagram for the supported types (Type). Strings are stored as binary with a ConvertedType set to UTF8.

The recommended row group size is 512 MB to 1 GB with a larger corresponding HDFS file block size of the same setting. This allows an entire row group to be read with one file block retrieval. The Parquet file extension is `.parq`.

Avro

Avro is an Apache open source data serialization system project. The system processes data into a resulting container file that has some useful properties. It uses binary data format to keep the file size small and compact. This also results in faster read times.

Avro logo

The structure of the data is stored in the file container. Rich data structures are supported. Avro file structures, or schemas, are defined using JSON. This is a schema-on-write process as far as file creation is concerned. This has the benefit of client applications not having to generate code to define the data structure. This makes using Avro files for analytics purposes much simpler since you do not need to discover and define the file schema in your analytics code.

There are Python and Java libraries that can be used to create and read Avro files. Most likely, you will use something such as Hive (discussed later in the chapters) to store data into Avro files. Avro supports primitive data types of null, boolean, int, long, float, double, bytes, and string. It also supports complex data types such as arrays, record, and enums. The following is an example JSON schema definition:

```
{"namespace": "iotexample.avro",
 "type": "record",
 "name": "Sensor",
 "fields": [
     {"name": "sensor_id", "type": "string"},
     {"name": "temperature",  "type": ["double", "null"]},
     {"name": "recorded_time", "type": ["string", "null"]}
 ]
}
```

Data records are converted to binary during serialization and can also be compressed to reduce size further. The file extension for Avro files is `.avsc`.

Hive

We now move on from file storage formats to data processing and retrieval components. Apache Hive is a project in the Hadoop ecosystem that fits within the analysis interaction area. It allows you to write queries in a SQL-like language, called **Hive Query Language** (**HiveQL**), which it interprets into processing commands for execution over HDFS. HiveQL is very similar to SQL and will be instantly usable to any SQL developer.

Hive architecture consists of a **User Interface** (**UI**), a metastore database, a driver, a compiler, and an execution engine. These components work together to translate a user query into a **Directed Acyclic Graph** (**DAG**) of actions that orchestrate execution and return results utilizing Hadoop MapReduce (usually) and HDFS.

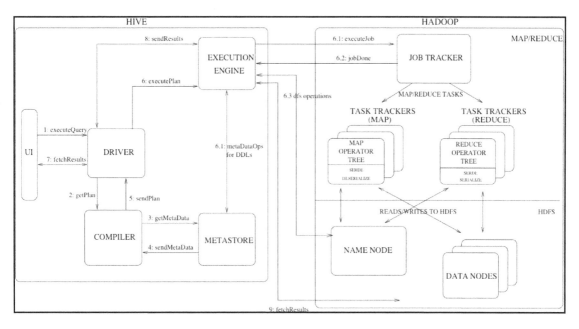

Hive architecture. Source: Apache Hive project documentation

The UI allows you to submit queries. It also supports other actions such as commands to create Hive tables. You will most probably not use it directly. An an IoT analyst, you are more likely to interact with it through a web-based interface, such as Hue, or through another application that uses a Hive ODBC driver, such as a programming IDE or visualization software such as Tableau.

The **metastore** database holds information about Hive tables. Hive tables are very similar to relational database tables where the structure is defined ahead of time. Hive tables can be managed by Hive in HDFS or they can be defined to point to data files not managed by Hive (called **external** tables). External tables are not necessary in HDFS. Amazon S3 is a common example where structured files can be stored and still be queryable through Hive as long as a Hive table definition has been created for it.

The metastore database can be housed inside the cluster or remotely. If you are creating transient Hadoop clusters for temporary use, such as through Microsoft HDInsights, the remote database can be useful as the metadata can persist beyond the life of the cluster. This allows it to be used by future incarnations of clusters. This is more common when Hadoop is being used for batch processing jobs or for a temporary use case, such as experimental analytics jobs. Hive metastores can also be used by other Hadoop ecosystem projects, such as Spark and Impala.

The **driver** serves as a coordinator. It creates a unique session ID for the query, sends it to the compiler for a query plan, and then sends it to the execution engine for processing. Finally, it coordinates the fetching of result records.

The **compiler** communicates with the metastore to get information on the tables in the query. It checks type and develops an execution plan. The plan takes the form of a DAG of steps, which can either be a map or reduce job, a metadata operation, or an HDFS operation. The execution plan is passed back to the driver.

The **execution engine** submits actions to the appropriate Hadoop components based on the execution plan. During the execution steps, data is stored in temporary HDFS files to be used by later steps in the plan. The final results are retrieved by the execution engine when the driver sends a fetch request.

Here is an example table creation statement:

```
CREATE TABLE iotsensor (
                sensorid BIGINT,
                temperature DOUBLE,
                timeutc STRING
                )
STORED AS PARQUET;
```

Hive tables can support partitions and other performance enhancing options. Query statements are very similar to SQL, typically not distinguishable for most simple queries. This is an example query statement:

```
SELECT stdev_samp (temperature) FROM iotsensor WHERE TO_DATE(timeread) >
'2016-01-01'
```

Here are some tips for using Hive for IoT analytics:

1. **Avoid too many table joins**: Keep less than five tables joined in a single query. If this is not possible, break the query up into multiple successive queries that build intermediate pieces into temp tables.
2. **Experiment with Hive using execution engines other than Hadoop MapReduce**: Hive on Tez and Hive on Spark are two newer implementation projects that promise faster, more efficient query processing by minimizing disk I/O and leveraging more in-memory processing.
3. **Store data in Parquet files**: The columnar storage better supports the types of query commonly run for analytics. File compression can reduce disk space requirements for IoT data.

Serialization/Deserialization (SerDe)

You will see **SerDe** mentioned often in Hadoop-related documentation. SerDe is short for Serialization/Deserialization. The serialization and deserialization refers to how files are transformed from the saved state into a standardized readable format. Serialization is part of creation of the file when writing and deserialization happens when a file is read. This allows files to be compressed and structured. Metadata about the file contents and data structure can also be saved as part of the file.

It is a way of *abstracting* away the details of decoding a file format from the client applications. It also allows multiple different formats to work seamlessly in the same environment. Some of these formats can even be invented later and it all still works.

A SerDe in Hadoop would point to the application that handles the encoding and decoding of the file. This is often a setting in the hive table creation script that will be stored in the metastore and later referenced by a client when reading the schema.

Hadoop MapReduce

Hadoop MapReduce is a core component of the Hadoop framework. It is a software framework that enables in-parallel processing distributed across nodes in the cluster. The topic can get confusing as people tend to refer to the *concept* of MapReduce and the Hadoop component interchangeably, as if they were all one and the same.

The concept of Map and Reduce will be covered in the Spark section later on in this chapter. It is not tied to any specific framework or project. You may read articles that imply that MapReduce is going away, to be replaced by something else. It may not be clearly spelled out (and often it is not), but they are referring to the Hadoop component and not to the concept.

The concept of Map and Reduce is not going anywhere; it has been around for a while and is even a key part of many newer distributed processing frameworks. We will always refer to the component in this book as Hadoop MapReduce to avoid any confusion.

In the Hadoop component, the MapReduce job normally divides the input dataset into independent chunks. The chunks are processed by the map tasks in parallel across the nodes. The output of the map tasks is then sorted and is input into the reduce tasks. Hadoop MapReduce handles task scheduling, monitoring, and will re-execute tasks if they fail.

Unless you are a professional Java programmer in the big data space, it is unlikely you will be interacting with Hadoop MapReduce directly. In analytics, you are far more likely to be using other higher level tools, which use Hadoop MapReduce under the covers. For this reason, we will not spend much time on this component even though it is a core part of the Hadoop ecosystem.

Yet Another Resource Negotiator (YARN)

Despite its whimsical name, YARN is the resource allocation component that most Hadoop components rely on. The idea behind YARN was to split resource management away from job scheduling and monitoring. In YARN, these are separate processing units.

As represented in the following diagram, there is a single **ResourceManager** for the cluster and **ApplicationMaster** for each job or set of jobs represented by a DAG, which runs on the nodes. The job or DAG of jobs is called an application. There is also a **NodeManager** for each node in the cluster. It is the job of the NodeManager to monitor the CPU, disk, memory, and network usage of the **container** on the node where the applications running on it are executed.

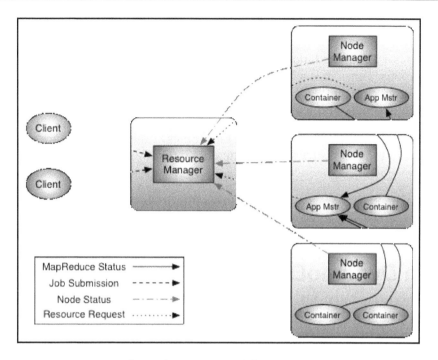

YARN architecture. Source: Apache Software Foundation

Containers are self-contained environments operating on top of the underlying OS; think of it like a system within a system. They allow for consistent operation of applications running inside the containers even if the underlying OS configuration and software differs between nodes. NodeManager also reports usage information back to the ResourceManager.

The ApplicationMaster has the job of negotiating resources with the ResourceManager and operating with NodeManagers to execute and monitor application tasks. The ApplicationMaster can interact with containers on different nodes to execute its application.

The ResourceManager handles the scheduling and allocation of resources to the running application based on the resource constraints of the various nodes. The ResourceManager can also restart individual application masters if there is a failure.

HBase

Apache HBase is a distributed, non-relational database built to handle very large tables with quick response times. It is a NoSQL type database, which means it is non-relational and does not support the full SQL language for query processing. It is constructed on top of the Hadoop environment and uses HDFS for data storage.

However, unlike HDFS, it has very fast response times and is built for random, real-time read/write access. It does this trick by putting data into indexed files that are then stored in HDFS.

HBase is useful if you have large (in the realm of hundreds of millions of records or higher) datasets and need fast single record lookups.

Amazon DynamoDB

DynamoDB is very similar to HBase in its operation and use cases. It manages underlying resources and storage for you, and you pay only for what you use. It is useful under many of the same conditions as HBase.

Amazon S3

Amazon S3 is not just a place to dump files. You can use it like a data warehouse as it is highly available and extremely fault tolerant. File durability is 99.999999999% over the span of a year. S3 is also a Hadoop-compatible filesystem. And you do not have to keep three copies of the data as it already has data replication built in.

S3 is not good for data that is updated frequently, but it is great for data that is appended frequently. IoT data tends to fall squarely in the latter category so S3 works well. Many companies that are advanced in analytics keep large datasets in S3 and create temporary Hadoop clusters for processing and analytics. Results are then stored, and the temporary Hadoop clusters are terminated to save costs.

Apache Spark for data processing

Apache Spark is a new-ish project (at least in the world of big data, which moves at warp speed) that integrates well with Hadoop but does not necessarily require Hadoop components to operate. It is a *fast and general engine for large-scale data processing* as described on the Spark project team welcome page. The tagline of *lightning fast cluster computing* is a little catchier: we like that one better.

Apache Spark logo

What is Apache Spark?

Good question, glad you asked. Spark was built for distributed cluster computing, so everything scales nicely without any code changes. The word *general* in the general engine description is very appropriate for Spark. It refers to the many and varied ways you can use it.

You can use it for ETL data processing, machine learning modeling, graph processing, stream data processing, and SQL and structure data processing. It is a boon for analytics in a distributed computing world.

It has APIs for multiple programming languages such as Java, Scala, Python, and R. It operates mostly in memory, which is where the speed improvement over Hadoop MapReduce mainly comes from. For analytics, Python and R are the popular programming languages. When interacting with Spark, you will probably be using Python, as it is better supported. The Python API for Spark is called **Pyspark**.

The descriptions and architecture discussed in this chapter are for Spark 2.1.0, the latest version at the time of writing.

Spark and big data analytics

Spark operates across nodes in the cluster in a similar way as Hive. The job or set of jobs that you are executing over Spark is called an application. Applications run in Spark as independent sets of processes across the cluster. These are coordinated by the main component called the Driver. The key object that operates in the Driver is called SparkContent.

The following diagram is a very simple architecture diagram of Spark. Spark can connect to different types of cluster managers such as Apache Mesos, YARN, or its own simple Spark standalone cluster manager. YARN is the most common implementation.

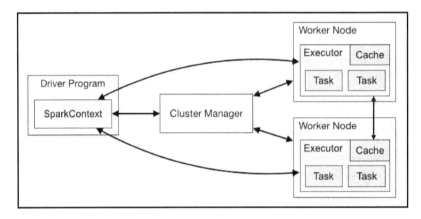

Apache Spark architecture. Source: Apache software foundation

Through the cluster manager, the driver program acquires resources on each worker node, which runs computation and stores data in support of executing the application. These are system processes that are called Executors. An **Executor** will process one or more tasks as instructed by the driver program.

SparkContext is created for each user session, and it is isolated from other SparkContexts. This means applications are isolated from one another. This adds to overall robustness but also means it is not easy for different SparkContexts to share data. In practice, this is not much of an issue.

The Executors acquired by an individual SparkContext are also isolated from each other. Each Executor runs on its own **Java Virtual Machine** (**JVM**) on the worker nodes. The Driver program sends the executors the application code in the form of Java JAR files or Python files. Then, it sends the tasks to be executed.

The Driver program must be able to listen and accept incoming communications from its executors. Executors must be able to talk to each other. All components should be "near" each other in the cluster. For this reason, it is not a good idea to be running a Driver program (Spark instance) on your laptop that is connected directly to the cluster.

It is common and recommended practice to install Spark on the same cluster nodes as HDFS. This puts the processing close to the data and results in improved performance.

It is very important to understand what portion of your application runs on the Driver and what portion runs across the worker nodes. The Driver is located on a single node and is limited to the CPU and memory available to it on that node. For this reason, data, memory, and computer requirements for operations must fit within those limits or the application will fail. What will run fine across the cluster, which has a much higher set of distributed resources, will crash and burn if unintentionally pulled back to the driver node.

Thinking about a single machine versus a cluster of machines

Designing distributed computing analytics requires that you think what can be run in parallel and what has to be run one step after another. Running computations in parallel is where a lot of the speed advantage comes from in cluster computing systems such as Spark. But it does require a little different thinking.

Think in terms of how to split up an analytics job into actions that can be run either record by record or on a small subset of records, without needing to know what is going on elsewhere in the full dataset. A simple example is a word count exercise.

Imagine you have millions of rows of survey results and need to analyze the survey question:
"Comment about the insightfulness and literary poetry that is the book *Analytics for the Internet of Things*".

The responses are stored as a free form text field in each data row. You want to do a word count to see what are the top words respondents use. Hopefully, words such as **fantastic** and **educational** are on top and words such as **fraud** and **time wasting-junk-pile** are further down in the list.

The first step is to break up the text string for each row into a list of words. This can be done across many different nodes all at the same time. You would write Python code that does this, and then provide it to Spark to send to each executor so it can use it. This would be the first **Map** step. The next step would be to take each word and put a number next to it, so it can be summed up later. The form would be (**fantastic, 1**). At this point, the number would always be 1 as the same word will be in the dataset as often as it is present. This is the second map step, and you would use the same procedure as we discussed earlier.

Next, the results should be ordered by the word across the cluster so it can be counted easier. This is a shuffle step. Then, each executor can add the numbers attached to each of the words together to get a total for the words it has on its plate. This reduces the rows to an individual word subtotal for each executor. Hence, this is called a **Reduce** step. Finally, all the subtotals are added together for an overall total for the cluster by each individual word in the final reduce step.

Taken together, this concept is called **Map/Reduce**. This is a very simple example, and in practice, systems such as Spark handle much of the details for you. But, the overall concept holds even at higher-level applications where map and reduce is not directly called upon. You should think how to break apart the work so it can be distributed, then aggregate it into a much smaller result set for further analytics.

Using Spark for IoT data processing

Using our conceptual diagram from earlier in the chapter, Spark fits into both the analysis interaction and the execution engine areas. You can write code directly on the core Spark objects and also make use of the programming modules that come along with it. The following image helps to visualize the Spark module stack:

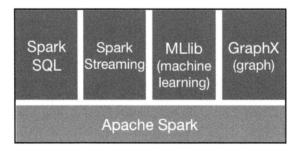

Spark Module Stack. Source: Apache Spark

Spark SQL is included with the SparkSession when it is created and allows you to write standard SQL that is interpreted into Spark actions and executed (using a DAG, of course). You can use it intermixed with other Spark code. This allows you to leverage the power and knowledge of SQL when appropriate and use code where it is appropriate, all without needing to switch languages.

Spark Streaming is a set of libraries that allow the processing of stream data. Stream data is a high throughput, consistent feed of data from one to many sources. Spark Streaming provides higher-level abstracts to make it easier to analyze this type of data. The stream input is broken down into smaller batches of data for analytic operations using the Spark engine. Results can then be stored for additional longer-term analysis.

MLlib is a set of machine learning libraries and commands that are optimized to run in parallel. This allows you to use very large datasets for training and run them much faster than other Hadoop-based projects. Machine learning algorithms are highly iterative which requires a lot of disk I/O for Hadoop MapReduce-based components. Spark operates mostly in memory, which greatly speeds up the iterations versus disk I/O.

GraphX is a set of libraries designed for graph processing. The term *graph* used in this context is not about charts but is a branch of analytics specializing in network analysis. This is what is used to identify influential people in social networks as one example. A graph consists of **nodes** and **edges**, with the edges representing the connections between nodes.

All of these modules can be used together and in a single application. This allows for a wide variety of applications and flexibility all within the same tool and programming construct. And everything scales with the size of the cluster.

Spark works well as an ETL tool due to its scalability, speed, and flexibility. IoT data needs all three, so it is a good match. The incoming IoT data can be cleaned, processed, and enhanced using Spark. It can also create a machine learning pipeline to train algorithms as part of the same process.

A common use case is to have a Spark job, most likely written in Pyspark, handle the initial ETL for long-term storage. Then, a separate set of jobs run on a daily or other regular schedule to enhance and further analyze the data. Finally, a visual analysis tool such as Tableau and statistical analysis libraries in either R or Python are linked to the resulting data for more advanced analytics.

The Spark SQL module is also fully compatible with HiveQL and can use the Hive metastore, Hive **User Defined Functions** (**UDF**), and SerDes. There is a **HiveContext** object that natively supports the integration when Spark is installed alongside Hive on the cluster. Spark also natively reads and writes to the Parquet format. The Parquet file could be in HDFS, S3, or another filesystem that Spark can access. Since Parquet includes schema information with the file, it is very simple to load and set up distributed datasets for analytics.

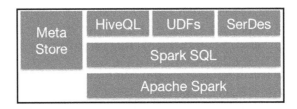

Spark Hive compatibility architecture. Source: Apache Spark

To stream or not to stream

Streams are datasets that continuously update as each new data message arrives with little to no latency. Streaming analytics operate on this continuously updating dataset at much shorter intervals than batch processing. Real-time analytics is a little bit of a misnomer when applied to streaming analytics as intervals are typically in minutes rather than continuously ongoing. The frequency affects processing and technology requirements, so intervals should be set for longer time periods if possible in order to save costs.

Stream datasets normally keep data for a window of time, and then discard it. There are specialized technology and processing options to handle streams, which are, for the most part, in addition to requirements for long term big data store technology we have focused on in this chapter. Amazon Kinesis is an example of a specialized data streaming technology service.

The technology and the programming code base needed to support analytics are (usually) different for streaming than that needed for long-term historical analytics. This means that two systems and code bases are required for most use cases. There are multiple efforts underway to consolidate this into one; Spark 2.1 is a notable example with the Spark Streaming module, but this area is still maturing.

For IoT analytics, it is important to consider the use cases and what datasets you will need to support before deciding real-time streaming analytics is what is actually needed. When you are looking for insights and new business opportunities, you will almost always be using datasets will long term history. Data from the latest hour or minute adds little incremental value for those use cases.

Even though the lure of real-time analytics is tempting, you have to consider if the additional cost and maintenance of streaming technology is worth it. In most cases for IoT analytics, it is not and could be better served by increasing the batch processing frequency. You also have limitations in what you can do with streaming analytics versus batch analytics when incorporating additional datasets. Unless those datasets are also real-time, they are only usable for less frequent batch processing.

While this is the case for *exploratory* analytics to find insights, it may not be the case for *productionalizing* the insights from those analytics. You may want near real-time analytics processing in some cases, such as when applying a predictive model to streaming sensor data to predict an equipment failure. You may want real-time streaming analytics for reporting dashboards that are monitored by fast reaction customer support teams.

These are separate decisions, however. The recommendation is to avoid the overhead of adding streaming analytics unless there is a strong business case to do so. *Real-time* sounds good, but you need to make sure the incremental gain is worth the additional expense in both time and resources.

Lambda architectures

Lambda architectures consists of an arrangement of data and processing technologies intended to serve both regular batch processing activities and near real-time streaming activities, in a way that allows results from both to be combined into a single view. The following descriptions and diagram highlight the conceptual components that make up the three layers to the architecture:

- **Batch**: This layer keeps the master dataset and regular batch processing of the data to create views to support analytics, dashboards, and reporting linked to the Serving layer. The master dataset is immutable, meaning the data does not change once incorporated, and it is appended with new data as time goes on. A long-running Hadoop cluster would be an example.

- **Speed**: This layer is focused on recent data only (the streaming data). It handles requests that have low-latency requirements in terms of recency of data. Algorithms need to be fast and incremental to operate in the speed layer. Amazon Kinesis would be an example technology that operates in the speed layer.
- **Serving**: This layer indexes batch views so they can be served up with low latency. This includes batch views from both the Batch and Streaming layers.

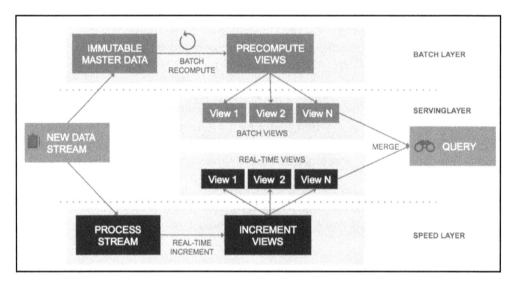

Lambda architecture. Source: MapR technologies

Handling change

Change is constant, as contradictory as that sounds. The architecture, data model, and technology will constantly evolve over time. You will need to decide how to handle change in order to keep flexibility in your data storage and processing architecture. You will want to use tools that are decoupled from each other to allow future analytics to be easily integrated into the data processing stream.

Fortunately, components in the Hadoop ecosystem were intentionally designed to be decoupled from each other. They allow the mixing and matching of components and were built to be extensible for new frameworks not even invented yet. Cloud infrastructures allow for easy testing and incorporation of new technologies and software.

You will need to design a process that takes your analytics and data processing code from experimentation, to development, to production. This holds true for your overall infrastructure as well. A common practice is to keep three separate environments: one for development, one for testing, and one for production.

In order to save costs, you may decide to reduce this to two: a hybrid development and test environment, and a production environment. Either way, you will need a structured process to move your insights from initial ideas to fully-fledged parts of your standard operation.

Summary

In this chapter, we discussed several cloud infrastructure technologies specific to IoT and processing incoming data from devices in the field. We also reviewed some strategies to collect and store IoT data in order to enable analytics. The Hadoop ecosystem and architecture was introduced with some detail on the key components for IoT analytics.

You also learned when and why to use Spark for data processing. We discussed tradeoffs between streaming and batch processing. The Lambda architecture was introduced. Deciding how to handle change was discussed to build in flexibility to allow future analytics to be integrated with data processing.

6

Getting to Know Your Data - Exploring IoT Data

"Yes, I know the three-month average is 45.2, but what does it mean? We have over 2 terabytes of data now. But what does it tell us?"

Your boss is in one of his moods again. He is peppering you with questions, and you are not sure how to answer. Your first instinct was to spit back numbers from the weekly reports, but it obviously did not work.

"Is the data even any good?" he continues, "Are we building up value or just cluttering up the basement with junk?"

You start to shrug but wisely stop yourself. You think the data is very valuable, but you actually do not know much about the dataset beyond the numbers that are included in the reports you have been asked to develop. You realize you are not even sure what the individual data records look like. You know that averages can hide a lot of things, but no one has ever asked you to look any deeper.

You straighten your shoulders and say confidently, "There is value in the data. We are just not looking at all aspects of it. I will show you there is more to it."

You do not feel confident at all. You are not sure how you are going to show where business value is buried just waiting to be discovered. But you hide it well.

Your boss lets out a harrumph-like noise, clearly not really buying what you are selling. He turns around and walks off down the hallway muttering to himself.

> *Data is the sword of the twenty-first century, those who wield it well, the samurai.*

> *-Eric Schmidt and Jonathan Rosenberg in How Google Works*

This chapter is focused on exploratory data analysis for IoT data. You will learn how to ask and answer questions of the data. The first part of the chapter will be on understanding the data quality. Then, we will move on to getting to know the data better and what it represents. We will use Tableau and R for examples. You will learn strategies for quickly assessing data and starting the hunt to find value.

This chapter covers the following topics:

- Exploring and visualizing data
- A quick Tableau overview:
    - Techniques to understand data quality
    - Basic time series analysis
    - Getting to know categories in the data
    - Analyzing with geography
- Looking for attributes that have predictive value
- Using R to augment visualization tools
- Industry-specific examples:
    - Manufacturing
    - Health care
    - Retail

Exploring and visualizing data

The first step in any analytics, *especially* IoT analytics, is getting to know your data. Like a future spouse, you need to know everything you can about it. Know its flaws and its strong points. Know which attributes can be annoying and make sure you are able to live with them. Get to know its future earning potential. And find all this out before it is too late and you are bound to it.

In this chapter, we will use a couple of tools to quickly learn quite a bit about a sample dataset. Examples will follow along with methods to dive into the data in order to find its strengths and weaknesses. For exploration and visualization, we will use Tableau. For more statistical evaluations, we will use the statistical programming language R.

The Tableau overview

Tableau is a business intelligence and analytics software tool that allows you to connect to dozens of different database and file types, drag and drop to build visualizations, and easily share them with others. There are two main versions, desktop and server. The desktop is a high-powered tool you install on your laptop to connect and manipulate datasets. A server is a web-based component where you publish your desktop visualizations for others to easily interact with them.

We will only focus on the Tableau desktop in this chapter as our mission is to explore data versus communicating analytic findings. It is free to try for a limited period. You can download it from the company's website (`https://www.tableau.com/products/desktop/download`).

The first step in working with your data using Tableau is to connect to your dataset. Tableau has many different connectors able to link to a wide variety of databases and file formats. Think of Tableau as a window into your data, a way to link to it and explore it. It is separate from your data though, keep them distinct in your mind.

After you connect to your data, there are four main sections of the workspace. They are highlighted in the following screenshot:

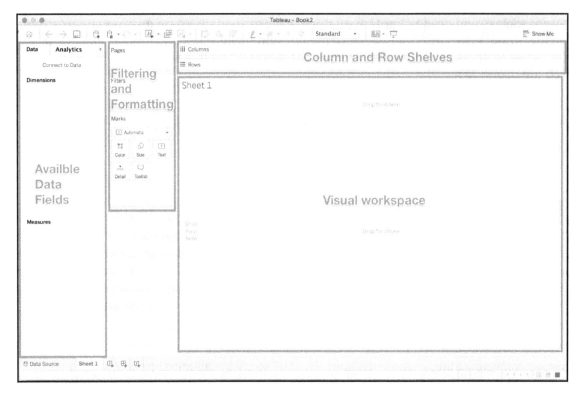

Tableau desktop main view

We will describe each section in detail next.

- **Available data fields** (Data pane in Tableau terminology): This section shows the fields in the linked dataset. You can also create additional fields calculated from other data fields. You can create your own category groupings and hierarchies here. Data fields are split into two types.
    - **Dimensions:** A dimension is a field that holds categories or labels. A way to determine if a field should be a dimension is to think if it would make any sense to sum up or average its values. If the answer is no, it is better used as a dimension. Examples are customer names, segments, ID fields, phone numbers, state names, and dates.

- **Measures:** A measure is a number that does not represent a category and is from a continuous range of values. These are numbers that you would sum or average. Examples are units sold, temperature, and the lengths of time.

- **Filtering and formatting** (the **Filter** shelf, the **Pages** shelf, and the **Marks** card): This is where you filter data records and determine the format of the charts and tables in the visual workspace.
- **Column and row shelves** (the **Columns** shelf and the **Rows** shelf): This is where you drag fields to build your view in the visual space. Fields listed here are on deck in the interactive view.

- **Visual workspace**: This shows the results of your manipulations in the other sections. You can also dig directly into the data records behind the points or numbers shown in this area.

Techniques to understand data quality

The dataset we will use for examples in this chapter is from the United States **National Oceanic and Atmospheric Administration** (**NOAA**). It is a subset of the U.S. 15 Minute Precipitation Data, which is available on the NOAA website (direct link: `https://www.ncdc.noaa.gov/cdo-web/search?datasetid=PRECIP_15`).

We are using the dataset from January 1, 2013 to January 1, 2014 for the U.S. state of Colorado. You can download it from NOAA or from the Packt website for this book. Make sure to check all the available fields when downloading the data from NOAA. Also download the documentation on the dataset, which has descriptions of the fields (`https://www1.ncdc.noaa.gov/pub/data/cdo/documentation/PRECIP_15_documentation.pdf`).

For this exercise, you can save reading the documentation until the end of the chapter to see how it lines up with what we observe. For any other situation, you should scour the documentation first and take notes as if you are studying for a final exam in a class where you want the top grade.

Look at your data - au naturel

The very first thing you should always do with unfamiliar data is to look at a good sample of it in raw form. This is a very important and an often overlooked step, even by experienced analysts. Your first instinct will be to run averages and standard deviations to look for trends. Resist the impulse.

You want to view the file first without any formatting or interpretations, so you need to use a software tool that does not apply any formats to it. If you have a Windows laptop, Notepad is a good one to use as long as the file is not too large. Excel is not good to use for this, as it applies its own formatting and interpretations to text files, such as `.csv`.

On a Mac or a Linux machine, use a command-line text viewing tool. On a Mac, you can open Terminal and navigate to the directory with the file, and type the command `cat filename.csv | less`. Pressing the spacebar will advance the screen; type `q` to exit. You can do the same from a Linux command line. The following shows how the raw data looks on a Mac or Linux machine. Windows will show a very similar format:

```
STATION,STATION_NAME,ELEVATION,LATITUDE,LONGITUDE,DATE,QGAG,Measurement Flag,Quality Flag,Units,QPCP,Measurement Flag,Quality Flag,Units
COOP:053579,GREENLAND 9 SE CO US,2279.9,39.1044,-104.7286,20130101 00:00,0.44,   ,HT,999.99,),,HT
COOP:053579,GREENLAND 9 SE CO US,2279.9,39.1044,-104.7286,20130101 00:15,0.00,g,,HT,0.00,g,,HT
COOP:053579,GREENLAND 9 SE CO US,2279.9,39.1044,-104.7286,20130130 14:15,0.45, ,,HT,-9999,,,
COOP:053579,GREENLAND 9 SE CO US,2279.9,39.1044,-104.7286,20130131 11:45,0.46, ,,HT,0.10, ,,HT
COOP:053579,GREENLAND 9 SE CO US,2279.9,39.1044,-104.7286,20130201 00:00,0.45,N,,HT,-9999,,,
COOP:053579,GREENLAND 9 SE CO US,2279.9,39.1044,-104.7286,20130201 00:15,0.00,g,,HT,0.00,g,,HT
COOP:053579,GREENLAND 9 SE CO US,2279.9,39.1044,-104.7286,20130201 09:45,0.46, ,,HT,-9999,,,
COOP:053579,GREENLAND 9 SE CO US,2279.9,39.1044,-104.7286,20130212 12:00,0.47, ,,HT,0.10, ,,HT
COOP:053579,GREENLAND 9 SE CO US,2279.9,39.1044,-104.7286,20130222 13:00,0.48, ,,HT,0.10, ,,HT
COOP:053579,GREENLAND 9 SE CO US,2279.9,39.1044,-104.7286,20130222 15:00,0.49, ,,HT,0.10, ,,HT
COOP:053579,GREENLAND 9 SE CO US,2279.9,39.1044,-104.7286,20130223 11:00,0.50, ,,HT,0.10, ,,HT
COOP:053579,GREENLAND 9 SE CO US,2279.9,39.1044,-104.7286,20130227 10:30,0.51, ,,HT,0.10, ,,HT
COOP:053579,GREENLAND 9 SE CO US,2279.9,39.1044,-104.7286,20130228 23:45,0.51, ,,HT,-9999,,,
COOP:053579,GREENLAND 9 SE CO US,2279.9,39.1044,-104.7286,20130301 00:00,0.51, ,,HT,-9999,,,
COOP:053579,GREENLAND 9 SE CO US,2279.9,39.1044,-104.7286,20130301 00:15,0.51,N,,HT,0.00,g,,HT
COOP:053579,GREENLAND 9 SE CO US,2279.9,39.1044,-104.7286,20130325 12:15,0.52, ,,HT,0.10, ,,HT
COOP:053579,GREENLAND 9 SE CO US,2279.9,39.1044,-104.7286,20130401 00:00,0.52, ,,HT,-9999,,,
COOP:053579,GREENLAND 9 SE CO US,2279.9,39.1044,-104.7286,20130401 00:15,0.52,N,,HT,0.00,g,,HT
COOP:053579,GREENLAND 9 SE CO US,2279.9,39.1044,-104.7286,20130403 09:00,0.53, ,,HT,0.10, ,,HT
COOP:053579,GREENLAND 9 SE CO US,2279.9,39.1044,-104.7286,20130414 08:15,0.54, ,,HT,0.10, ,,HT
COOP:053579,GREENLAND 9 SE CO US,2279.9,39.1044,-104.7286,20130414 09:15,0.55, ,,HT,0.10, ,,HT
COOP:053579,GREENLAND 9 SE CO US,2279.9,39.1044,-104.7286,20130418 13:45,0.56, ,,HT,0.10, ,,HT
```

Example raw data from NOAA U.S. 15 Minute Precipitation Data

From this initial look, you can learn a few things about the makeup of the data and areas you will need to investigate. Some examples are listed next:

- **The first row has the names of the fields in it**: This is good as you will not have to figure it out and enter the names yourself. However, you will need to make sure that when the file is loaded into a data store such as HDFS, the first row is not considered a data row.

- **There are two fields each with the name of Measurement Flag, Quality Flag, and Units**: This could be duplicate data, or it could be that the order of the field has meaning in relation to another field. You will need to know what each means and which one is which when you are ready to analyze the dataset. The order may be different in the analysis tool than it is in the text file. To prepare for this, find some rows that have different values in each of the fields, then note the fields that uniquely identify it (such as **STATION** and **DATE**). You can use those in the analysis tool to verify which field is which.

- **Values in the QPCP field are either very small positive numbers or -9999**: -9999 appears to signify something other than a measurement. Good thing you did not run averages using it.

- **There are quite a few missing values in the Measurement Flag and Quality Flag fields**: You will definitely need to review the documentation to understand what this means.

- **The date time values are not in a common standard format**: You might need to do some parsing to get your analytic tools to recognize the value as a date. Note the structure (`yyyymmdd hh:mm`).

- **There may not be a record for every 15-minute interval**: The rows appear to be in date and time order, but there does not appear to be a record for every 15-minute interval in a day. This may not be the case when the entire file is sorted, but you should note it as something to investigate.

Scan through several screens worth of data and look for any patterns. If the dataset seems to be sorted, scan through at least one transition to another source device to see how values change. We are not attempting to be very scientific at this stage in getting to know your data. The goal is to look for any obvious patterns and data quality issues.

Data completeness

Due to the nature of low-power sensors and unreliable connectivity, IoT data often has missing and incomplete values. You will want to get a sense of how often this occurs and if there are any patterns to it. For an initial look, we will use Tableau to connect to our sample dataset. It is recommended to go through the introductory training on the software website to familiarize yourself with it.

The first step is to connect to the `.csv` file that holds the weather data. In the starting screen, click on **Text file** as the data source type. Then, browse to and select the file to link to it.

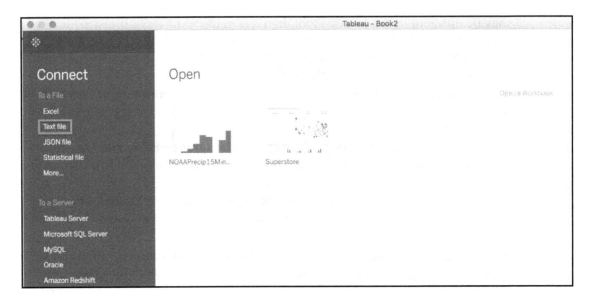

Review the field types assigned to the columns in the file. Note that the **Date** field is assumed to be a string format instead of a date-time format. If you attempt to change this, it will not be recognized due to the uncommon format. You will need to parse the date (as suspected during the raw file review):

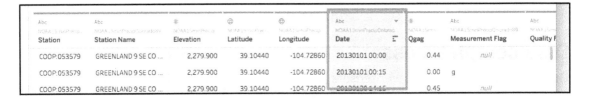

Click on the **Sheet1** tab to start building views into the data. We will need to do a little modification to the data fields to make exploring them a little easier. Right-click on the **Date** dimension and create in the pop-up menu and select the **Calculated** field. Call it `Measurement Date` and input the calculation, `DATEPARSE("yyyyMMdd hh:mm",[Date])`. This will take a string in the format described and interpret it as a date:

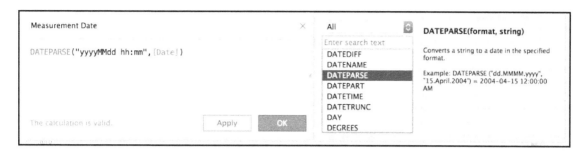

Next, we need to distinguish between the duplicate field names. You can give a field an alias name by right-clicking on it and selecting **Rename**. Rename the fields without a **1** at the end so that **Qgag** is after the name. Rename the fields *with* a **1** at the end with **Qpcp** after the name.

Use the unique identifiers you noted earlier to verify the field names are referring to the correct measurement.

1. Drag the **Station** field to the **Filter** shelf, and select one of the stations you noted.
2. Drag the **Measurement Date** field over and select the corresponding date and time.
3. Drag # of Records from measurements to the text box in the **Marks** card. There should only be the number 1 in the view, which verifies that the record is unique.
4. Right-click on the number and select **View Data** to look at the record. Verify that the field values for the renamed columns match what you noted earlier:

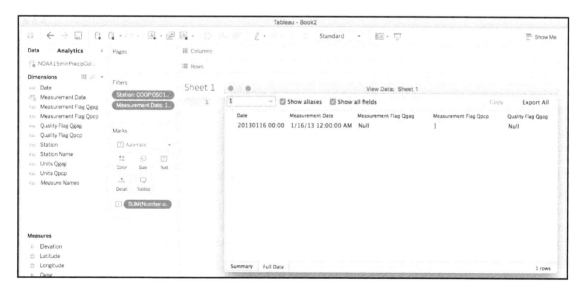

5. Move the **Number of Records** value from the **Marks** card to the **Rows** shelf.

6. Remove everything from the **Filter** shelf.

We will now fast forward a bit on the assumption you have went through the online training and know your way around Tableau. Any of the methods we will review could be done with other visualization software as well.

Completeness is not just about missing values but also about the continuity of data records. Even if all the values are complete, entire records could still be missing. Check for this by lining up record counts by date and time. Break out by station to look for periods when no data was recorded. If a data record was captured every 15 minutes, you should find 96 rows every day ((60 min/15 min) * 24 = 96):

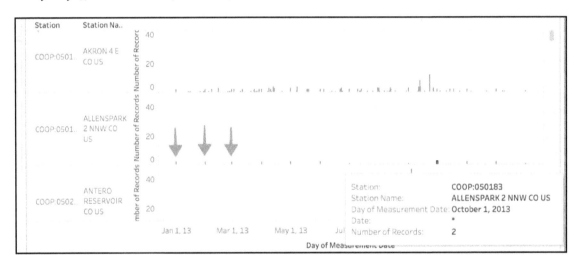

Record count by weather station and date

As can be seen in the preceding visual, there are not 96 records every day for each station. The record varies per day and some days have no records at all. Some weather stations are only reporting once a month on the first day. When you look into these records, it appears to be test records without usable precipitation values.

This would be the time to call your engineering and field service teams to understand if the station is reporting as intended. If so, you will want to know how to identify stations that report only test data, so they can be handled differently for analytics. If not, you may have just stumbled on a service you can provide. Your analytics team can create an algorithm to identify this pattern and automatically notify your customer that the station is not reporting data.

Select a bar for one of the stations that is sending frequent records, such as **Akron 4 E CO US**. Look at the individual records and review the values in the **Qgag** and **Qpcp** measurement fields. **Qgag** is a measure of the volume of precipitation in the measurement vessel at the time the record was captured. **Qpcp** is a measure of the amount of precipitation that occurred during the 15-minute time period. Look at the times to see if they are actual 15-minute intervals. It is possible that data records are only sent when there is something to report (in other words, it was raining).

Again, verify that conclusion with the people who developed the device and software. If this is the case, you may need to create artificial records for the intervals where it was not raining. This will depend on the analytics being explored. If you are predicting the probability of rainfall, you will need data for when it is not raining as well as when it is raining.

This is where understanding the dataset completion is important. If the device was functioning properly with no networking issues, then it would be safe to assume that no record means it was not raining. However, if the device was offline for some reason, it is not safe to assume this. Doing so will make accurate predictions very difficult.

Look through several other stations and note anything unusual. For example, you may notice some weather stations where record counts dramatically change frequency levels after a certain date. This can happen when a device had not been reporting correctly and the problem was fixed. You will need to adjust for this also; the records prior to the date when the device was corrected will probably need to be ignored for analytics:

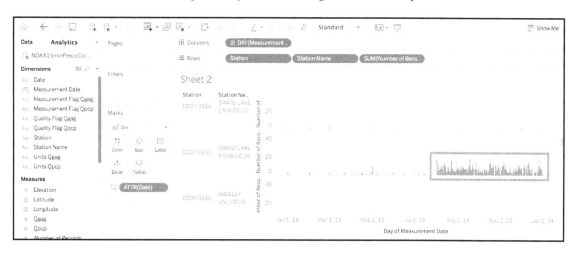

An example of a weather station with an increase in record counts

Note any unusual spikes in record counts. If this happens at multiple weather stations at the same time, it could indicate a data problem such as record duplication. It could also be real, so you need to verify it one way or another. Even if it seems odd, do not assume for certain that it is a data problem. In the example dataset, note the big increase that occurred during September 2013 at the Boulder 2 CO US station:

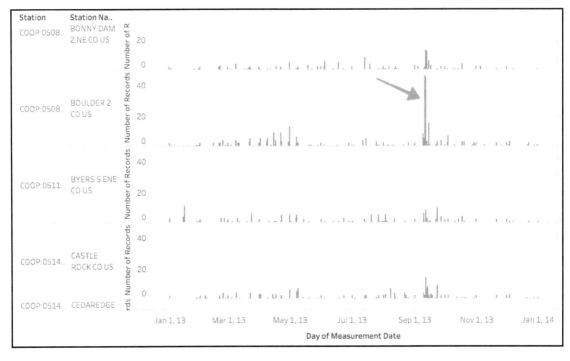

The record count spiked during September 2013 at Boulder 2 CO US weather station

The record count is well outside the range of any other period for the station. You also note that other stations are showing an increase at the exact same time. Note this for further exploration. We will come back to it later in the chapter.

Data validity

After finishing your completeness checks, it is important to check the validity of the data in the records that you do have. For each field in the measurements shelf, look for outliers well beyond any other data point. Also check for specific values that show up at a high frequency. The first could be either an error value or is serving as an indicator of an event other than a measurement. The second could be a default value that was intended to be overridden by the actual measurement value. There can be multiple explanations for unusual values; the goal is to identify the values and the approximate frequency of occurrence.

Looking at the **Qgag** values on a scale, it is apparent that there is a common outlier value on the negative side (**-9999**) and another one on the positive side (**999.990**, which may be rounded to 1,000 in the view). Select points in each of the outlier areas to review individual records. See if the actual values are consistently the same or have some variation. Consistent values are likely serving as intentional indicators. Variation could be due to a calculation error or conversion error that has the decimal point in the wrong place:

Qgag values on scale

Check the same view on a station by station basis. All stations have at least one **-9999** value but not all have **999.99**.

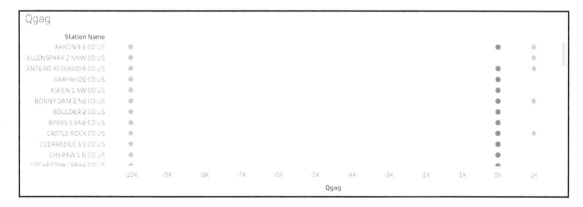

Qgag values by station

Since the extreme values do not appear to be actual readings, filter out both the high and low, by filtering to values between 0 and 900. Then, review the results to get a feel for typical ranges across weather stations. The values range between 0 and 2.4:

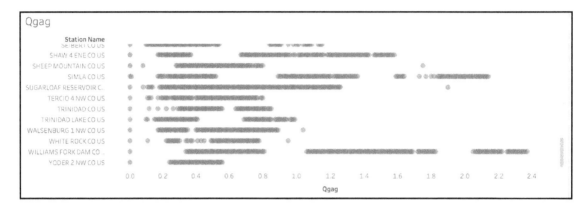

Filtered Qgag values by station

Repeat the same process with the other measure in the dataset, **Qpcp**. You will see that it also has the same extreme values (**-9999** and **999.990**) with the exception that some stations do not have a **-9999** record. Another difference is that where **Qgag** values are along a continuous scale, **Qpcp** appears to be reported in the increments of 0.1:

Filtered Qpcp values by station

Select some points and review individual data records to see if the **Qpcp** values are precise to the tenths digit or if there is some variation that is not visible on the chart. In this case, all values are precisely at the tenths digit.

We have shown some ways to look into data validity, but do not limit yourself to only what has been demonstrated. Continue exploring the data by slicing and dicing it in as many ways you can brainstorm. Talk with your design engineers on what range of measurement values should be expected and compare observations to that range. Refer back to your IoT device diagram in Chapter 1, *Defining IoT Analytics and Challenges* and use it to look for inconsistencies or distortions in the data.

Assessing Information Lag

Data from IoT devices does not always arrive into your dataset in the same intervals of time. Some records maybe included quickly as the devices are located closer or are in more populated areas with better connectivity. Remote locations may have more of a lag between the device capturing the observation and the data records becoming a part of your dataset. There could also be differences between groups of IoT devices in the data transportation route, or in the ETL jobs which process it into the dataset used for analytics.

Assessing the variation in lag times, which we will call **Information Lag**, is important to understand before applying more advanced analytics to the data. There could be significant bias in the faster arriving data records that does not exist after all records for the time period have been included. The following diagram shows variation in the Information Lag time for events that occurred at the same time. If the dataset were to be analyzed today, only the bottom event would be included:

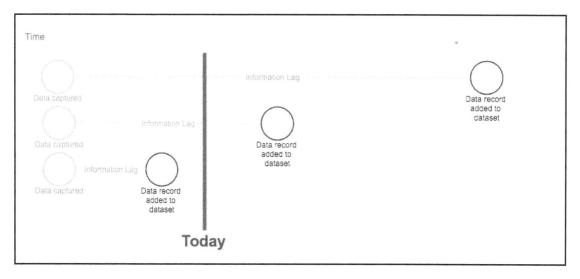

Information Lag time variation

In order to understand the variation in Information Lag, for each record used for analytics, subtract the time the record was added to the dataset from the time the observation was captured. Create a histogram (a binned bar chart) of the result to view the distribution of lag times.

Compare the data from the low lag time bins against the full dataset to look for differences in values. Pay special attention to geographic locations. Differences in averages and standard deviations are clues that the faster arriving data records are not good representatives of the full dataset. You will need to build in a wait time filter when analyzing recent data records to make sure most of the records needed for valid conclusions have arrived in the dataset.

Representativeness

Do the observed data values represent the real world? IoT devices should record values that are not only within the range of the sensors but also line up with what they are measuring in the real world. For example, a healthcare IoT device that measures pulse rate should report a distribution similar to what is observed at physician's offices for the same patient population.

A pulse rate of 120 is valid, but a distribution with an average of 120 does not represent a normal patient population. Unless the device is only attached to people during strenuous activity, there is probably something wrong with the data.

Basic time series analysis

Another way to get to know your IoT data is to explore observation values over time. Reviewing data records in order by the time and date recorded can allow you to discover patterns you may not otherwise find. We have done some of this already by reviewing record counts by date.

What is meant by time series?

Time series analysis is very common; you run across it every day from stock market price trends to GDP graphs. It is intuitive and so pervasive that it feels awkward even giving it a name. Time series is simply ordering data values chronologically and analyzing the results for patterns. The order should be at equally-spaced intervals even when there is no data for the interval.

Patterns can be discovered by the time of year (seasonal), by the business cycle, from values increasing or decreasing over time (trends), and even by the time of the day. Identified patterns can then be used in forecasting future values over time. We will look at the time series forecasting technique later in the book.

Applying time series analysis

The first step in time series analysis is deciding which time interval to use when exploring the data. You can choose several, and it is good practice to do so when getting to know your IoT data. You can start with monthly trends, then weekly, then daily, and even to the minute.

For our analysis, we will continue with the daily interval. Start with the **Qpcp** measure and view it by station to graph a daily summed **Qpcp** value. Filter out the extreme values that are almost certainly not actual measurements (you can use a 0 to 900 range in the filter). We have already identified an unusually high record count for the **Boulder 2 CO US** station that occurred in September 2013.

You also learned that there is not a data record for every 15-minute time period and have theorized that the data is sent primarily when there is a precipitation amount to report. If the assumption is correct, the sum of **Qpcp** values for a day should indicate the amount of precipitation for the day:

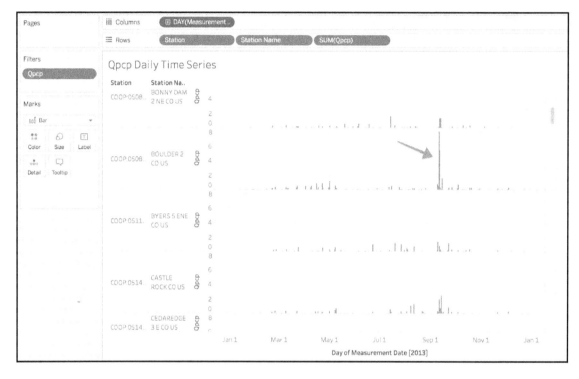

Qpcp sum spike during September 2013 at Boulder 2 CO US weather station

The preceding graph shows that the summed precipitation for the day is also at an unprecedented high during a few days in September 2013. Select the period and review the data records behind the bars. Checking the values and the recorded date-times, there does not appear to be record duplication:

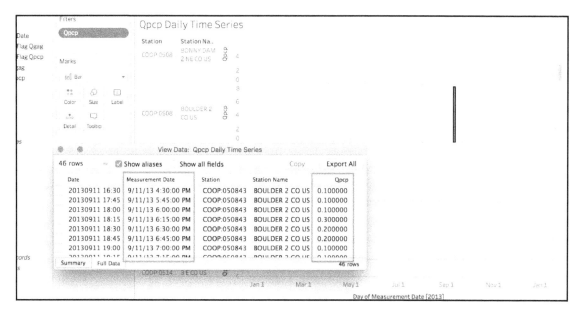

Data records sample from September 11-12th 2013 period for Boulder 2 CO US weather station

So far, there is not an indication of flawed data, despite the highly unusual number of records and summed precipitation values. Fortunately, weather is monitored by multiple news outlets and environmental agencies. If the values in the IoT data are real, it should be easy to confirm using external sources.

We will turn to one of an IoT analytic expert's most powerful tools, **Google search**, to see what we can find. All joking aside, web search skills are important to IoT analytics, whether it is researching a machine learning model or understanding sensor functionality.

External confirmation of unusual patterns in IoT data is also an essential data validation practice. We are using it here as a fun example, but it is something you should do on a regular basis:

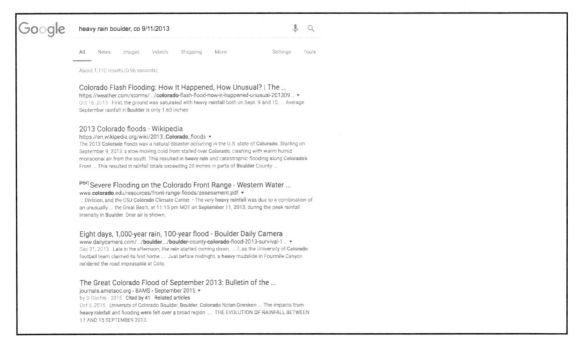

Google search results for heavy rain boulder, co 9/11/2013

From the search results, we can see there was, in fact, an extreme weather event in the Boulder, Colorado area at that time, rainfall so severe as to be referred to as a 1,000 year rain. This adds a lot of confidence that the reported results are indeed accurate.

Now, we can explore the **Qgag** value as a time series. Recall that **Qgag** is the measure of precipitation accumulated in the measure device. Here is the graph of **Qgag** by station over time (with the extreme values filtered out):

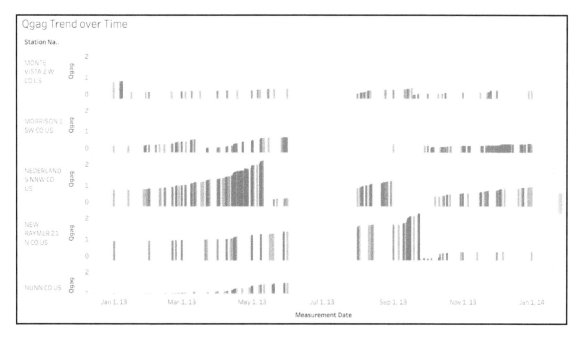

Qgag values over time

We can note a couple of interesting patterns. The first is that **Qgag** values are missing across all stations for a period around July 2013. This would warrant some phone calls to find out why. There are data records during that period; however, all have the **-9999 Qgag** values so are filtered out in this view.

The second is that the **Qgag** values for a station increase over time and at irregular intervals suddenly drop to a significantly lower value. Knowing that the values indicate accumulated precipitation, the drop could be an indication that the vessel on the device that holds the precipitation was emptied.

Identifying patterns like this can be value opportunities for your company. You can develop an analytic process that identifies both when a vessel needs emptied and verification that the task was completed. This could be valuable to a customer that has to send technicians to remote locations to perform the work. They could be very willing and quite happy to pay your company for this service. This means a path to increased revenues for your company with little additional cost to do so.

Get to know categories in the data

Now, explore the data by identifying categories and missing values. Drag various **Dimensions** to the **Rows** and **Columns** shelves to view categories, record counts, and missing values (Null). Compare some dimensions against each other to understand how they interact. Are both Null at the same time, or do they appear unrelated?

Tableau allows you to interact this way quickly, so take advantage of it. An example is shown in the following screenshot comparing the **Measurement Flag** fields for **Qgag** and **Qpcp** against each other. You can see that they are frequently Null at the same time:

Qgag versus Qpcp measurement flags using record counts

Bring in geography

Geography is a very powerful aid in understanding IoT data when devices are located in a variety of places. A thousand devices centered in Denver, Colorado are likely to provide different data values than a thousand devices spread evenly across the state. Patterns that are not obvious from statistical analysis of the data can become very obvious when shown on a map.

Look at the geographic location of the weather station precipitation data on a map. Are there clusters of stations in certain areas? If the locations are not evenly distributed, would an average rainfall calculation for the state based on device readings represent the actual average rainfall for the state? Probably not.

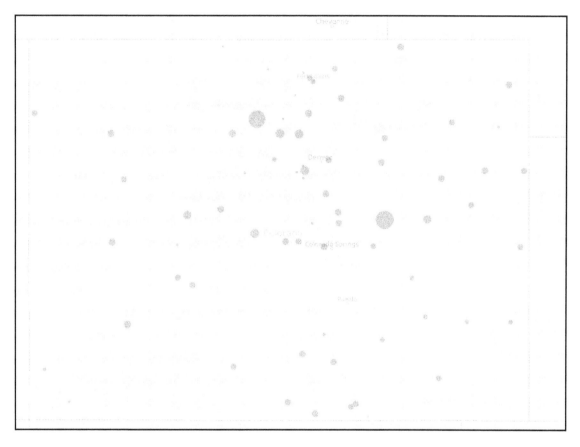

Geographic distribution of sample data on a map of Colorado. Size of the circle represents record counts.

If the latitude and longitude of the IoT devices are not available, use State/Province, phone number area codes, postal codes, or country. View data at different levels of resolution for geographic region (from state to postal code for example).

Also view how values and record counts change over time on the map. In Tableau, this can be done by dragging the date value, **Measurement date**, to the **Pages** shelf. Change the aggregation level to **Month with Year** and move through the months to observe how the data changes.

Look for invalid location data as well. If you have data filtered to the country code for Mexico yet see points in Canada, there is probably some data cleanup to perform.

Look for attributes that might have predictive value

Attributes is another name for data fields. It is commonly used when discussing predictive analytics and machine learning (**Features** is another synonym). When first exploring datasets, it is a good idea to look for attributes that could have predictive value if machine learning techniques are applied.

These are fields or categories that seem to influence the measurement values. Keep an eye out for them and take notes on what you find.

R (the pirate's language...if he was a statistician)

R is an open source statistical programming language. It has a wide variety of powerful libraries that are simple to download and plug into your analytics code. The packages are developed and maintained by a large community of statisticians and data scientists. It is very powerful and is continuously enhanced with new packages, which are released frequently.

Installing R and RStudio

If you do not have R, install the latest version from `https://cran.rstudio.com/`. Then, install RStudio, an **Integrated Development Environment** (**IDE**) for R, from `https://www.rstudio.com/products/rstudio/download/`. Both are open source and free to download and use. **RStudio** is managed by the RStudio company, based in Boston, which also offers paid support and an enterprise version of the software.

Using R for statistical analysis

For this example, we will use the *datasets* package, which has a wide variety of sample datasets. In RStudio, use the **Packages** tab to verify the *datasets* package is in the list and has a checkmark next to it. The **Packages** tab is in the interface in the lower-right quadrant.

Import the NOAA 15 minute Colorado precipitation dataset that we have been working with by clicking on the **Import Dataset** button and selecting **From CSV....** Navigate to the file, review the data column preview and code preview, and then click on the **Import** button.

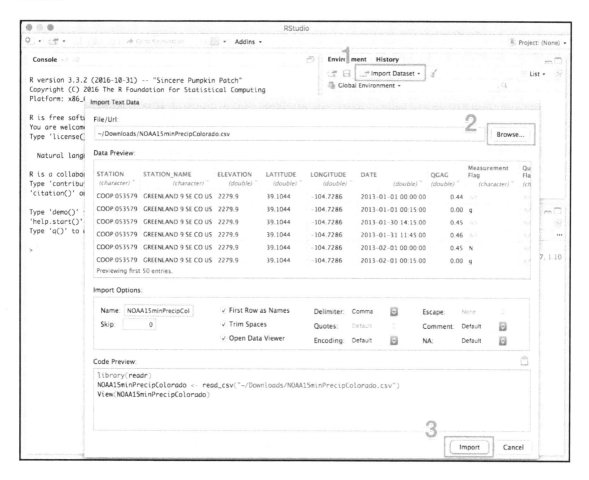

Note the code that was generated for you, which loads the data. You can also use this as a template to load in data files without going through the GUI menu:

```
#Bring in the code library for reading in text files
library(readr)

#Load the 15 minute precipitation dataset
NOAA15minPrecipColorado <-
read_csv("~/Downloads/NOAA15minPrecipColorado.csv")

#Show the dataset in an RStudio window
View(NOAA15minPrecipColorado)
```

The code loads in the data file, and then executes the `View()` function to display it in a table window. You will see the data in the upper-left pane. In the bottom-left pane (console), review any errors that occurred during the loading and parsing of the dataset. This will also have useful information on how R interpreted the data columns. You will need to decide whether the data errors are tolerable for the analysis you are doing. If not, some additional formatting and parsing will be needed.

Run the following code to generate summary statistics on each column in the dataset:

```
#Run summary statistics on the data frame the file was loaded into

summary(NOAA15minPrecipColorado)
```

The resulting summary will look like the following:

```
Console
> summary(NOAA15minPrecipColorado)
   STATION          STATION_NAME        ELEVATION
Length:11805       Length:11805       Min.   :1062
Class :character   Class :character   1st Qu.:1579
Mode  :character   Mode  :character   Median :1885
                                      Mean   :1993
                                      3rd Qu.:2469
                                      Max.   :3051
                                      NA's   :15
    LATITUDE          LONGITUDE           DATE
Min.   :37.07     Min.   :-109.0     Min.   :2013-01-01 00:00:00
1st Qu.:38.90     1st Qu.:-105.9     1st Qu.:2013-04-18 13:00:00
Median :39.25     Median :-105.1     Median :2013-07-29 20:15:00
Mean   :39.30     Mean   :-105.1     Mean   :2013-07-09 21:05:57
3rd Qu.:40.04     3rd Qu.:-104.1     3rd Qu.:2013-09-15 16:30:00
Max.   :40.93     Max.   :-102.1     Max.   :2014-01-01 00:00:00
NA's   :15        NA's   :15
     QGAG          Measurement Flag    Quality Flag
Min.   :-9999.00  Length:11805       Length:11805
1st Qu.:    0.33  Class :character   Class :character
Median :    0.72  Mode  :character   Mode  :character
Mean   :-1609.72
3rd Qu.:    1.09
Max.   :  999.99

    Units               QPCP          Measurement Flag_1
Length:11805       Min.   :-9999.0    Length:11805
Class :character   1st Qu.:-9999.0    Class :character
Mode  :character   Median :    0.1   Mode  :character
                   Mean   :-3211.8
                   3rd Qu.:    0.1
                   Max.   : 1000.0

Quality Flag_1       Units_1
Length:11805       Length:11805
Class :character   Class :character
Mode  :character   Mode  :character
```

Note the extreme values for **Min.** and **Max.** that we have already discovered in **Qgag** and **Qpcp.** We decided they are probably an indicator flag and not actual measurements. We can remove those values by some data manipulation. If you do not already have the R package *dplyr*, you can install it by either running the following code or using the RStudio GUI. The *dplyr* package is very useful for data manipulation and is used frequently for analytics with R:

```
#Install the package for dplyr on your laptop
install.packages("dplyr")
```

After *dplyr* is installed, run the following code to filter out data rows that have the extreme values for either **Qgag** or **Qpcp.** The code will also rerun the summary statistics:

```
#Bring in the code library for dplyr
library(dplyr)

#Filter records with the extreme value out of the dataset
NOAAfiltered <- filter(NOAA15minPrecipColorado, QPCP > 0, QPCP <900, QGAG
>0, QGAG<900)

#Run summary statistics on the filtered copy of the dataset
summary(NOAAfiltered)
```

The summary should now look like the following. Note the averages, medians, and quartiles are now more representative of real-world precipitation values:

```
> summary(NOAAfiltered)
    STATION           STATION_NAME         ELEVATION          LATITUDE          LONGITUDE
 Length:5076        Length:5076        Min.   :1062      Min.   :37.07      Min.   :-109.0
 Class :character   Class :character   1st Qu.:1532      1st Qu.:38.85      1st Qu.:-106.4
 Mode  :character   Mode  :character   Median :1885      Median :39.41      Median :-105.1
                                       Mean   :1935      Mean   :39.27      Mean   :-105.2
                                       3rd Qu.:2352      3rd Qu.:40.04      3rd Qu.:-104.1
                                       Max.   :3051      Max.   :40.93      Max.   :-102.1
       DATE                     QGAG          Measurement Flag    Quality Flag
 Min.   :2013-01-11 05:30:00   Min.   :0.0100   Length:5076        Length:5076
 1st Qu.:2013-04-18 10:56:15   1st Qu.:0.4600   Class :character   Class :character
 Median :2013-08-12 01:15:00   Median :0.7400   Mode  :character   Mode  :character
 Mean   :2013-07-13 06:10:00   Mean   :0.8376
 3rd Qu.:2013-09-18 20:15:00   3rd Qu.:1.1500
 Max.   :2013-12-30 03:30:00   Max.   :2.4000
    Units              QPCP          Measurement Flag_1 Quality Flag_1       Units_1
 Length:5076        Min.   :0.1000   Length:5076        Length:5076        Length:5076
 Class :character   1st Qu.:0.1000   Class :character   Class :character   Class :character
 Mode  :character   Median :0.1000   Mode  :character   Mode  :character   Mode  :character
                    Mean   :0.1095
                    3rd Qu.:0.1000
                    Max.   :1.2000
```

In practice, when you have missing or invalid values, you need to carefully review the dataset and decide whether it is better to remove the entire data record or to replace the value with something else. When you filter out the row, you will lose other fields, which may hold valid values. Your decision will depend on the type of analysis you are doing. Think carefully.

Summing it all up

So, what have you learned so far just by some quick slicing and dicing of the data? You learned that the dataset does not have a complete history for every weather station over the period. We identified that records are probably sent when there is something to report, and there is not a record for every 15 minutes of every day. We found some stations that only report once a month on the 1st day.

We detected a potentially useful pattern with the accumulated level of precipitation over time. An extreme event was identified in the data and was externally verified as an actual occurrence. You learned the statistical distribution of values for each field in the data using R.

The geographical distribution of stations was also explored. You learned that stations are not evenly spaced across the state of Colorado (although not too bad for the range of area covered). We also identified some data values that appear to be acting as an indicator instead of a measurement (**-9999**, **999.990**). All in all, you learned quite a bit about an unknown dataset.

Now, we will review the dataset documentation to find out whether we were correct about the extreme values. This is what would normally be done first, but saving it to last makes the chapter a little more interesting.

Reading through the documentation, we see that there is a value that indicates the beginning and end of precipitation accumulation. According to the document, this value is **99999** and coincides with a measurement flag of either **a** or **A**.

However, we know from looking at the data, that there are no **99999** values anywhere in the dataset. There is also no measurement flag of **a** or **A**, although the other categories listed seem to be present. The values we did observe, though, seemed to be representing the intent as there is no other special value mentioned anywhere in the document.

This is an important lesson for IoT data. Documentation can be wrong. Always check into what the data is telling you, trust but verify. Logic can also be implemented inconsistently across devices resulting in a mix of values, which may be the case here.

Solving industry-specific analysis problems

We will touch on a few industries to discuss special consideration for IoT data exploration and analysis.

Manufacturing

For IoT data generated during the manufacturing process, the accuracy of recorded values is especially important. Explore the data for outliers and analyze distributions carefully. Verify all the data ranges and distributions that you see with the experts on the manufacturing process.

The benefits of making sure the measurement values are clean as possible are two fold. First, any machine learning models created to detect problems will be significantly more accurate. Secondly, false positives due to invalid data can have a high penalty. The manufacturing line and product deliveries may be halted while the issue is investigated. In manufacturing, this can get expensive quickly. More perniciously, the long-term effect of false positives tends to be the complete rejection of the analytics by company management, when they no longer trust the numbers. This can cause even more expense to your company in the long run.

For IoT data generated from the product after it is delivered and in operation, the age of the product is key. Many issues are tied to how long the product has been in use, whether it is early in life (infant mortality) or late in life (wear out) problems. Age will need to be tracked carefully and investigated closely in your exploratory analytics.

Something else to watch out for: many inexperienced analysts calculate problem rates by grouping populations by production periods and comparing them by dividing the number of failures by the number of units built. Failures are typically determined by an IoT device communicating a fault code or by an abnormality in a measured value. There is a problem with this though, and it is a big one.

Since units built earlier have had more time in operation, they have more opportunity to experience a failure. Newer built units have had less opportunity. Units will continue to age, and the average time in operation for a production period will only grow over time. They are at uneven points in their operational life, as the datasets are not complete.

Populations with the same real failure rate will appear to have a declining failure rate when comparing older groups to newer groups. The conclusion from viewing the charts displaying these trends tends to be that the issue must have been corrected; the failure rate is down. This is a big problem as actions to correct the issue will not occur, as the management believes it is not needed. This can end up being a very expensive mistake.

To avoid this issue, you will need to normalize failure rates by the amount of operational time when comparing different production periods. If you measured by operating hours, you would compare failure rates by equivalent operating time. Only include failures up to that time in the calculation and make sure units included have been in use for at least that long.

There are other techniques that take time in operation into account such as **Weibull analysis** and the **Time-in-Service matrix** method (beyond the scope of this book). The key message here is to pay close attention to time in operation when calculating failure rates.

Healthcare

Healthcare IoT analytics have a lot in common with manufacturing IoT analytics. The accuracy of reported values is extremely important, and the age of the unit is a key factor linked to multiple health issues. However, unlike manufacturing, which strives to make consistent and repeatable processes, nature values variation in the units (people).

This makes environmental factors, location, and population demographics more important. Maybe counter-intuitively, it also makes the production period (when people are born) less important. In manufacturing, a change in the process could affect everything immediately. In life, variation protects against this, and trends take longer to affect the full population. This makes the detection of problems more difficult and complex statistical techniques more valuable to health care analytics.

The more accurate the IoT device records values and the more consistent the data sampling period, the better the performance of advanced analytics. Pay extra attention to the data value distributions compared to what would be expected for the population of people being measured.

Retail

Analysis problems in retail will focus on location, demographics, and time, among other factors. Exploring data using geography (latitude and longitude of locations) in a software such as Tableau increases the likelihood of finding patterns that can be exploited for business value.

When you can explore by geography, you can also integrate data with economic indicators for the region. Datasets about population in the area can be explored in combination with the IoT data. Date and time values for retail data needs to be especially accurate. Foot traffic during the day can impact sales. The IoT time values need extra analysis to ensure the accuracy.

Knowing the location combined with accurate time values can allow you to calculate the correct local time along with whether it is dark or light outside. Incorporating local traffic patterns and the amount of daylight could end up being key predictive features for a predictive model. The model could lead to increased sales.

Seasonal impact is also be a key factor for retail analytics. With accurate time and location, you can analyze IoT data for patterns related to the weather at the time the IoT data was captured.

Summary

In this chapter, you learned steps to explore IoT data in order to get to know and understand it well. The importance of reviewing raw data was discussed. Tableau was introduced, along with some walk-through on how to use it to explore and visualize data.

We introduced R and RStudio as a powerful way to do some statistical analysis of datasets. The chapter also discussed some industry-specific considerations for IoT analytics.

7

Decorating Your Data - Adding External Datasets to Innovate

"What if rich women like their houses colder than poor women?"

Oh no, you think. Your boss just asked an odd question and this usually means one thing. He has been assigned a SEWOTI, which means you have been assigned a SEWOTI (Stupid Executive Waste Of Time Idea). How would you even answer a question like that? Would that not require some extensive marketing surveys?

"Interesting question, how did it come up?" you ask.

"John, the Senior Vice President of Sales, was talking about how cold his wife likes to keep the house in the summer," he answered, "So we got to thinking that maybe wealthy women just like it colder. And if that was the case, maybe we should market the new top of the line thermostat to women instead of men."

You nod your head like it is a great idea. But you do not think it is a great idea, certainly not without the marketing data that backs it up.

"We were even talking about changing the color scheme on the faceplate to make it more feminine. Anna is working on pricing it right now," he continued, "And with the great work that you've done with analyzing and mapping the data from the field, I figured this would be an easy question for you to answer. So I told John we'll take the ball and run with it!"

How are you going to answer the question? You just have the data on the devices, not on the income level of the people pushing the buttons.

This chapter is about dramatically enhancing value by adding additional datasets to the stored IoT data. Valuable additions come from both internal sources, such as manufacturing or **Customer Relationship Management** (**CRM**) data, and external data sources, such as economic or demographic datasets. You will learn how to look for valuable datasets and combine them to enhance future analytics in the search for untapped business value.

This chapter covers the following topics:

- General strategies on extracting value from combining datasets
- Internal datasets:
    - Which ones and why?
- External datasets - geography:
    - Elevation
    - Weather
    - Map APIs
    - Transportation
- External datasets - demographic:
    - Census statistics
    - World factbook
- External datasets - economic:
    - Global economic data
    - Federal Reserve US time series
    - Using code and APIs to add data

Adding internal datasets

IoT data by itself is only part of the story. There is a multitude of useful data already available to you that could be a store of hidden value. Internal datasets can be overlooked as a way to quickly enhance IoT data. They are an excellent place to start. IoT data should not be viewed in isolation; think of it as a continuation of data already stored about your company's products, customers, and processes.

Data should be combined into a 360-degree view of your business to maximize the opportunity of finding new value in it. The fastest and easiest place to start is usually (but not always) the internal datasets that you already have available.

The reason it may not always be the fastest and easiest comes from internal data security and legacy system hurdles; which can sometimes make it difficult to extract internal data to combine with IoT data. This may be a stumbling block for internal datasets, which, perhaps counter-intuitively, is not the case with external datasets. External datasets tend to be easier to obtain and have less security concerns, since they are publicly available. Either way, the potential value is still worth the effort of overcoming these hurdles.

Which ones and why?

When deciding on which internal datasets to integrate with IoT data, think about which ones would help explain unusual changes in sensor values or would correlate with patterns in the data. These datasets are more likely to help uncover business value. There are many internal company datasets that will help you unlock value; we will discuss four areas to consider next.

Customer information

As obvious as it may be, it bears pointing out how important incorporating information about the customer is to uncovering value from your IoT data. Information such as customer address can be geocoded to get the latitude and longitude coordinates. This can be used to establish a device location, which will allow you to build another layer of analytics.

Understanding things such as sex, age, or income level can help identify patterns not visible otherwise. For industrial customers, knowing industry and application of the equipment where your device is located can be the key that unlocks hidden patterns in the data. For these and many other reasons, customer information should be at the top of the list of internal datasets to combine with IoT data.

Production data

Production information about the equipment that is the source of your IoT data is also valuable to throw into the mix. Failures are often linked to the manufacturing date, plant, and line where the equipment was assembled. Subcomponents and third-party parts are tied to the equipment identifier.

Production data can also be used to estimate time in the field if that is not directly available. This can be done by using manufacturing date as a starting place and estimating time to sale and in field operation. Different equipment configurations may also end up being key attributes that you can use to make assumptions for other data that you may not have.

For example, if a company builds vehicles, and red flashing lights are only included on vehicles built as fire trucks, you can probably classify the customer of these vehicles as fire departments even if you do not have this information directly in the customer data.

Field services

Bringing in datasets from technician repair visits, maintenance records, and call center logs is another great place to start tapping value from your data. There will be key events such as repair work or complaint calls that can be linked to unusual patterns in IoT data.

Maintenance records will be useful in developing predictive maintenance models. It may also tie into equipment failure predictive models. Call center logs could be mined to develop attributes of IoT data events beyond just reported numerics or categorical values. **Natural Language Processing (NLP)** can be used to extract attributes from text data.

For a utility company that provides natural gas, for example, the phrase *rotten egg* in call log texts, corresponding to a pattern in the IoT data for low gas pressure, could be a tip off that a gas leak is occurring. Analytics could then be developed to recognize the pattern in future IoT data records for proactive investigation.

Financial

The difference between revenue and cost is profit. The anticipation of profit is the driver for most investments in IoT systems. Linking customer payments (revenue) and company expenses (costs) to IoT datasets can shed light on potential value opportunities.

You may find that customers spend money on your products after certain events identifiable in IoT data. This could be extended warranty purchases or service parts. You may also find that they do not spend money when you would expect they should. An example is IoT data indicating part failures but with no corresponding part purchased by the customer. This implies the service parts were bought from someone else. You will want to identify both the situations.

Adding external datasets

There is a wide variety of useful external datasets available to download and integrate into your IoT analytics, often for free. There are far too many of these to do an exhaustive tour, but we will touch on some useful examples. Using these datasets is a great low-cost way to enhance the value of your IoT data.

External datasets - geography

You have IoT devices distributed across many locations. Location is now an attribute that can allow you to find patterns in the data, which you can then monetize. The environment, the demographics in the area, the local economic conditions, and the weather can all be tied to the geographic location of the device. Use geographic datasets to enhance the potential value of your IoT data.

Elevation

Elevation can be an important attribute in many situations as it is tied to the operating conditions of the device and the surrounding environment. Even if your device does not move, it can still be valuable to know its elevation. The maker of a smart oven, for example, would surely want to know elevation as it affects baking time and characteristics.

SRTM elevation

In February 2000, the U.S. Space Shuttle Endeavor was launched specially equipped with two radar antennas on a mission to map the topography of most of the globe. As depicted in the following image, one of the radar antennas was inside the shuttle bay and the other was at the end of a 200 foot (60 meter) mast. The mast was extended once the shuttle was in the orbit. The combined radar swept the earth as the shuttle orbited in a pattern over the globe.

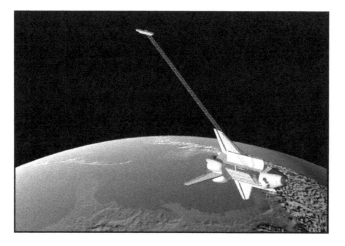

The artist rendering of SRTM in operation. Courtesy NASA/JPL-Caltech

The mission was called the **Shuttle Radar Topography Mission** (**SRTM**) and in its 10 days of operation, it collected the most complete near-global dataset of high-resolution elevation mapping to date. This was an international mission led by the National Geospatial-Intelligence Agency (NGA) and the National Aeronautics and Space Administration (NASA).

The data was captured using two sets of radar equipment: one referred to as C-band and the other as X-band. The C-band data was processed over two years by the Jet Propulsion Laboratory in California. The slightly higher resolution X-band data was processed by German Aerospace Center (DLR). Global data was fully released in 2015.

The resolution of the data is at 90 meters globally and 30 meters within the United States. The dataset can be downloaded from the **U.S. Geological Services** (**USGS**) website (`https ://lta.cr.usgs.gov/SRTM`). There are also R and Python packages (*SRTM.py* on GitHub is an example) built to handle downloading and manipulation of the SRTM dataset. The author recommends using one of these instead of the full dataset, unless you have a very large set of locations that you want to add elevation data for, all at once.

National Elevation Dataset (NED)

The NED is a high-resolution elevation dataset covering the United States, including Alaska, Hawaii, and territorial islands. It is managed by the USGS, which updates it about every 2 months to include new and improved data. The data is assembled from a diverse set of sources and transformed to a common coordinate system and elevation scale (meters).

The resolution ranges from 90 meters down to 3 meters (1/9th arc-second) in some areas. Processing and interpolation techniques are used to produce a seamless dataset for full coverage. The size of the total set of data files is quite large; the USGS has a map viewer to help identify regions to download the subsets of the data.

NED includes the following sets of products:

- **NED 3**: This data has the highest resolution (1/9 arc-second, which is approximately 3 meters) but has limited coverage.
- **NED 10**: This data has high resolution (1/3 arc-second ,which is approximately 10 meters) and is created from multiple **Digital Elevation Models** (**DEM**). Sources can include LIDAR and aerial photography.
- **NED 30**: This dataset has wide coverage and moderate resolution (1 arc-second, which is approximately 30 meters). It is assembled from multiple DEMs resampled to 1 arc-second.
- **NED 60**: This is the lowest resolution data (2 arc-seconds, which is approximately 60 meters). It adds coverage for some areas of Alaska.

NED is useful for higher-precision elevation data needs. The downside is that it is limited in coverage to the United States. The author recommends using SRTM when possible as long as the resolution is acceptable for your use case. The elevation values will differ between the datasets, but in general, the author has found them to be fairly comparable.

NED data can be downloaded using the map viewer tool at `https://viewer.nationalmap.gov/basic/`. The following screenshot shows the coverage of the NED 10 data. Data files are in GIS format, which we will discuss further in a later chapter. Files are also available for a direct download from an FTP site (`ftp://rockyftp.cr.usgs.gov/vdelivery/Datasets/Staged/Elevation/`). The following image shows the map and download interface:

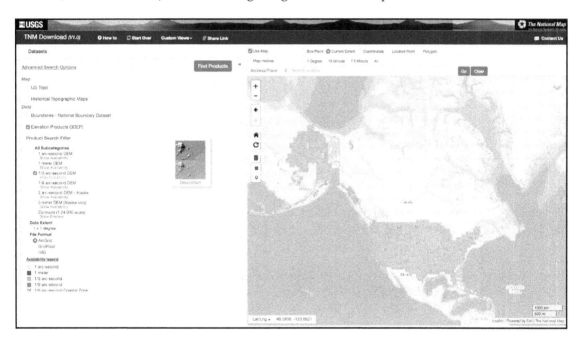

National map viewer data download tool. NED 10 coverage shown in orange.

Weather

There are many sources for weather-related data, both paid and free. The **National Oceanic and Atmospheric Administration** (**NOAA**) has multiple free datasets available for download. From climatic data to daily averages, there is a lot of useful information to choose from.

The Integrated Surface Global Hourly dataset can be useful for many IoT analytics projects. This dataset includes weather attributes such as air quality, atmospheric pressure, temperature, dew point, wind speed and direction, clouds, and precipitation from over 20,000 global stations. The digital observations are forwarded from various operation centers or decoded directly at the Federal Climate Complex in Asheville, North Carolina, USA.

All the data is stored in a single ASCII format that conforms to **Federal Information Processing Standards** (**FIPS**). The data files are sorted by the weather station, year, month, day, hour, and then minute. An example of the dataset is shown in the following screenshot:

```
 AWS   WBAN  YR--MODAHRMN  DIR SPD GUS CLG SKC  L M H  VSB  WW  WW WW  W  TEMP DEWP   SLP   ALT   STP MAX MIN PCP01 PCP06 PCP24 PCPXX SD
722280 13876 200301010053  140  11 ***  49 OVC  * * * 10.1 00  ** ** *   59   54 1003.8 29.65 ****** *** *** ***** ***** ***** ***** **
722280 13876 200301010153  140  13 ***  25 OVC  * * *  2.5 63  10 ** *   57   54 1003.7 29.65 ****** *** ***  0.03 ***** ***** ***** **
722280 13876 200301010253  170  14  21  14 OVC  * * *  3.0 63  10 ** *   57   55 1003.7 29.65 ****** *** ***       T ***** *****  0.22 **
722280 13876 200301010316  160   9  16  79 BKN  * * * 10.1 00  ** ** *   57   54 ****** 29.65 ****** *** ***       T ***** ***** ***** **
722280 13876 200301010353  150   9 *** 108 BKN  * * * 10.1 00  ** ** *   57   54 1003.7 29.65 ****** *** ***       T ***** ***** ***** **
722280 13876 200301010453  170   9 ***  59 BKN  * * *  4.0 10  ** ** *   57   54 1003.4 29.64 ****** *** ***       T ***** ***** ***** **
722280 13876 200301010553  170   6 ***  60 OVC  * * * 10.0 00  ** ** *   56   53 1002.6 29.62 ******  60  56 *****  0.22 ***** ***** **
722280 13876 200301010609  170   8 ***  19 OVC  * * *  7.0 61  ** ** *   55   54 ****** 29.62 ****** *** ***       T ***** ***** ***** **
722280 13876 200301010617  160   8 ***  20 OVC  * * *  7.0 00  ** ** *   55   52 ****** 29.61 ****** *** ***       T ***** ***** ***** **
722280 13876 200301010653  160   5 ***  36 OVC  * * *  7.0 61  ** ** *   55   52 1002.2 29.61 ****** *** ***       T ***** ***** ***** **
722280 13876 200301010700  160   5 ***  37 OVC  * * *  7.0 61  ** ** *   55   52 1002.2 29.61 ****** *** ***  0.00 ***** ***** ***** **
722280 13876 200301010753  170   6 ***  17 OVC  * * *  6.0 51  45 10 *   54   52 1002.0 29.60 ****** *** ***  0.00 ***** ***** ***** **
722280 13876 200301010823  150   5 ***  13 OVC  * * *  4.0 61  10 ** *   54   52 ****** 29.60 ****** *** ***  0.01 ***** ***** ***** **
722280 13876 200301010853  190   6 ***  13 OVC  * * *  3.0 61  45 10 *   54   52 1002.2 29.61 ****** *** ***  0.00 ***** *****  0.03 **
```

Sample NOAA integrated surface global hourly data. Source: NOAA

The dataset can be downloaded in multiple ways, including with a map viewer. You can also get data definition and other useful documentation from `https://data.noaa.gov/dat aset/integrated-surface-global-hourly-data`.

If you know the latitude and longitude of your IoT devices, you can download the location information for the weather stations from the web page. This information is compiled in a KMZ file. Use this to link to the nearest weather station in order to add the weather attributes at the place and time of IoT data records.

Geographical features

Elevation and weather conditions are valuable datasets to add when you know the location of your devices, but incorporating geographical features in relation to your device can also be a way to unlock hidden value through analytics. This becomes especially important when your device moves, such as when attached to a shipping container.

Planet.osm

OpenStreetMap is a free and editable map of the world created and maintained by volunteers. It has important features such as roads, places of interest, country borders, and ports. It is released with an open-content license, so it is free to use.

Geographic data was compiled from many sources, including the public submission of GPS traces. The following screenshot shows an example of the level of detail available and some of the volunteer submission of GPS traces:

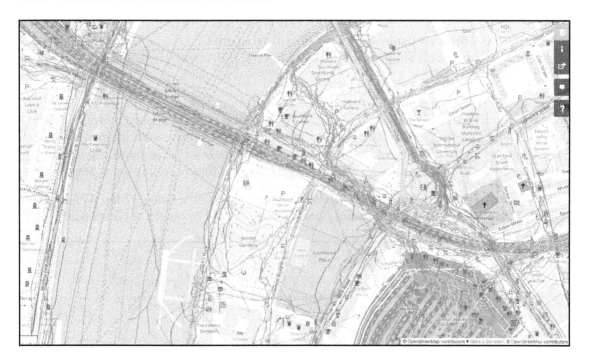

OpenStreetMap closeup view of London with GPS traces layer turned on.

Planet.osm is all of the OpenStreetMap features in one file. The file in total is about 750 GB when uncompressed, so it is a mouthful. You can also download files for individual countries or continents (called extracts).

Information on the **planet.osm** file and download locations is located on the OpenStreetMap wiki site (`http://wiki.openstreetmap.org/wiki/Planet.osm`). There are two file format options, PBF or compressed OSM XML. PBF is a binary format. It is smaller, so it is faster to download and process. OpenStreetMap recommends using it when possible.

You will need GIS tools to open and process the data. These will be discussed in a later chapter. Having a full dataset with details about roads (name and type of road for example) and points of interest (restaurant or gas station for example) can be especially useful for transportation-related IoT data. Incorporating a full-scale dataset into your Hadoop environment, for instance, allows you to operate geospatial analytics at scale.

Google Maps API

Location data from IoT devices can also be decorated as needed versus integrating a full dataset into your environment. Third-party APIs are a good way to do this while leveraging the expertise of other companies that specialize in geospatial analytics. There are many good ones available, including APIs from Google, Bing (Microsoft), Esri, and OpenStreetMaps.

Although mainly intended for web and mobile application developers, the web service APIs for Google Maps can be used to quickly add location identifiers, turn addresses into latitude and longitude coordinates, or calculate driving times between locations. The APIs can add many useful attributes to a dataset. Using them makes a lot of sense when your data record flow is in the tens of thousands per day versus tens of millions per day.

The following screenshot shows the variety of currently available Google Map APIs. Each API has its own set of functionality and options, putting a lot of power at your fingertips:

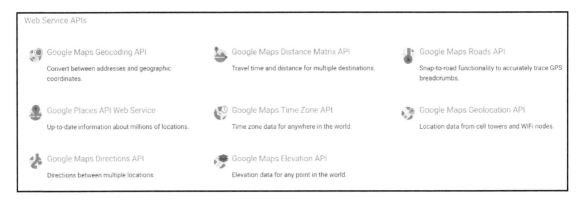

Google Maps web service APIs. Source: Google

Leveraging the web service APIs to add attributes to IoT data can be done easily in R or Python. Google provides a Python Client Library to simplify the use for the programming language. There are packages available on CRAN, such as a googleway, that simplify Google Maps API calls for R.

To start using Google Maps API, you will need to obtain a developer key to use in your API calls that authenticates the code and sets up billing. There are links on the Maps API website to help you set this up.

Here is a sample R code using the *googleway* package. You will need to install it first using the RStudio GUI or the code, `install.packages ("googleway")`. Insert your Google Maps API key and run the code to get the time zone offset for the latitude and longitude coordinates:

```
#Load googleway package (assuming it is already installed)
library(googleway)

#Get the timezone offset information for a pair of latitude and longitude
coordinates
tz <- google_timezone(location = c(41.882702,-87.619392),timestamp =
as.POSIXct("2017-03-05"),key = "< Replace everything between these quotes
with your API Key >")

#view results
View (tz)
```

This is a very simple example, but shows how easily it can be used to do something that would be quite complex to develop by yourself.

USGS national transportation datasets

The **United States Geological Survey** (**USGS**) national transportation dataset is a collection of datasets that includes railroads, trails, airports, roads, waterways, and other transportation-related geographical features. The data was provided through U.S. Census Bureau sources and supplemented with road data from a specialist mapping company, HERE.

Data not only includes the shapes of roads and railways but also tables of information about them. The coverage is limited to the United States but has standardized classification codes and descriptors. The dataset was compiled to support geospatial analysis related to traffic safety, congestion, disaster planning, and emergency responses.

The dataset is available to download at no cost in either Esri File Geodatabase or Shapefile format. The following screenshot is a subset of the available data tables in the dataset:

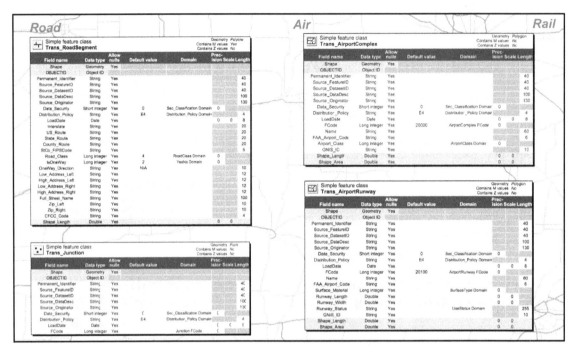

Partial view of USGS Best Practices data table definitions. Source: USGS

External datasets - demographic

Another way to enhance the value of IoT data is to add demographic information based on time and location. Attributes such as healthcare coverage rate, average income in the area, and population ages could have predictive values when combined with your IoT data.

The U.S. Census Bureau

For the U.S., the Census Bureau maintains demographic datasets down to the state and county level. Many other countries have similar government bodies with the same mission. There are multiple datasets available, but a great place to start is the QuickFacts dataset.

QuickFacts maintains statistics for all U.S. states and counties, along with cities and towns that have a population of 5,000 or more. It includes statistics on population size and density, age and sex, race, housing, education, economy, income, business, and health. The dataset uses the **Federal Information Processing Standards** (**FIPS**) code as the identifier. The FIPS code is normally what you would use to link to your IoT data.

The FIPS code is a five-digit identifier that identifies counties (or county equivalents) in the United States. The first two digits signify the state and the last three identify the county. A list of FIPS codes can be downloaded from `https://www.census.gov/geo/reference/code s/cou.html`.

The U.S. Census Bureau also maintains some useful geospatial datasets that have demographic information already integrated. Information about the **Topologically Integrated Geographic Encoding and Referencing** (**TIGER**) datasets is available at `https ://www.census.gov/geo/maps-data/data/tiger.html`:

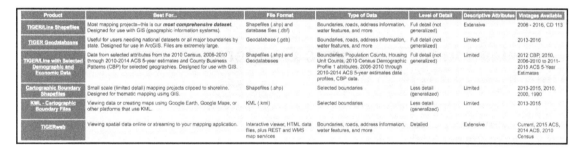

Product	Best For...	File Format	Type of Data	Level of Detail	Descriptive Attributes	Vintages Available
TIGER/Line Shapefiles	Most mapping projects—this is our *most comprehensive dataset*. Designed for use with GIS (geographic information systems).	Shapefiles (.shp) and database files (.dbf).	Boundaries, roads, address information, water features, and more	Full detail (not generalized)	Extensive	2006 - 2016, CD 113
TIGER Geodatabases	Useful for users needing national datasets or all major boundaries by state. Designed for use in ArcGIS. Files are extremely large.	Geodatabase (.gdb)	Boundaries, roads, address information, water features, and more	Full detail (not generalized)	Limited	2013-2016
TIGER/Line with Selected Demographic and Economic Data	Data from selected attributes from the 2010 Census, 2006-2010 through 2010-2014 ACS 5-year estimates and County Business Patterns (CBP) for selected geographies. Designed for use with GIS.	Shapefiles (.shp) and Geodatabases	Boundaries, Population Counts, Housing Unit Counts, 2010 Census Demographic Profile 1 attributes, 2006-2010 through 2010-2014 ACS 5-year estimates data profiles, CBP data.	Full detail (not generalized)	Limited	2012 CBP, 2010, 2006-2010 to 2011-2015 ACS 5-Year Estimates
Cartographic Boundary Shapefiles	Small scale (limited detail) mapping projects clipped to shoreline. Designed for thematic mapping using GIS.	Shapefiles (.shp)	Selected boundaries	Less detail (generalized)	Limited	2013-2015, 2010, 2000, 1990
KML - Cartographic Boundary Files	Viewing data or creating maps using Google Earth, Google Maps, or other platforms that use KML.	KML (.kml)	Selected boundaries	Less detail (generalized)	Limited	2013-2015
TIGERweb	Viewing spatial data online or streaming to your mapping application.	Interactive viewer, HTML data files, plus REST and WMS map services	Boundaries, roads, address information, water features, and more	Detailed	Extensive	Current, 2015 ACS, 2014 ACS, 2010 Census

TIGER products description. Source: U.S. Census Bureau

CIA World Factbook

The Central Intelligence Agency (CIA) of the United States maintains a free, useful, no-strings-attached (that we know about) database of information about the countries of the world. Despite the reputation of daring spywork, CIA also has the comparatively boring role of compiling useful information about places all over the world.

The agency makes some of this information available to anyone that can use a web browser. If anyone from the agency is reading this book (hopefully through a purchase and not directly from the author's laptop - but we kid, we kid), the author would like to thank you for making this great source of global information available for free. It is available as public domain, which means no worries about copyright or reserved publication rights issues.

The World Factbook includes information about over 260 world entities (as they term it, but think countries). The information is on things such as the history, people, government, economy, geography, communications, transportation, and military for each country.

However, the World Factbook is not available in machine-readable form from the website; you can find a JSON version on GitHub. It is a useful reference for understanding various countries of the world if your IoT devices are globally distributed. It is available at `https ://www.cia.gov/library/publications/the-world-factbook/`.

External datasets - economic

Economic data and changes in trends can also be a source of predictive value when combined with IoT data. This information can help explain buying patterns for retail use cases, energy consumption for utility monitoring, and machinery utilization rates in manufacturing.

Organization for Economic Cooperation and Development (OECD)

OECD is a forum where 34 democratic market-economy countries work together along with over 70 non-member countries to promote economic growth, prosperity, and sustainable development. As part of this mission, the organization compiles a database of economic and related statistics, which it makes available to everyone.

> *The Organization provides a setting where governments can compare policy experiences, seek answers to common problems, identify good practice, and coordinate domestic and international policies.*

The database is available on **OCED.Stat** (`http://stats.oecd.org/`). It has datasets that range from agriculture and fisheries to industry and services. Data is included for OECD member countries and some selected non-member economies. Since the information for all the countries follow the OECD statistic guidelines, they are much more comparable than when collected through different sources, which may have different statistical methods.

Each theme has subcategories and multiple measures within each of them. There are methods to export the datasets into machine readable form (such as **.csv**) and an API that can be used to grab the data with code. The site has functionality to create template API queries, which simplifies using it. The following screenshot is an example of what statistics are available in the **Monthly Economic Indicators** theme:

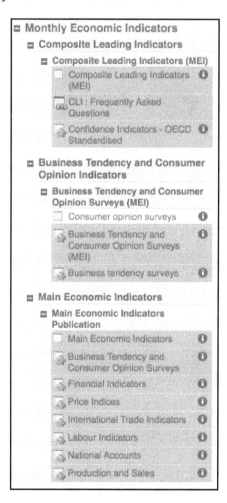

OECD Monthly Economic Indicators Available Datasets. Source: OECD.Stat

Federal Reserve Economic Data (FRED)

In the United States, the Federal Reserve Bank of St. Louis maintains a huge set of economic related time series data, mostly covering the U.S., but some are international. This collection is referred to as FRED. FRED is your friend, he knows a lot.

He knows the Consumer Price Index For All Urban Consumers, by month. FRED knows the Civilian Unemployment Rate and Real Median Household Income. He knows the Estimate of People of All Ages in Poverty for United States and the number of internet users in the world.

There are over 470,000 U.S. and international time series from over 80 different sources in FRED. FRED has useful tools such as a Microsoft Excel Add-in and some mobile apps for your smartphone. FRED even has a forecasting game you can play called FREDcast. FRED is located at `https://fred.stlouisfed.org/`.

FRED has a geospatial component called GeoFRED. You can use it to create a map version of the time series data or to download shapefiles. The following screenshot is an example showing the 2014 90% Confidence Interval Lower Bound of Estimate of Median Household Income by County:

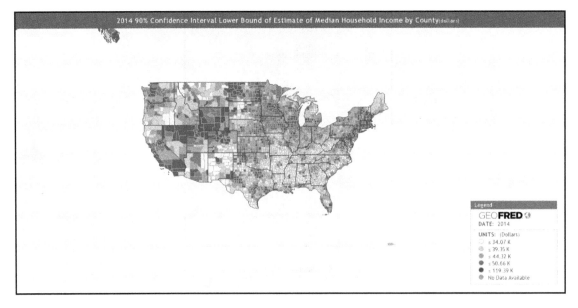

2014 90% Confidence Interval Lower Bound of Estimate of Median Household Income by County. Source: GeoFRED

FRED has three developer APIs:

- **FRED APIs**: This can be used to programmatically retrieve time series data from the FRED datasets.
- **FRASER APIs**: This API can be used to retrieve metadata from the **Federal Reserve Archival System for Economic Research** (**FRASER**). FRASER holds historical documents and archives.
- **GeoFRED APIs**: This allows programmatic access to GeoFRED data and shapefiles.

You will need to obtain an API key from the FRED website to use them. Another way to grab FRED data is from using an R package such as *Quandl*. Install the package from RStudio GUI or the `install.packages` function. You can then use it to get data from several financial data sources including FRED. The following is some sample R code that gets the U.S. GDP time series data:

```
#load Quandl library
library(Quandl)

#Grab US GDP time series data from FRED
gdp_ts = Quandl("FRED/GDP")

#Display
View(gdp_ts)
```

Using code libraries in R allows you to automate the process to incorporate the data on a regular basis into your analytics environment.

Summary

In this chapter, we discussed how to enhance your IoT data with both internal and external datasets. This can greatly enhance the opportunity to find value. By adding this additional data, you can develop attributes to develop and test theories about your data.

All theories should be tested with data. IoT data allows you to have a giant lab where you can run virtual experiments by segmenting and comparing the data you already have. By adding in external datasets, you can magnify the ability to find valuable patterns with IoT analytics.

8
Communicating with Others - Visualization and Dashboarding

It has been a few months since your analysis prevented the bright pink thermostat cover debacle. Your boss has been promoted to Director, IoT Analytics due to his leadership in developing the capability to use IoT field data to answer business questions. You, however, have the same job just more responsibilities.

Your analytics is being used throughout the company. You are excited about it, but are now spending a lot of time pulling together standard reporting to be sent to various groups every week.

"Klineman in Finance wants to see the active devices trend chart you do, but he wants it in a table. I don't know why, but can you do a version like that for him?" your boss asks with an upbeat tone in his voice. He seems to get happier the more charts and graphs that people want. You get busier and busier.

"Okay, that's it!" you say as your anger slips out, "They need to get their own charts somehow. I can't handle all these versions and questions that come back. I didn't take this job to spend all my time doing basic reporting and answering basic questions. They need to be able to answer it themselves."

Your boss is taken aback by your response; he probably assumed you were as happy as he was. "Okay, okay. We'll figure this out. You just need to create some dashboards so they can answer their own questions. See, easy! I'll back you up and make them do it, no worries."

You are not sure how to do that, but definitely want to free up your time to do more advanced analytics.

After talking with Jim Klineman in Finance, you discover he only wants a table because he wants to average the count over the fiscal year. He is using it for financial planning purposes. The sales technicians, however, want to see charts, since they use it day to day as a quick check on increases and declines.

You will have to think about this carefully. You do not want to create a different dashboard for everyone, but you also want each of them to be able to get effective use from whatever you create. And not bug you with follow-up questions.

This chapter is about designing effective visualizations and dashboards for IoT data. Once you find valuable patterns in data, you will need to communicate them with others. Visualizations are an effective way to quickly communicate complex data.

As your analytics develop, other people will be monitoring the data to identify patterns and track trends over time. Designing useful dashboards allows them to quickly identify patterns to investigate and also answer their own follow-up questions. Think of it as another type of communication.

We will be using Tableau to build both visuals and dashboards. You will learn how to take what you have learned about the data and convey it in an easy to understand way. This chapter covers both internal and customer facing dashboards.

This chapter covers the following topics:

- Common mistakes when designing visuals:
    - Tips to avoid them
- The hierarchy of questions method:
    - Mapping out end user thought processes
    - Developing question trees
    - Aligning visuals with a hierarchy of user questions
- Designing visual analytics for IoT data:
    - Using position to convey importance
    - Using color effectively
    - Tips for creating effective charts
- Creating a dashboard with Tableau:
    - Walk-through example using weather station data
- Quickly create and visualize alerts:
    - Alert principles
    - Organizing alerts for Tableau dashboards

Common mistakes when designing visuals

Charts and dashboards tend to be done as an afterthought to analytics. The interesting work (to the analyst) has already been finished at this point. There is a rush to put together some visuals so one can move on to the next challenge.

The rush to throw together a visual is a mistake in itself, as the first impression your audience, the people at the meeting or the users of your dashboard, will make on the quality of your analytics is determined by what they see first - your visuals. In this chapter, we will use the word *audience* to refer to both the end users of a dashboard and the viewers of an analytics presentation.

This makes it far more important to get it right than you may think. Analytics for the sake of analytics is pointless. Someone needs to actually use it, for it to have value. For someone to be willing to use it, they must understand it and be engaged by it.

It is easy to design bad visuals; we see examples of it all the time - especially in marathon powerpoint meetings. Watch out for these common mistakes when you design yours:

- **Assuming others know the data intimately**: You know it well, and it can be easy to forget others do not. Here are some ways to address this:
    - **Always, always, always (always) label chart axes so your audience know what is being measured**: Some charting software makes this difficult as the default setting inexplicably does not show axis labels (*I'm looking at you, Microsoft Excel*).
    - **Avoid using abbreviations and acronyms**: Make this clear in order to minimize opportunities for misinterpretation. The acronym ETD can mean Estimated Time of Departure or Explosive Trace Detection, both would mean very different things when analyzing airport data.

- **Focusing on the analytics instead of the conclusions**: You did great work and want to show it off, nothing wrong with this. But your audience wants to know what to do with it more than they want to know all the methods and techniques you used to get there. They want to know what actions they need to take based on the analysis. Here are some ways to help them:
    - **Make the conclusions obvious**: Highlight, circle, and point a big arrow at the important information. Do not make them have to figure it out for themselves. In a dashboard, the important information should draw the eye first.

- **Hide the complexity**: If it does not add information useful to drawing a conclusion, hide it.
- **Start with the end**: Show your conclusions first, then follow up with the explanation of what led you there. The same is relevant with a dashboard; make the most prominent visual the one that will drive a user to make an action. Follow it up with the supporting information.

- **Not considering how the analytics will be used**: Will the analytics and visualizations be used to update an executive team once a month? Or will it be used by support technicians on a daily basis? Very different visuals would be created for either circumstance, even if it is the same information. Here are some things to think about:

  - **Simplify for management reporting**: Executives have a lot of information thrown at them every day, from a variety of sources. Make yours simple to understand with clear trend lines and red, yellow, and green symbols indicating status.
  - **Add more detail for daily operations users**: They will need as much relevant information as you can display in single view without it being too busy to interpret. Find the right balance, but lean toward showing more useful data.

- **Making it difficult to answer follow-up questions**: Follow-up questions from a visual should be easy and natural to answer. What caused this spike in the data? This should be simple to answer for a user of a dashboard. Here are some suggestions to avoid this mistake:

  - **Anticipate the follow-up questions**: Have the answer either already visible or just a simple click away.
  - **Layer the views**: Have the capability to drill into the data behind the visual elements. Link simpler summary visuals to more detailed visuals, such as tying a top 10 Pareto chart to monthly trends.

To illustrate how to transform a bad visual into a good one, we will start with a horrid example that would give Edward Tufte heart palpitations (Google him - then read his books):

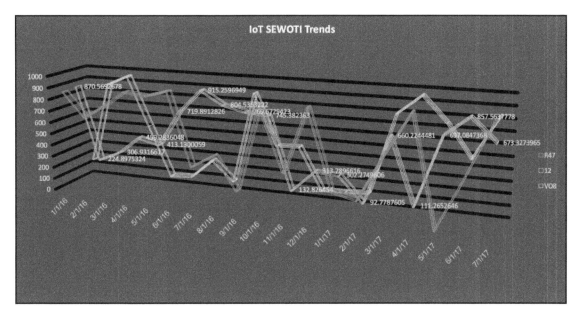

An example of a putrid chart. Don't do this

There are multiple problems with this visual. Dark backgrounds are distracting unless the entire theme of a presentation or dashboard is dark. Neither of the axes are labeled. It is unclear which line is more important, so the chart gives the impression to the audience that all are equally important.

A character code is used in the legend instead of a more descriptive name. If someone is not intimately familiar with the code, they will have to look up the descriptions for them. 3D was used in a way that does not provide any informational value. It distracts attention away from the key data.

Labels are applied to values without any rounding. This makes the chart cluttered and implies a precision that may not be accurate. If this is a chart reviewed monthly, the historical trend is important, but the exact values are not - with the exception of the current month.

The chart is both difficult to interpret and visually confusing. Now, let's look at an improved version of the same chart:

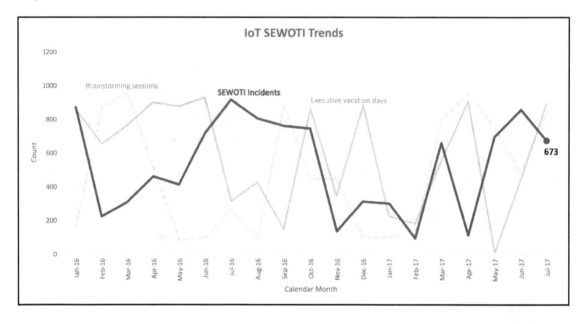

Much better visual, the key trend is obvious and the current month value is clearly stated

This visual is much more clear about which trend line is the most important one. Lines are also clearly labeled so the audience does not have to reference a legend. The current month value, which is the number reported on each month, is clearly visible without an implied extreme precision.

Both axes are labeled so that the audience does not have to guess at what is being measured. The axis labels for the month are perpendicular, which visually aligns with the value for the month. It takes a little more work to format a visual in this way, but the audience will understand the information faster and more clearly. This makes it worth the effort.

The Hierarchy of Questions method

When designing visuals and dashboards, instead of just replicating the same charts and tables that you created for yourself when exploring the data, take a minute to think about things from the point of view of the audience. Think about how their perspective and needs differ from yours.

In your situation as an analyst, you know the data and environment well already; you do not need labels and descriptions on your charts. What you want is as much information as you can fit into one place, so you can easily find patterns. The people who will be either interacting with dashboards or viewing your presentation have different needs.

They will want to be able to orient themselves visually with minimal effort. They want the key conclusions to be obvious. They do not want to have to spend a lot of time trying to figure it out, or have to ask a lot of questions just to understand what is being shown. They want simple and familiar, but with enough detail that they feel confident that the data is backing up their interpretation.

It is useful to follow a framework when designing analytics interactions for others. This will help to organize your thoughts and plan out what visualizations and dashboards are needed to support analysis by other people.

The Hierarchy of Questions method overview

Here, we will introduce a process to plan out visualizations, which we will call the **Hierarchy of Questions method**. Instead of starting with requirements and mockups, you start with mapping out the thought process of the audience.

After this, you pull together the data needed to answer the questions identified in the mapped thought process. The data should be in a form that can be queried efficiently and in multiple different ways. We will discuss ways to do this in a later chapter.

Finally, visuals are created which are aligned to the mapped thought process. The same data will probably be used multiple times in different ways. The benefit of following this process is that it puts the needs of the audience first, without anchoring to a starting visualization - which is likely to be whatever was easiest to create. The tendency, in that case, is to do what is simplest for the developer (you) to create and maintain, as opposed to what is best for the audience. Freeing yourself from a set starting place for a visualization allows you to be open to innovative ways of interacting with the analytics.

Remember, you are one person while the audience is many; and, in the case of dashboards, each person will have to use it many times over. The sum benefit of getting it right can be large, especially for customer-facing dashboards, which could have thousands of users.

General process for the hierarchy of questions method

Developing question trees

The first step in the process is to brainstorm a list of questions that the visualizations in a presentation or dashboard should answer. If at all possible, do this with a small group of end users. If it is not possible or you are preparing a small presentation, start by putting yourself in their shoes. Try to forget what you know about the data. Think what questions you would want answered, if you were in their place. List them out.

The next step is to generalize the list of questions into the underlying concepts of what is really being asked for each one. For example, the question *Is the temperature sensor reading under 21 degrees in the summer?* would be turned into *Is the temperature sensor reading significantly different from the average at this time of year?*. Some questions may get consolidated together. The idea is to get to a concept that can be applied over many situations versus a specific situation.

Then, review the list and identify the questions that are the starting points. Starting points are the reasons that would motivate one to initially go to a dashboard or sit through a presentation in the first place. Then, identify which questions are really follow-up questions to the starting point question. The example question *Is the temperature sensor reading significantly different from the average at this time of year?* is probably not a starting point question. It is more likely to be *What is the average temperature reading trend for a region?*, followed up by *Are there any outlier readings?*, and then *Is the temperature sensor reading significantly different from the average at this time of year?*.

Arrange the questions in a hierarchy with the starting points at the left linked to their follow-up questions out to the right. If the same follow-up question relates to multiple starting point questions, duplicate it for each. It may be subtly different in each scenario. We will refer to the resulting diagram as a **question tree**. This can then be used as a reference when building the datasets and visualizations.

To illustrate how this process works, we will use movie time information to walk-through the process. Most people can easily relate to it. The first step is to list out the questions that would lead you to want to know your movie time information:

- When is *Transformers 12* playing?
- What theaters are playing *Rocky Horror Picture Show*?
- Is the cinema sold out for *Avengers vs. Justice League* at 8:10 pm tonight?
- How many seats are left?
- How much does a ticket cost at that theater?
- How far away is Cineblast 128?
- How long will it take to get to Cinema Cheap-o?
- What movies are at Luxury Cinema tonight?
- What movies are playing at around 9 pm tomorrow night?

The next step is to generalize the questions and consolidate:

- What times can I see the movie I want to see?
- What theaters are playing the movie I want to see?
- Will I be able to get good seats at a specific theater and time?
- Will I be able to get good seats at a specific theater and time? (consolidate)
- What is the price of a ticket at a specific theater and time?
- What is the travel time to a specific theater at a specific time?
- What is the travel time to a specific theater at a specific time? (consolidate)
- What movies are at the theater I want to go to?
- What movies can I see at a certain time?

Then, identify the main starting point questions. It is helpful to start documenting your reasoning for choosing the questions. In this example, there are three variables: movie, place, and time. You generally have decided on one of those already and need information to help you decide on the other two:

- What times can I see the movie I want to see?
  - *I know the movie I want. I'm dying to see Transformers 12; I just need to know which times I can see it. Then, I'll want to know where it is playing and whether I can still get good seats for me and my friends. Ticket price and how long it will take to get to the theater would be helpful too.*

- What movies are at the theater I want to go to?
  - *I know the place I want. I love going to Luxury Cinema; it is such a great experience. I just want to know if there are any movies there that I want to see. Then, I'll want to know the times and whether I can get good seats; I don't want to pay top dollar and not even be able to sit next to my girlfriend.*

- What movies can I see at a certain time?
  - *I know the time I want. We're going out to dinner with reservations at 7 pm, and I want to see if there are any movies in the area I can see afterwards. I'll want to know the price and whether I can get good seats, and how long it will take to get there from the restaurant.*

The final step is to organize the questions into a question tree. The following diagram shows a question tree for the movie time example:

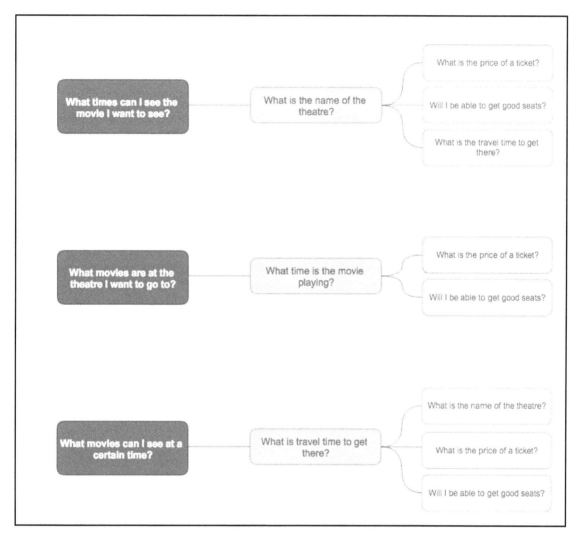

Movie time information question tree example

Here's a summary of the steps in creating your question tree hierarchy:

1. List the questions the audience wants to ask of the analytics.
2. Generalize the questions and consolidate.
3. Identify starting point questions.
4. Organize the questions into a question tree diagram.

Pulling together the data

IoT data is typically stored using big data technology such as Hadoop (HDFS specifically). Joining together tables in SQL statements for dashboards typically decreases performance, sometimes significantly in these systems.

Pull together the data into as few tables as possible, so the table joins are only done during batch processing instead of every time a dashboard is used by someone. When considering what information to include in the dataset, reference the question tree and include what is needed to answer the questions.

Aligning views with question flows

When designing visuals, align them with the question tree hierarchies. The first and most visible visual should answer the starting point question. The follow-up questions should be addressed in the same visual, if possible, but less prominently. If this is too unwieldy, then the follow-up should be a simple click away for a user to answer his question. The same is applicable with the follow-up question to the first follow-up question, and so on.

You may need to do a different dashboard for each hierarchy tree if it is too cumbersome to answer in the same dashboard. The test here is to think what is easiest and most natural to a user. The goal is for the dashboard or presentation order to follow the thought processes of the audience.

We will walk through a full example using an IoT data set later on in the chapter.

Designing visual analysis for IoT data

We will review some important considerations when designing visual analysis with special attention for IoT data.

Using layout positioning to convey importance

Layout position implies what is important and primary; you should take advantage of this to help communicate more effectively with your audience. In Western cultures, the eye starts in the upper-left position of a view. This is due to years of habit reading from left to right and top to bottom. This is where one's eye goes first by habit. Put the key message here: the answer to your starting point question.

As you travel right and lower in a view, put the visuals (including tables and text) in order of its position in the question tree. This will follow along with eye movement and the audience's thought process:

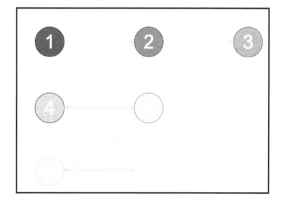

Recommended layout order when showing multiple visuals in same view

In other cultures, apply the same concept but follow the position order that aligns with reading order. For example, in Pakistan the language Urdu is written right to left - so the most important information should be in the upper right.

Use color to highlight important data

Color is also a powerful way to communicate to an audience what they should interpret as important. Use it sparingly, however, as too many colors in the same view are confusing and diminish the impact.

The impact of using a single color to communicate importance

In order to reiterate how powerful color (or shades of gray if only grayscale is available) can be, we will look at an example. In the following image, look through the numbers and count how many 6s you see. What was your count? How long did it take?

```
83291381337794749
91422691539122696
17946686489967647
35594183184243557
62144473513428797
96375323638591958
```

A random set of numbers. Count the number of times 6 is shown.

Now, let's take the same image and put the important information (the 6s) in the foreground using color and the less important information (the other numbers) in the background by lightening to a shade of gray.

Looking at the changed image, how many 6s do you count? How long did it take you? You will find that it is far easier and faster to do with the key data highlighted with color. Do the same for your audience, and you will make it easier for them also to understand the key information:

```
83291381337794749
91422691539122696
17946686489967647
35594183184243557
62144473513428797
96375323638591958
```

The same random set of numbers with the number 6 highlighted in color. Adapted from Cole Nussbaumer Knaflic's book *Storytelling with Data*.

Be consistent across visuals

In a presentation or in a series of dashboards, make sure to keep your colors and formatting consistent. If the average temperature is shown as a solid blue line in the first chart, make sure it is also a solid blue line in all following charts. Keep colors consistent even if the type of chart changes. If a pressure sensor trend in a line chart is blue, make sure that in a following scatter plot, the points are also blue.

This consistency saves your audience from having to reorient themselves between views. It also helps prevent misinterpretations as it is easy to assume the same color has the same meaning.

Make charts easy to interpret

For IoT data, time series analysis is very common. Analyzing trends in IoT sensor values over time is useful for people in roles such as technical support, marketing, quality, and engineering. Time series charts communicate trend data more effectively than pareto charts or pie charts. Since you will be employing them quite a bit, it is important to make them as effective as you can. When creating charts, keep some things in mind to help make it easy for your audience to draw the conclusions that you intended.

In most cases, you have looked at the data in far more ways than you will be making available to your audience. You picked the charts that best convey what you have learned from your analysis of the data. Make it easy for your audience to grasp.

Here are some ways to help:

- **Accentuate the key data**: Make the key trend line in a chart bright and bold. In a table, bold the row you found to be the most important. Make it obvious. You are not insulting their intelligence, you are saving them time and minimizing misinterpretations.
- **Label chart items clearly**: Give the chart a clear title and make the font big enough to read easily. Make sure chart axes are labeled and avoid abbreviations.
- **Point out key information**: Circle an area on a chart you want to make sure the audience notices. Draw an arrow pointing to it and add text that states how they should interpret it. If there is a spike in average temperature in December due to record high regional temperatures, and not due to a system issue, circle it and add a note. It will save the audience from having to ask the question or investigate it themselves.

Creating a dashboard with Tableau

Tableau makes it easy to assemble a dashboard from the visual analysis tabs you have already created. We will use it to build from the weather station data example in `Chapter 6`, *Getting to Know Your Data - Exploring IoT Data*. We will also walk-through the hierarchy of questions process in the course of building the dashboard.

The dashboard walk-through

There is also web server software for Tableau, called **Tableau Server**, that allows you to easily publish a dashboard from the desktop software so that it is viewable through a browser. Other users can then easily interact with it. Although Tableau Server is outside the scope of this book, you would most likely want to publish the dashboards you create to it.

Hierarchy of Questions example

For this simple example, let's assume the audience is a government water use planning group for the State of Colorado. The group wants to understand how many weather stations are reporting precipitation information and a sense of how well the information is being captured. The following steps show how this can be made into a question tree:

- **Step 1: List out questions the audience wants to ask of the analytics**:
    - Did the number of stations reporting precipitation change from last month?
    - How many stations in total have sent precipitation numbers?
    - Where are the stations located?
    - How many have reported a significant rainfall?
    - Is there anything weird in the daily sums for each station that might indicate a problem?
    - Which areas of the state had some good rain last month?
- **Step 2: Generalize the questions and consolidate**:
    - What is the trend of stations reporting usable precipitation data?
    - How many stations report data?
    - Where are the stations that reported usable data in the period?
    - Did a station report significant rainfall in the period?

- Are there abnormal precipitation values for a specific station?
- Where are the stations that reported usable data in the period? (consolidate with the similar question earlier in the list)

- **Step 3: Identify starting point questions**:
    - Based on conversations with the water planning group, you determine their first thought is to simply check the number of stations that report 15-minute precipitation data.
    - Starting point question: How many stations report data?
- **Step 4: Organize the questions into a question tree diagram**:

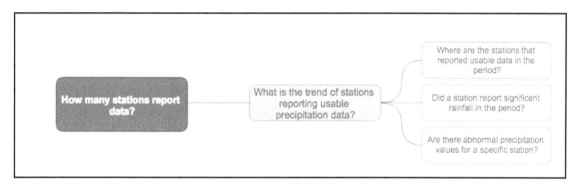

Weather station question hierarchy

Aligning visuals to the thought process

Think through what visuals are needed and how to arrange them before creating them in Tableau. The most important thing, the starting point, should be the first thing the audience views. If there are to be multiple visuals in the same dashboard, it should be in the upper-left part of the screen.

Since a simple count is all that is really needed to answer the question, this can just be a number. No chart is necessary. You should make it large, so it is instantly noticed. Make it what may feel uncomfortably large, and it will be obvious to the audience without needing to point out that it is the most important piece of information in the view.

A trend of the number of reporting stations is needed so the audience can understand if more or less are reporting usable data over time versus the total number. This aligns with the first follow-up question. A monthly trend should work.

Then, for any given period, the water planning group wants to know where the reporting stations are located and whether there was significant precipitation for the period at the stations. They also want some idea of locations in the state with significant reported precipitation. A map is a good way to fit in a lot of spatial information in a way that can be easily comprehended. This aligns with the secondary follow-up question.

For any station or group of stations in an area, the planning group wants to be able to see daily trends, so anything unusual can be detected quickly for additional investigation. This aligns with the last follow-up question. Now, we can start building the views one at a time, then assemble them into a dashboard.

Creating individual views

For the first view, use Tableau to connect to the 15-minute precipitation dataset from Chapter 6, *Getting to Know Your Data - Exploring IoT Data*. The starting point question can be answered by counting the number of unique stations in the dataset regardless of the validity of the values. Set up a calculated field called **Number of Stations** using the formula, COUNTD([Station]), which will aggregate based on a distinct count of unique stations. Drag the **Number of Stations** aggregation to the text box in the **Marks** shelf. Make the number big and bold, so it will be seen first.

Total stations count view

The next view should align to the follow-up question on the trend in the **Number of Stations** reporting valid values. Since the audience is interested in longer-term trends, a monthly grouping is appropriate. At this point, let's rename **Qpcp** to a better description. From the dataset documentation, the value represents the amount of precipitation measured in inches. We will rename **Qpcp** to **Amount of Precipitation (inches)**. Also filter out records with the extreme values in either **Qgag** or **Qpcp** (the latter now called **Amount of Precipitation (inches)**).

Set up the measurement date to show month and year. Drag the **Number of Stations** field to **Rows** shelf to show the trend. There is an implicit comparison to the total **Number of Stations**, so make the values visible by dragging **Number of Stations** to the **label** box in the **Marks** shelf.

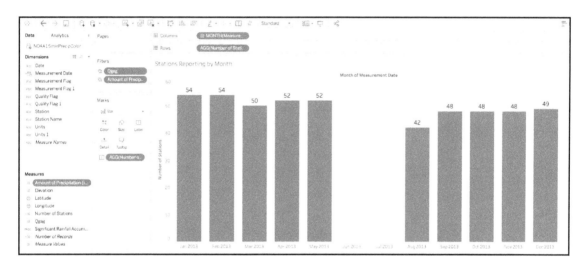

Monthly trend view

The next follow-up question in the question hierarchy is about the location of the stations. Use the mapping functionality to convey location information. You can also answer the other follow-up question about which stations reported significant precipitation for the period in the same view using color. Create a calculated field using the following formula, and drag it to the color box in the **Marks** shelf. The value to use as the breakpoint for what is considered significant should be determined with the audience. We will use **0.2** inches for this demonstration:

```
IF SUM([Amount of Precipitation (inches)]) >= 0.2 THEN
    "Yes"
ELSE
    "No"
END
```

The resulting view should look similar to the following screenshot. Make sure to use the same principles of color and arrangement for the tooltips in each view so that important information is clear:

Map view

Finally, answer the last question in the hierarchy on abnormal precipitation values by showing daily summed values for each station. You learned from the data investigation in `Chapter 6`, *Getting to Know Your Data - Exploring IoT Data,* that unusual values can be found easily in a daily bar graph by station. The resulting visual should look similar to the following screenshot:

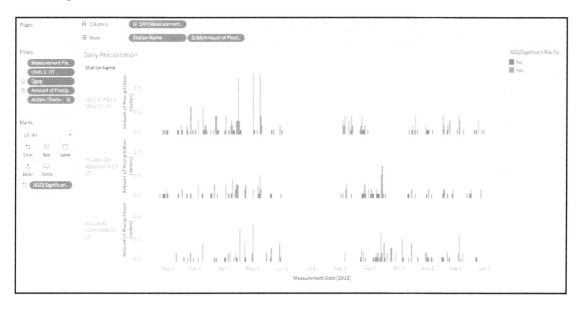

A daily trend by a station view

Assembling views into a dashboard

The next step is to create a new dashboard tab. Set the size to **Generic Desktop (1366 x 768)**. Add the four views in the priority order discussed previously in the chapter. The initial dashboard should look like the following screenshot:

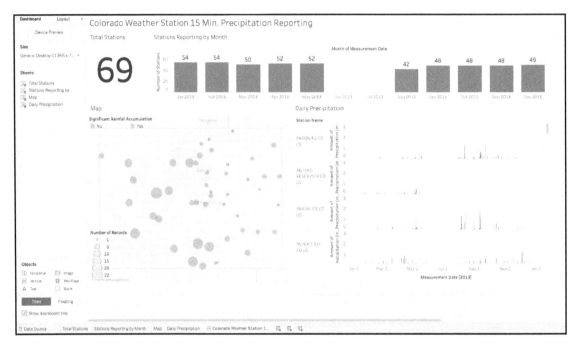

The initial dashboard

With Tableau, you can add dashboard actions that allow a user to filter other views based on what they click in a source view. Following the question hierarchy, a click on a monthly station count bar in the monthly trend view should filter the map view. A selection of stations on the map view should filter the daily trend view.

Go to dashboards in the menu bar and select **Actions…** to add a couple of actions to the dashboard view. Add a filter from the the monthly trend view to the map view linked by the **MONTH([Measurement date])** field when a bar is selected. Do the same for the **Map** view targeting the daily trend view linked by the **Station** field:

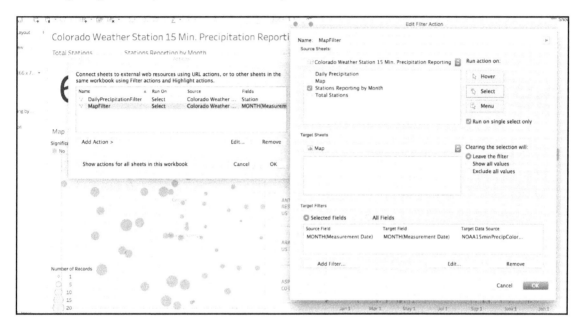

Add dashboard actions

Now, a user of the dashboard can investigate a measurement month to quickly understand which weather stations are reporting data. They can also view one station or groups of stations by the daily summed precipitation values to identify unusual results. The example of following screenshot shows the mapped location for November 2013 reporting stations and the daily trend for a few stations in the Denver area:

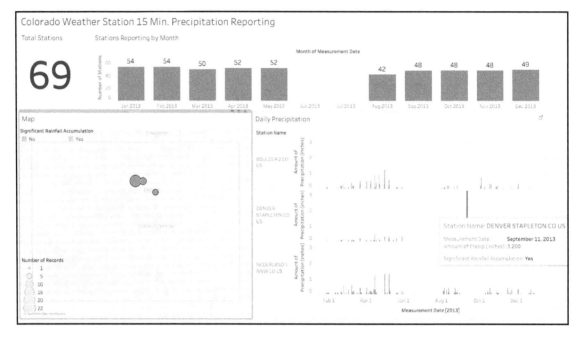

Example of dashboard interaction

Creating and visualizing alerts

IoT data is inherently noisy. There are often cases of invalid and missing values. This requires constant vigilance to identify and correct data issues when they occur. The correction could then be handled in the transformation of the raw data or in the software and design of the device.

Either way, the faster an issue is detected, the quicker it can be resolved. For IoT data, consider bad data as lost money that can rarely be recovered. Minimize the loss by identifying and correcting issues quickly.

Dashboards can also be created for this purpose by following the same process we introduced in this chapter. Think about what you want to watch out for and set up an alert view to identify it for you.

Alert principles

There are some principles to follow when designing an alert system, even a simple one that will be part of a dashboard:

- **Balance alert sensitivity to minimize false positives**: People will learn quickly to ignore alerts if they rarely identify an actual problem. This has to be balanced against missing too many real issues though. A cost benefit calculation can be used to help in this decision.
  *[cost of investigating a problem] * [number of alerts] < [cost of actual problem] * [probability of true positive]*
  The left side of that equation should be noticeably less than the right side.
- **Be wary of alert fatigue**: A long list of continuous alerts is daunting, and human brains tend to become conditioned over time to recognize it as a normal situation. Alerts will start to become background noise and will not get a response. Anyone with an Android smartphone knows how this feels - too many alerts are exhausting. There does not need to be an alert for every problem. Keep it to a manageable amount for the big ones.
- **Make alerts like a to-do list**: A user should not have to search for where the problem is; it should be listed out for them if there are any. If there are no issues discovered, a blank list can be comforting - like leaving work an hour early!
- **Incorporate a tracking system for alert responses**: Nothing is more frustrating than spending a couple of hours investigating a problem someone else has already discovered and corrected.

Organizing alerts using a Tableau dashboard

A simple example can highlight how to use a dashboard for alerting purposes. Tableau server has an email functionality that a user can subscribe to that will email an image of the dashboard at a regular interval with an embedded link back to the interactive dashboard. This can then be read and digested like a morning newspaper.

You learned while investigating the 15 minute precipitation dataset that there were measurement values that represented a state instead of an actual reading. In these cases, the value was either **-9999** or **999.99**. What we would want to see, if we were relying on this data on a daily basis, is that a station reports valid precipitation measurements and little to no non-measurement values. We can organize a simple question hierarchy to represent our thinking process:

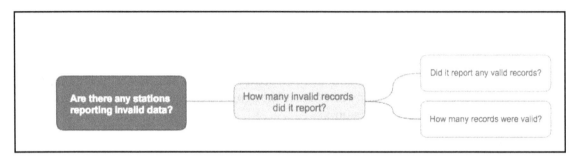

Alert question hierarchy for stations reporting invalid precipitation data

We can create an alert dashboard to monitor this on a daily basis. This will allow quick identification of a problem. We will start by creating four additional calculated fields in the following order:

Name: **Precip Accumul Value Validity**

Calculation:

```
CASE [Qgag]
    WHEN -9999 THEN
        "Invalid"
    WHEN 999.990 THEN
        "Invalid"
    ELSE
        IF [Qgag] >= 0 AND [Qgag] <20 THEN
            "Valid"
        ELSE
            "Invalid"
        END
END
```

Name: Precip Value Validity

Calculation:

```
CASE [Amount of Precipitation (inches)]
   WHEN -9999 THEN
       "Invalid"
   WHEN 999.99 THEN
       "Invalid"
   ELSE
       IF [Amount of Precipitation (inches)] >= 0 AND [Amount of
Precipitation (inches)] <20 THEN
           "Valid"
       ELSE
           "Invalid"
       END
END
```

Name: Invalid Count

Calculation:

```
IF [Precip Accumul Value Validity] = "Invalid" AND [Precip Value Validity]
= "Invalid" THEN
   1
ELSE
   0
END
```

Name: Valid Count

Calculation:

```
If [Invalid Count] = 0 THEN
   1
ELSE
   0
END
```

As a little bonus, here is a trick in Tableau to create a dynamic bar chart within a tooltip. You can use the ASCII character for a fixed in square to create what looks like a dynamic length bar. Create the following calculated field and drag it to the **Tooltip** box in the **Marks** card:

Name: **Valid Count Bar**

Calculation:

```
LEFT("■ ■ ■ ■ ■ ■ ■ ■ ■ ■ ■ ■ ■ ■ ■ ■ ■ ■ ■ ■ ■ ■ ■ ■ ■ ■ ■ ■ ■ ■ ■ ■ ■ ■
", SUM([Valid Count]))
```

Now, arrange the calculated fields into a view that looks like the following screenshot. Make sure to edit the tooltip card to arrange information in the appropriate order. You can move the bar chart formula to be after the valid count field. Add a measurement date filter, so the list is for a single day only:

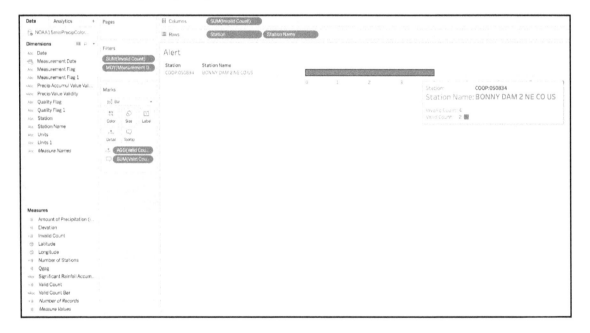

Alert view

And, voila! Now, you have an alert view to put into a dashboard. If this were a live feed, you can change the date filter to be a relative date and set it to yesterday. Then, in Tableau server, set up the users to receive daily emails of the alert view. Now you have a list of stations that need reviews sent to their inbox every morning.

Summary

In this chapter, we discussed common mistakes when creating visuals for IoT data. Some tips were given to avoid making them. We introduced a method to develop dashboards and visualizations to communicate analytics to an audience. The method has the goal of aligning the visuals to the thought process of the person interacting with them.

We reviewed the use of position on a dashboard to convey importance. The most important piece of information should be in in the upper-left part for cultures that read left to right. Color can also be used effectively to highlight key information to the audience.

Tableau was used to demonstrate how to quickly create a dashboard to communicate your analytics in an interactive way. We walked through an example with the IoT weather data continued from a previous chapter. Some principles of alerting were reviewed along with an example using Tableau.

For further exploration, not discussed here but worthwhile for you to learn, there are also some great visualization packages in R and Python. The author recommends *ggplot* for R and *Seaborn* for Python.

9

Applying Geospatial Analytics to IoT Data

"I know it has been tough since Willard left, but I have some good news; we will be getting you some help." These words are coming to you accompanied by a concerned, paternal look from the Vice President of Connected Product Development, who is standing in your cubicle.

Willard was your boss, now your former boss. He left recently to join another company as Head of their IoT division. They were highly impressed with his accomplishments building up a cloud-based IoT analytics capability, which was all your idea, of course, but *c'est la vie*.

Now, with your boss gone, the VP and other executives are worried about the momentum stalling. You are a little bit miffed at this since you had to twist your boss's arm to get him to go along with everything in the first place. *Look on the bright side*, you tell yourself, *at least you are getting some help*.

He continues, "We want to up the ante, none of the competition is aggregating their thermostat data and selling it to power companies. Maybe the new guy can figure out how to do that."

Ha, the new guy. "I got this, I developed what we have so far. I can certainly handle this," you state confidently, holding his gaze. "I've been looking for an excuse to do a little geospatial anyway."

You feel capable now; it is time they started giving you some credit. But you are not quite sure how to do it, as it seems a little daunting. The power companies are going to have service areas that do not stick to state boundaries or zip codes. You will need to somehow draw the service areas on a map and then find the devices in the area. This sounds like a lot of manual work.

"Well, we will see. I have lots of ideas if you can pull this one off," he replies. With this, he turns around and strolls assuredly down the hallway on his way to the next meeting. You hesitate for a second wondering if he knew all along that you were the brains behind the IoT analytics and just manipulated you into putting all your energy into his project. Then you shake your head thinking *surely not*, and get back to work.

This chapter is about leveraging the field of geospatial analysis to enhance IoT analytics. IoT devices are sometimes attached to equipment that moves around geographically. Even if this is not the case, devices will probably have diverse geographic locations when deployed. This creates an opportunity to find patterns and develop valuable services by using location based analysis. We will introduce some key concepts and technology for geospatial analytics.

This chapter covers the following topics:

- The benefit of geospatial analytics for IoT
- Geospatial analytics basics:
    - Welcome to Null Island
    - Coordinate Reference Systems
    - Python for geospatial analysis
- Vector-based methods:
    - A bounding box
    - Contains
    - Buffers
    - Simplify
    - The vector summary
- Raster-based methods
- Storing geospatial data:
    - File formats
    - Spatial extensions for relational databases
    - Geospatial data in HDFS
    - Spatial indexing

- Processing geospatial data:
    - Geospatial analysis software:
        - ArcGIS
        - QGIS
        - ogr2ogr
    - PostGIS spatial functions
    - Geospatial and big data
- Solving the pollution reporting problem

Why do you need geospatial analytics for IoT?

Imagine that your company sells a device that measures airborne pollutants. It is internet-enabled and reports data back to your company at regular intervals using MQTT. The target market for this product is environmentally-minded consumers who want to both measure pollutants near their home and contribute to the collective monitoring of the environment.

The value proposition is that they get free analysis of their local air quality in exchange for donating their data to support a cause they probably believe in anyway. Your company is planning to aggregate and package analytics of high-quality air pollution data to sell it to government and private organizations.

Since the device is sold to consumers indirectly through various retail outlets, your company is not initially aware of the location of the devices. The consumer connects the device to the internet after it is purchased, and then enters their addresses. At this point, the location can be determined.

The device has multiple sensors that measure the level of different contaminants in the air. One of the sensors measures the level of nitrogen dioxide (NO_2). NO_2 is not only a toxic gas by itself but has even more damaging side effects. It facilitates the creation of acid rain and photochemical smog and is a precursor to other harmful secondary air pollutants such as ozone.

The following image shows an example of a Nitrogen Dioxide Sensor and Nitrogen Dioxide Analyzer Module made by the company, Aeroqual:

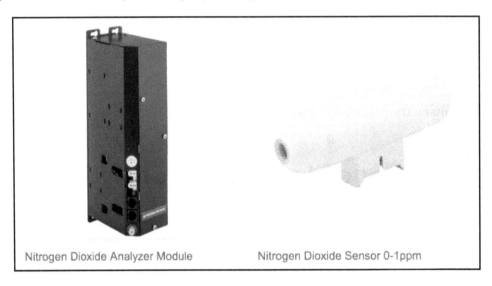

Nitrogen Dioxide Analyzer Module   Nitrogen Dioxide Sensor 0-1ppm

Nitrogen Dioxide Sensor and Analyzer. Source: Aeroqual

NO2 is produced by the burning of fossil fuels. The main contributor in urban areas is typically motor vehicle exhausts, but the gas can also come from power plants, manufacturing facilities, and welding work.

Your company wants to build and sell a data package summarizing NO2 levels by distance from Interstate highways. It also wants to aggregate the resulting data by each of the 115 congressional districts in the United States. The company believes congressional lobbyists would pay well for this information.

This task may seem daunting at first, as all you know about device locations is the address registered by the customers. The first thought may be a manual process of reviewing each device location on a map and categorizing it based on its distance to the nearest Interstate highway. This would be very labor intensive and cost prohibitive when you have 500,000 devices.

Thankfully, geospatial analytics can do this type of analysis efficiently. We will introduce several concepts, and then revisit this example and show how it can be solved.

The basics of geospatial analysis

Before we jump into the fun stuff, we will cover some basic concepts. This will give context to how the analytics work behind the scenes.

Welcome to Null Island

If you have devices that report GPS location data, you will soon start to notice that many are visiting an area off the west coast of Africa. A new vacation destination, perhaps? Turns out this is a place called Null Island. If you have not heard of Null Island, it is located at precisely 0 latitude and 0 longitude. There is even a tourism website for it where you can get to know the culture and buy a T-shirt, as shown in the following screenshot:

Null Island location and website. Source: www.nullisland.com

But the place does not exist; it is an inside joke in the geospatial community. Missing coordinate values or null values are stored as 0 and 0 (latitude and longitude). Besides it giving insight into the sense of humor of the geospatial community, Null Island helps to introduce a key concept for geospatial analytics.

All the locations are based in reference to some other starting point. To accurately represent a location, you need to know where the starting point is located and the framework on how position is determined from that starting point. There are many representations on how to do this. This is where **Coordinate Reference Systems (CRS)** come into play.

Coordinate Reference Systems

A Coordinate Reference System, also referred to as **Spatial Reference System (SRS)** or a **map projection**, identifies what method was used to convert the three dimensional sphere-like Earth into a flat X,Y coordinate surface. In other words, it explains what method was used to project three dimensions onto a two dimensional surface.

There are literally thousands of defined ways to do this, each with its own pluses and minuses. Each defined method is a separate CRS, the most common being **World Geodetic System 1984** or **WGS 84,** which is used by the **Global Positioning System (GPS)**.

In order to correctly identify a position and accurately calculate things such as surface distance between two points, the CRS for a set of spatial data must be known. It is typically identified and stored as part of the file or geospatial database. One CRS can be converted into another CRS as long as both are known.

The Earth is not a ball

The world is not a perfect sphere. It is an ellipsoid and like a middle-aged man, it bulges in the center. This means that using simple geometry calculations for a sphere on geospatial data will not be entirely accurate.

Using methods for calculating distance across a sphere, such as the haversine formula for great circle distance calculation, will become more and more inaccurate as the distance between two points increases. You can still use the haversine method for calculating short distances without much loss in accuracy, but avoid it for longer distances.

$$\boxed{\mathrm{hav}(\theta) = \sin^2\left(\frac{\theta}{2}\right) = \frac{1 - \cos(\theta)}{2}}$$

The haversine formula. Source: Wikipedia.org

The following R code can be used to calculate the haversine distance for two points on the Earth. Remember that it is not entirely accurate over long distances. Instead, leverage code packages and database systems that are aware of the CRS, and are able to use it to calculate spatial data with precision. The R code uses two points that are far apart to give you an idea of the relative inaccuracy of the method. The actual distance between the points is 12,935 km:

```
#code adapted from RosettaCode.

#Coordinates for the two points
#Chicago, USA O'Hare airport (ORD)
Point1Lat = 41.978194
Point1Long = -87.907739

#Coordinates for Chhatrapati Shivaji International Airport near Mumbai,
India airport (BOM)
Point2Lat = 19.0895595
Point2Long = 72.8656144

#convert decimal degrees to radians
degrees_to_rad <- function(deg) (deg * pi / 180)

# Volumetric mean radius is 6371 km for the Earth, see
http://nssdc.gsfc.nasa.gov/planetary/factsheet/earthfact.html
# The diameter is thus 12742 km

#function to calculate great circle distance using haversine method
great_circle_distance <- function(lat1, long1, lat2, long2) {
  a <- sin(0.5 * (lat2 - lat1))
  b <- sin(0.5 * (long2 - long1))
  12742 * asin(sqrt(a * a + cos(lat1) * cos(lat2) * b * b))
}

#calculate distance for the two points
haversine_distance <- great_circle_distance(
  degrees_to_rad(Point1Lat), degrees_to_rad(Point1Long),   # Nashville
International Airport (BNA)
  degrees_to_rad(Point2Lat), degrees_to_rad(Point2Long))  # Los Angeles
International Airport (LAX)

#result shown in kilometers
haversine_distance
# 12,942.77km
```

There are different methods to adjust for the actual shape of the Earth. WGS 84 CRS uses a few parameters in order to increase accuracy of the projections. The following table summarizes the parameters:

Parameter	Notation	Value
Flattening Factor of the Earth	1/f	298.257223563
Geocentric Gravitational Constant	GM	3986004.418 10^8 m^3/s^2
Nominal Mean Angular Velocity	ω	7292115 10^{-11} rad/s
Semi-major Axis	a	6378137.0 m

WGS 84 defining parameters. Source: United Nations Office for Outer Space Affairs

Although you will mostly come across two dimensional coordinates for the WGS 84 CRS, it is a three dimensional representation of the Earth. The starting point is based on the Earth's center of mass. The following image from the Defense Mapping Agency shows how this is represented:

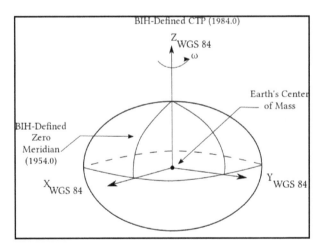

WGS Reference Frame By Defense Mapping Agency - Section 1-5 PDF of the DMA TECHNICAL REPORT TR8350.2-b - (Second Printing, 1 December 1987) Supplement to DoD WGS 84 Technical Report Part 2 - Parameters, Formulas, and Graphics. http://earth-info.nga.mil/GandG/publications/tr8350.2/TR8350.2-b/Sections%201-5.pdf, Public Domain, https://commons.wikimedia.org/w/index.php?curid=41796676

The point of highlighting this detail is to not only give an idea of the complexity behind map projections but to convince you to leverage the centuries of work already completed in this field. Do not attempt to duplicate it; take advantage of what has already been done.

A great way to take advantage of what has already been done in geospatial analytics is by using Python geospatial libraries. There are many great packages for R that can be used as well, but there are more options with Python. They tend to be more mature due to the long use of Python in the geospatial community.

Python also tends to scale better than R, so it can be a better fit for large-scale, compute-intensive processing. Geospatial calculations can get fairly intensive and IoT data, as we know well by this point in the book, becomes a large-scale effort in a short amount of time.

Due to these considerations, Python for geospatial analytics is a great fit. In this chapter, we will shift our focus from R code to Python code. For big data analytics, you should be comfortable with both. An easy way to get started with Python is to download the **Anaconda** package from `https://www.continuum.io/downloads`. Anaconda includes Python, R, and over 720 packages, including more than 100 of the most popular packages for data science.

It also includes both a Python IDE called **Spyder** and the browser-based notebook, **Jupyter**. Jupyter is important for IoT analytics as it can be run on a Hadoop cluster, allowing you to develop Python code in a distributed environment without having to run code through a console. It also can be used to develop Spark applications in Python, Scala, or R. The combination of Spark and Python geospatial libraries, installed across the cluster, provides the capability to scale geospatial analytics.

Vector-based methods

There are two main categories of geospatial analysis and file types, **vector** and **raster**. Vectors are all about shapes, while rasters are more about grids. Vector is more common due to flexibility and efficient storage. Vectors can be defined simply by using a set of points. There are three main types of vector geometry:

- **Points**: This can be defined in two or three dimensions. It is the common latitude, longitude pair you are probably very familiar with. The airport locations used in the R code previously are examples of points.

- **Lines** or **LineString**: A LineString is defined by a set of points and order is important. More than one LineString can be stored together; in that case it is called, unsurprisingly, a **MultiLineString**. A river system or roadways network is an example of a MultiLineString. A file that contains a MultiLineString for the US Interstate roadways network can be downloaded from the University of Iowa GIS Library (`ftp://ftp.igsb.uiowa.edu/gis_library/USA/us_interstates.htm`). The following image is a visualization of that file:

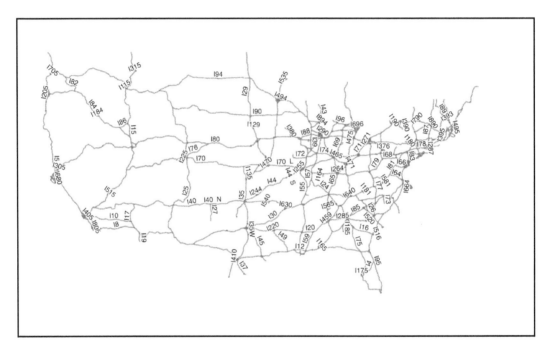

The US Interstate system. Source: Environmental Systems Research Institute, Inc. (ESRI)

- **Polygon**: A polygon is defined as a closed network of points. Order of the points is important and the starting point is also repeated as the ending point, thus closing out the shape. More than one polygon can be stored together, which is then called, you guessed it, a **MultiPolygon**. An example of this is a MultiPolygon representing the nation of Indonesia, which, according to the CIA World Factbook, consists of 13,466 islands:

A Multipolygon image of Indonesia

There are several Python packages developed for geospatial analytics. Two of the most popular related to vectors are *shapely* and *fiona*. *Shapely* has several computational geography algorithms while *fiona* interacts with vector files. You can install both packages using `conda` or `pip install` from the command line, as seen in the following code. Use `conda install` if you installed the Anaconda distribution:

```
conda install shapely
```

Or you can use the following:

```
pip install shapely
```

We will review some key vector concepts and the *shapely* code that implements them. There are many more than we cover here, but this should give you a good starting place. Use *fiona* to save the results into a file.

The bounding box

An important concept in vector-based analysis is the **bounding box**. This plays into many aspects of geospatial processing, including spatial indexing. A box shape is computationally much easier to search and manipulate than an irregular LineString or Polygon. Putting things into a box first and then fine tuning specific to its shape later is a common pattern for efficient searching.

A bounding box is simply the smallest rectangle that will contain the vector object in question. This is often called a **Minimum Bounding Rectangle (MBR)** and is the basis for many geospatial search algorithms. The following image shows an MBR for a collection of polygons:

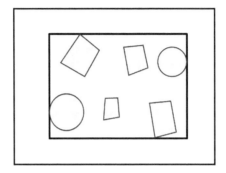

Minimum bounding rectangle for a set of polygons. Source: Wikipedia commons

An MBR can be determined with *shapely* using the bounds method:

```
#Import linestring class
from shapely.geometry import LineString

#create a linestring from a series of points
MBRline = LineString([(1, 0), (1, 1),(3,5),(2,2)])

#determine MBR bounding box
MBRboundingBox = MBRline.bounds

#output results
MBRboundingBox

#(1.0, 0.0, 3.0, 5.0)
```

Contains

You can also test if one spatial object contains another, such as a point in a polygon or a city in a state using the `contains` function. This can be used to determine if a location is in a postal code, province, or congressional district. The `within` function is the inverse and determines if the object is within another object:

```
#import polygon class
from shapely.geometry import Polygon
```

```
#create a square polygon
polysquare = Polygon([(0,0),(0,2),(2,2),(2,0),(0,0)])

#test if polygon contains the point
print(polysquare.contains(Point(1,1)))

#test if point is within the polygon
print(Point(1,1).within(polysquare))

#test if other point is within the polygon
print(Point(5,7).within(polysquare))
```

Buffer

A buffer expands a geometry object by a specified amount. If it is a LineString, a buffer will create a polygon in the shape of the LineString expanded on both the sides by the buffer amount. To illustrate this, the following screenshot shows a closeup of the US Interstate system near Chicago with a buffer of 1 km:

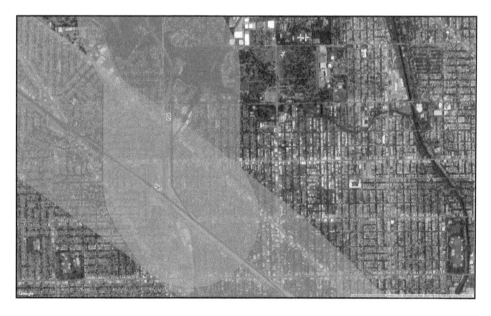

A closeup of US Interstates near Chicago with 1 km buffer

Dilation and erosion

With *shapely*, a positive buffer is a **dilation** and a negative amount is an **erosion**. A dilation works as previously described while an erosion shrinks a polygon by the buffer amount. *Shapely* also has some options for the shape of a cap (the buffer area at the ends of lines) and areas where the buffer joins to itself. The following shows the cap and join style options:

shapely.geometry.CAP_STYLE

Attribute	Value
round	1
flat	2
square	3

shapely.geometry.JOIN_STYLE

Attribute	Value
round	1
mitre	2
bevel	3

The following code shows a simple example of how buffering works:

```
#import linestring class, cap and join styles
from shapely.geometry import LineString, CAP_STYLE, JOIN_STYLE

unbufferedLine = LineString([(0, 0), (1, 1), (0, 2), (2, 2), (3, 1), (1,
0)])
dilatedBufferedLine = unbufferedLine.buffer(0.5, cap_style =
CAP_STYLE.square)
erodedBufferedLine = dilatedBufferedLine.buffer(-0.3, join_style =
JOIN_STYLE.round)

#Show the polygon detail.  This gets more complicated than a line!
print(erodedBufferedLine)
```

The following image helps to visualize the results:

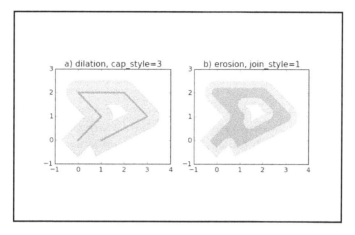

Buffer example. Source: Shapely documentation

Simplify

Sometimes, the exact detail is not necessary and a simpler version of a geometry object can be used to speed up computations. For our Interstates example, a line that follows a road precisely is probably not necessary for the use case. If the line is approximately close, it will work fine when a 1 km buffer is applied. The reduction in the complexity and size of the object can pay big dividends, especially in a parallelized big data environment. In that environment, the spatial objects could be held in memory on hundreds of nodes, so efficiency improvements can have a large impact.

Shapely provides the `simplify` method to reduce the size and complexity of a geometry object while retaining much of the original shape. The `tolerance` variable controls the amount of reduction with a higher number resulting in more simplification. The following Python code demonstrates how this works (this example is an extension of the previous buffer code):

```
#print area of polygon
print(erodedBufferedLine.area)
#show number of coordinates needed to define exterior of the polygon
print(len(erodedBufferedLine.exterior.coords))

#simplify
erodedSimplified = erodedBufferedLine.simplify(0.05,
preserve_topology=False)
```

```
print(erodedSimplified.area) #note minimal change in area
print(len(erodedSimplified.exterior.coords)) #big reduction in coordinates

print(erodedSimplified)
```

Vector summary

We have barely touched the surface of the functionality that is available to work with, manipulate, and analyze vector-based geometry. There are entire books on the subject, which are well worth your time for insight into ways to enhance your IoT analytics capability.

Raster-based methods

Raster consists of a grid of cells arranged in rows and columns. Think of raster like pixels on a screen, except each pixel is defined using a set ground distance. There is a lot in common between raster files and image files. Raster files are sometimes saved using the same formats as image files. Images are often created straight from raster files; you see such examples all the time, from weather forecasts to terrain maps.

The size of the cells in the grid is similar in concept to the resolution of an image. Unlike vector data, a raster contains information for the entire area it covers. It is useful for things that have values for an entire area, such as elevation and temperature. The downside is the resulting large file sizes.

Multiple values per cell can be stored as different **bands** in the dataset. This is similar in concept to RGB values for a color image. The SRTM and Digital Elevation Model (DEM) datasets discussed in Chapter 7, *Decorating Your Data - Adding External Datasets to Innovate*, are examples of raster data models.

The prime Python package for rasters is *GDAL*. It can interact with over 80 different raster file types and contains functions to read and transform raster data. Manipulating raster data can get complex and is outside the scope of this book. There are some great tutorials that can be found with a quick Google search. For the most part, you will be using vector-based methods for IoT analytics.

Raster and vector data layers can be used in combination. The following image, courtesy of NOAA, represents how they can be used to together in a representation of the real world:

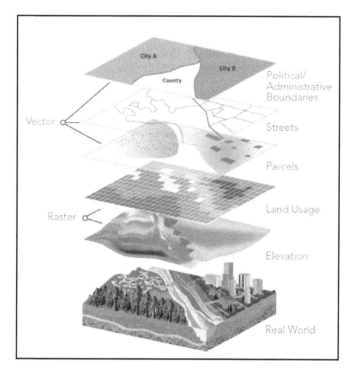

Geospatial data layers stack example. Source: NOAA

Storing geospatial data

There are many ways to store geospatial data. Depending on your intended use, a filesystem format or a relational database maybe the most appropriate. We will cover an introduction to both.

File formats

There are hundreds of file formats for storing geospatial data. The most common for vector data is **ESRI shapefiles**. A shapefile actually consists of multiple different files with the **.shp** extension for the main file. Most geospatially-aware software and Python packages know to look for the other needed files when given the location of the **.shp** file.

GeoJSON is another storage format that is human readable. It uses a defined JSON format to store vector data definitions as text. It is easily readable but can get large in size.

Another way to represent vector data, whether in a file or in code, is using the **Well-known text** (**WKT**) and **Well-known binary** (**WKB**) formats. WKT is human readable, while WKB is not. WKB offers significant compression in size, so is often a good choice for database storage. It can be converted into WKT upon reading. The following table summarizes the WKT formats for each geometry type:

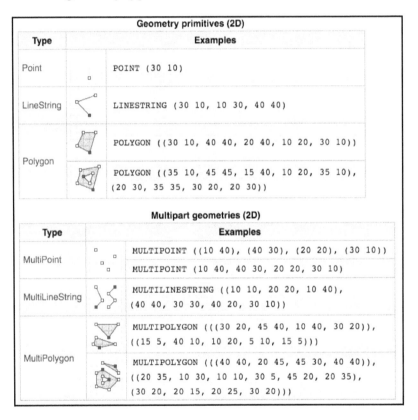

Well-known Text format examples. Source: Wikipedia

Raster data is most commonly stored in the **Tagged Image File Format** (**TIFF**) (**.tiff**) files. It can also be stored as ASCII grid files but file size is a concern. There are some compressed formats, such as **Multi-resolution Seamless Image Database** (**MrSID**) with the **.sid** extension and **Enhanced Compression Wavelet** (**ECW**) with the **.ecw** extension.

Spatial extensions for relational databases

With spatial extensions, relational databases can support storing geometry data in database tables and also perform some geospatial functions. These are typically not part of standard installation but can be enabled through administration settings or by installing software extensions.

For open source **Relational Database Management Systems** (**RDBMS**), **PostgreSQL**, and **MySQL** both support spatial functionality. PostgreSQL is the by far most popular and is most fully functional. When the spatial components are enabled for PostgreSQL, it is commonly referred to as **PostGIS**. You will see the terms used interchangeably. PostgreSQL is a supported RDS option on AWS. The spatial extensions can be enabled, turning it into PostGIS.

For closed source RDBMS, **Oracle** (**Spatial and Graph**), and **SQL Server** are popular. Oracle is generally considered as the most capable one. These are not the only options as more and more databases are supporting spatial data. **Amazon Aurora**, a MySQL-compatible managed RDS database on AWS, has recently added spatial support.

Storing geospatial data in HDFS

HDFS and Hive do not natively support spatial data types. All is not lost, though, as HDFS can store any type of file, including geospatial files. Geometry can be stored in string (WKT) and binary (WKB) forms. They can be converted using code upon retrieval. Hive tables are schema-on-read and support **User Defined Functions** (**UDF**). A UDF can be created to interpret geospatial data.

In fact, there are some open source projects that do just that. One is called **SpatialHadoop** and can be found at `http://spatialhadoop.cs.umn.edu/index.html`. Another is called **spatial-framework-for-hadoop** and can be found on GitHub (`https://github.com/Esri/spatial-framework-for-hadoop`). The downside is that these projects are not fully supported and are not a part of the Cloudera and Hortonworks Hadoop distributions.

A more robust method is to store spatial data as WKT or WKB and use geospatial Python packages to manipulate it.

Spatial indexing

The world is a big place. Imagine trying to find where someone lives if you do not know their house address, postal code, or even the country they live in. You would have to visit every home until you run into the person you are looking for, which will take longer than you have left and would not be very enjoyable anyway.

Thankfully, addresses allow a quick identification of where someone lives by identifying the country, the state or province within that country, the postal code, and the street name where you can drive, until you find their house number, which tends to follow an established order along the street.

Spatial databases can get very large, so an efficient method of searching for geometry is needed in order to improve response times. This is where spatial indexing comes into play. There are a variety of methods that are employed to do this. We will cover one of the more popular methods next.

R-tree

R-tree is a spatial indexing method used in both PostGIS and Oracle databases. It leverages the bounding box concept to create a hierarchical index tree. The tree is balanced in the sense that all branches have the same level of nodes. In order to understand how a basic R-tree index is built, we will walk through a simple example.

For a given set of geometries, the MBR for each one is defined. The MBR for each is what is retained in the index. The following image shows an example of these first steps:

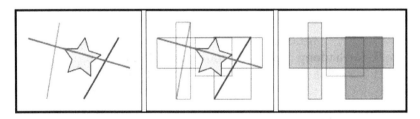

MBR for a set of shapes. Source: OSGeo project

The R-tree index is built from the MBRs so that larger bounding boxes contain groups of smaller bounding boxes with the goal of optimizing the search time for the lowest level MBRs. The resulting set of bounding boxes forms a tree hierarchy, which is stored as an index. The index tree is then used to quickly find the matching geometry by working down the hierarchy. The following image helps to visualize an example R-tree index:

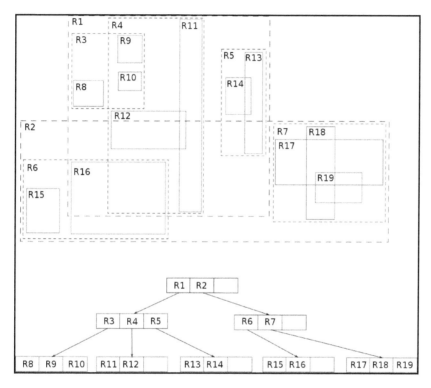

R-tree index. Source: Wikipedia

A spatial database such as PostGIS can easily create an index on a geometry field. A simple SQL statement such as the following for PostGIS will build an R-tree index. PostGIS builds it on top of a **Generalized Search Tree (GiST)** layer for robustness. GiST is a generic algorithm that can be used with several types of indexing methods. The example of GiST is shown in the following code:

```
CREATE INDEX [indexname] ON [tablename] USING GIST ( [geometryfield] );
```

There is also a Python package called *rtree* that can be used to build an index as part of a code module. This can be useful for some heavy duty geospatial processing where you need to repeatedly scan through a set of geometries.

Processing geospatial data

Specialized software can help in processing and visualizing geospatial data. This can be useful for small data and one-time analyses. Even if you have a big data solution, using these tools can help you communicate your findings more effectively to others.

Geospatial analysis software

We will review the most popular **Geographic Information System** (**GIS**) tools, so you have some familiarity with them. They are useful support tools for geospatial analytics.

ArcGIS

ArcGIS is the de facto standard for paid GIS software. It was developed and is maintained by the ESRI corporation. It has an awe-inspiring amount of functionality and is used by most professional geospatial analysts. It has world-class support by ESRI and many training options abound. It links to useful datasets and geospatial analytic capabilities, which are also maintained by ESRI.

ArcGIS is available as a desktop application or as a cloud service. You can sign up for a 60-day free trial (`https://www.arcgis.com/features/free-trial.html`). You can use ArcGIS to do many different kinds of analytics, including geocoding your own custom shapefile. The following example shows how ArcGIS can be used to define polygon areas within a 4-minute drive time of a set of location points on a typical Friday afternoon at 5 pm:

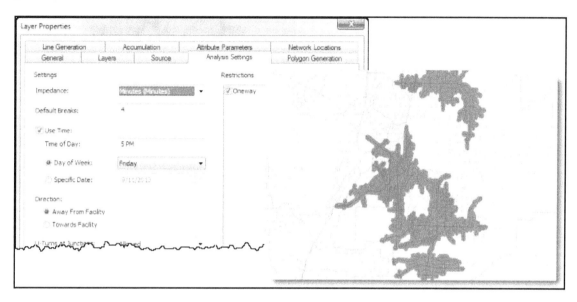

Drive time area analysis example. Source: ArcGIS

QGIS

QGIS is open source and very powerful desktop GIS software. It is similar to ArcGIS but not to the full scope of capability as the paid ESRI software. But the price is right, and it still has a wide variety of capabilities. It can also be manipulated with Python code. There is a vast trove of documentation on it and many useful books on how to use it.

You can download and install QGIS from the project site (`http://www.qgis.org/en/site/forusers/download.html`). If you are unable to get ArcGIS, make sure to keep QGIS handy. QGIS was used to create many of the images in this book. You can use both QGIS and ArcGIS to connect directly to geospatial databases, such as PostGIS and Oracle. The following image shows an example of what can be created with QGIS:

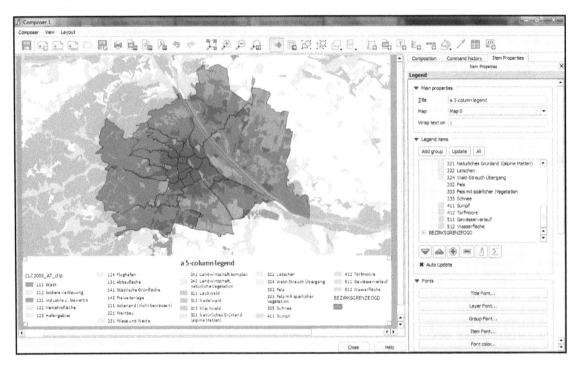

QGIS example screenshot. Source: anitagraser.com

ogr2ogr

`ogr2ogr` is part of the GDAL library. It is a command-line tool used to convert files from one **OpenGIS Simple Features Reference Implementation** (**OGR**) spatial format to another. It is a no-frills tool but is used heavily by geospatial analysts. The general format for a command-line conversion follows the following example:

```
ogr2ogr -f "file_format" destination_data source_data
```

You can use it to convert PostGIS data into shapefiles or load shapefiles into PostGIS for example. It supports conversion into over 90 file formats for vector data alone.

PostGIS spatial functions

PostGIS contains dozens of spatial functions that can be referenced in a standard SQL query. The following table provides an overview of some commonly used functions:

Function	Description
ST_GeomFromText	This returns a specified ST_Geometry value from WKT representation.
ST_GeomFromWKB	This creates a geometry instance from a WKB geometry representation and optional SRID.
ST_Buffer	This returns a geometry covering all points within a given distance from the input geometry.
ST_ConvexHull	The convex hull of a geometry represents the minimum convex geometry that encloses all geometries within the set.
ST_Intersection	This returns a geometry that represents the shared portion of geomA and geomB.
ST_Simplify	This returns a simplified version of the given geometry using the **Douglas-Peucker** algorithm.
ST_Boundary	This returns the closure of the combinatorial boundary of this geometry.
ST_Transform	This returns a new geometry with its coordinates transformed to a different spatial reference.
ST_Centroid	This returns the geometric center of a geometry.
ST_ClosestPoint	This returns the 2-dimensional point on g1 that is closest to g2. This is the first point of the shortest line.
ST_Contains	This returns true if and only if no points of B lie in the exterior of A, and at least one point of the interior of B lies in the interior of A.
ST_Covers	This returns 1 (TRUE) if no point in geometry B is outside geometry A.
ST_Crosses	This returns TRUE if the supplied geometries have some, but not all, interior points in common.

ST_Distance	For geometry type returns the 2D cartesian distance between two geometries in projected units (based on spatial ref). For geography, type defaults to return minimum geodesic distance between two geographies in meters.
ST_Intersects	This returns TRUE if the geometries/geography spatially intersect in 2D - (share any portion of space) and FALSE if they don't (they are disjoint). For geography, tolerance is 0.00001 meters (so any points that close are considered to intersect).
ST_Length	This returns the 2D length of the geometry if it is a LineString or MultiLineString. The geometry are in units of spatial reference and the geography are in meters (default spheroid).
ST_Touches	This returns TRUE if the geometries have at least one point in common, but their interiors do not intersect.

These functions can be used easily as part of a SQL query. The following example shows how to add a buffer to every LineString in the roads geometry field in the Interstates table:

```
SELECT ST_Buffer(Roads, 10, 'endcap=round join=round')
From Interstates;
```

Geospatial analysis in the big data world

Volume and velocity pose some challenges for geospatial analytics. The data size can easily be too large to analyze with a desktop GIS tool. It could even be too large to handle effectively in a relational database with spatial extensions. Due to the intensive computational requirements of geospatial functions, near real-time response can also be a challenge.

There are some options for geospatial analysis with tools built specifically with big data in mind. **Elasticsearch** is an open source distributed search engine. It can scale from one server to hundreds of servers, and it has some spatial search functions. You can search for locations within a certain distance of a latitude and longitude point, for example. AWS offers a managed Elasticsearch service where there is no need to worry about managing servers.

AWS also has a managed petabyte-scale data warehouse service called **Redshift**. This was introduced in Chapter 3, *IoT Analytics for the Cloud*. Redshift does not support geometry fields directly but does support Python UDFs. You can create UDFs using Python code and the *shapely* package, then call them from Redshift SQL statements. A similar strategy can be used for both Hive and Spark.

ESRI supports an open source project called **GP tools for AWS** that allows ArcGIS users to connect to Amazon EMR and S3 data sources. The project is hosted on GitHub (https://github.com/Esri/gptools-for-aws).

Solving the pollution reporting problem

From what you have learned in this chapter, you can now solve the IoT pollution sensor data by congressional districts problem introduced earlier. Follow these general steps using either Python code or spatial query functions in a database such as PostGIS:

1. Download a shapefile for U.S. Interstates such as the U.S. National Transportation Atlas Interstate Highways shapefile available from the University of Iowa (ftp://ftp.igsb.uiowa.edu/gis_library/USA/us_interstates.htm).

2. Download a shapefile for US congressional districts such as the TIGER/Line Shapefile available from the US Census (https://www.census.gov/cgi-bin/geo/shapefiles/index.php?year=2016&layergroup=Congressional+Districts+%28115%29).

3. Load the shapefiles into a geospatial database using ogr2ogr or into Python using the *fiona* package.

4. Add a 1 km buffer to the Interstates MultiLineString using the *shapely* package or ST_Buffer in PostGIS.

5. Use a mapping API such as Google Maps to geocode each device address in order to get the latitude and longitude point pairs. This was discussed in Chapter 7, *Decorating Your Data - Adding External Datasets to Innovate*.

6. Load the IoT device locations as Point geometries.

7. Optionally, apply R-tree indexes to the points and the congressional districts polygons to speed up calculations.

8. Find Points contained within the buffered Interstates roadways polygon. The contains function would be one way to do this. Tag those points as within the bounds. Tag the remaining points as outside the range so they can be used as comparisons.

9. For each point, search for the congressional district polygon that contains it and track the results. This would be a great place to leverage the spatial indexing created earlier.

10. Calculate the pollution values for each device and combine with the congressional district and the in/out of Interstates buffer tags.

11. Pivot and compare the data to compile the report.

12. Go ask for a raise, you have earned it!

13. You can also use the erosion option in the `buffer` function to create Interstate polygons that identify several distance ranges. Start with the largest range as the buffer, then erode your way back down for each range level. Create a buffered polygon for each range. Search the smallest buffered polygon first, the next biggest, then the next, and so on. The points that are not in any of those are outside the range.

14. Go ask for another raise!

Summary

In this chapter, you learned about how to use geospatial analytics to find insights and answer complex questions about IoT data. The importance of geospatial analysis for geographically distributed IoT devices was discussed. The concept of CRS was introduced along with haversine distance and its limitations.

The world is not a perfect sphere. Methods to adjust for that in order to accurately measure distance was covered. Python functions for geospatial analytics, such as `buffer` and `contains`, were discussed, along with some examples.

Storing and processing geospatial data requires some specialized handling. Some geospatial databases and GIS software tools were reviewed. PostGIS spatial functions were also reviewed. We went over some tips for leveraging geospatial analytics in a big data world.

Geospatial analytics offers a huge opportunity to analyze IoT data in new and innovative ways. It can help discover patterns in noisy data. New services can then be created as another way to extract value from your data.

10
Data Science for IoT Analytics

"Revenues are up 5% due to your little geospatial search trick," the VP of Connected Services says, "You know your former boss's position is still open. Maybe we should fill it from the inside..."

Your pulse quickens, you were hoping he might come to this conclusion. You deserve a promotion after what your analytics has brought to the company. You now have one person working for you focusing on geospatial analysis. You can just imagine what you could do with a whole team.

"There is something that we have been toying around with though," he continues, "With all this data we are collecting, we should be able to tap into machine learning models to predict equipment failures. Some think we should be hiring an outside consulting company to handle all of it. Sounds expensive to me. I sure wish we could coordinate this ourselves, work with data scientists of our own choosing... know anyone that might be up to it?"

He winks and walks off, hands behind his back, whistling a Brahms tune.

In this chapter, we introduce data science techniques such as machine learning, deep learning, and forecasting using ARIMA. Special focus is given on how to use these methods with IoT data. The core concepts for each will be reviewed along with examples in R. Deep learning will be described along with where to go to create an Amazon EC2 instance with TensorFlow.

This chapter covers a lot of ground, so hold onto your hats.

This chapter covers the following topics:

- Machine learning (ML):
  - Core concepts
  - Feature engineering
  - Validation methods
  - The Bias-variance tradeoff
  - Comparing models to find the best fit
  - Random forests
  - Gradient boosting machines
  - Anomaly detection
- Forecasting using ARIMA
- Deep learning:
  - Use cases with IoT data
  - Setting up and running a simple deep learning model using TensorFlow

Machine learning (ML)

As a wise uncle of a human-arachnid hybrid once said, With great power, comes great responsibility. This is very true of ML. There are many ways to go wrong. When in the hands of a skilled practitioner, it truly is a form of art. It can be used to do some incredible things on a grand scale, but it should come with a big caution sign. Use it carefully. Be paranoid and validate, validate, validate.

Although we will be going over some core concepts and providing code that you can take and run yourself, this is a big field with lots to learn. It takes years to skillfully and competently apply it. Each section in this chapter is really a book in itself. No, many books. If you plan to use it yourself on IoT data, read, read, read, and then read some more. This chapter is meant to able to provide you with a good foundation to have meaningful conversations with data scientists on the subject.

What is machine learning?

Ask a hundred experts for the definition of ML, and you are likely to get a hundred slightly different answers. Some will take a broad view and fully include deep learning, artificial intelligence, and some traditional statistical techniques, such as the sum of least squares linear regression. Others will be narrow and restrict their definition to a few modeling techniques, considering it separate from a related field called statistical learning.

Some will say it does not even exist in the real world, only in over-hyped media stories. They feel it is all the same traditional statistical analysis that has been done for decades. Some will consider the term ML as completely interchangeable with the term artificial intelligence, while others will consider them very separate things.

ML is an application of statistical techniques in an ordered set of steps (otherwise known as an algorithm). The statistical techniques are rarely new, many have been around for decades and some over a century. Many of the ML methods have also been around for several decades as well. What has changed is the dramatic decline in the cost of compute power along with a dramatic increase of computing capability. What would have taken months to calculate in 1980 now takes seconds or less.

With the availability of some strong open source statistical software libraries, such as R and Python, combined with the low cost and available speed of modern computing hardware, ML has become practical to implement in a large variety of applications. With an increased use of ML came refinements to the existing methods and developments of new algorithms. This has led to a significant increase in predictive capability and a golden age for ML.

We will use a (hopefully not overblown) analogy to help you think about this. With traditional statistical techniques, you are like a mechanical engineer, applying your expertise and knowledge of how things work to define a set of components that fit together. You use these methods to explicitly build your statistical model. You define the detail of each component based on testing and analysis of the data.

With ML, you become more like an agricultural engineer. A farmer of data models. In this chapter, we will define ML as a method that has three general components that, when combined, *grow* a program from the soil of the provided data. This set of statistical techniques *learn* a representation of the underlying function that determines the target values or categories. Learning, in this case, is adaptation and not cognition, as it would be with us humans. At no point does your computer have even an inkling of what it all means–it is all zeros and ones to it.

You as a ML practitioner.

Illustration: Jim Campbell; Inlander; https://www.inlander.com/spokane/farming-data/Content?oid=2136658

The true underlying function is never really known. So, the accuracy of the method can only be inferred from the error rates on new data examples. The goal of many of the ML algorithms (really a set of algorithms) is to iteratively find the right combination of levers to minimize these error rates. If the resulting ML model does a good job of this, then it is said to generalize well. More on this will be explained later.

Any ML model can be viewed as having three interrelated components:

- Representation
- Evaluation
- Optimization

We will cover each in the next sections.

Representation

Representation is how a model is formally constructed in a way which a computer can interpret. Examples are decision trees, support vector machines, and neural nets. ML models are commonly referred to by the name of the representation. A classifier is an instance in the set of possible models generated by the representation. When you make the choice of which representation to use, you are determining the possibilities of classifiers that your model is able to learn. The range of possibilities is known as the **hypothesis space**.

If the true (and remember, *unknown*) classifier model is not in the hypothesis space, it cannot be learned. Most representation models you will use have a large hypothesis space, so this is probably not going to be a problem. But you should be aware of it, as you may need to expand your choices of representation models in order to expand the collective hypothesis space. This may be necessary if you are getting poor predictive performance from your normal *go-to* set of ML models.

Evaluation

As the ML model *tunes itself*, there needs to be a way to evaluate how well it is doing. There needs to be a function that measures the performance to know which classifiers are good and which are bad. This is where the evaluation function comes into play. Some examples are accuracy, error rate, precision, recall, F-score, squared error, and information gain. These functions are also referred to as the **objective function** or **scoring function**.

Optimization

Most of the ML model representations have large hypothesis spaces. A sequential search of all possibilities would take longer than you would ever want to wait for an answer; months, years, or lifetimes, depending on the complexity of the model representation. The choice of the optimization method determines the efficiency of the learning process. There are several general methods to search for the optimal classifier. Some examples are gradient descent, greedy search, and linear programming.

Representation	Evaluation	Optimization
Instances	Accuracy/Error rate	Combinatorial optimization
K-nearest neighbor	Precision and recall	Greedy search
Support vector machines	Squared error	Beam search
Hyperplanes	Likelihood	Branch-and-bound
Naive Bayes	Posterior probability	Continuous optimization
Logistic regression	Information gain	Unconstrained
Decision trees	K-L divergence	Gradient descent
Sets of rules	Cost/Utility	Conjugate gradient
Propositional rules	Margin	Quasi-Newton methods
Logic programs		Constrained
Neural networks		Linear programming
Graphical models		Quadratic programming
Bayesian networks		
Conditional random fields		

The three components of ML algorithms. Source: A Few Useful Things to Know about Machine Learning by Pedro Domingos, University of Washington

Generalization

The fundamental goal of any ML project is to produce a model that operates well with datasets beyond what is available to you currently. You want it to predict, classify, or estimate with minimal errors. Not so much on the data you already have, but on data that you will have when the resulting model is implemented.

The data that you already have to develop your ML model is called the **training set**. The training set should be representative of what you expect to find in the datasets that you will be applying the model to in the future. Even if you have a very large training set, it is unlikely that future datasets will be precisely the same. This great big, complex world produces a lot of variation.

The ability of an ML model to work as expected with a variety of future examples is called **generalization**. It is a key concept in ML, deep learning, and most other predictive modeling techniques. You want your ML model to predict accurately on both the data you have today and the data you will have in the future. You want the model to *generalize* beyond the dataset it was grown from. You should be willing to sacrifice accuracy on the training set in order to increase the probability of accuracy on the future, as yet unknown, datasets. After all, this is the whole point of developing an ML model in the first place.

However, since the only data you have today is the training set and the underlying function that you are trying to approximate with the model is unknown, there is no choice but to use the error on the training data itself as a proxy for the error on the datasets of tomorrow, as the ML model optimizes itself. Yet this is dark and full of terrors – very dangerous!

Thankfully, there are some methods to protect yourself from falsely optimistic ML models. These will be covered later. For now, know that practical ML is based on a foundation of mistrust. This is one of the things that makes it so powerful. If done properly, ML models that pass the rigors of validation go on to very successful applications in the wild and woolly real world.

Feature engineering with IoT data

Beware of the siren call of the automated ML software tool, which takes all your data and determines what is important and automatically builds the best model from it–and all at the click of a button. Often, the raw data that you have is not in a form that ML models can be successful with. Using the data as it is can be a rocky proposition. Many an unaware ship has been wrecked on those rocks, lured by the lovely sound of automation.

One of the best ways to dramatically improve the predictive ability of your ML models is not in the algorithms themselves, but in how the data that they are grown from is presented to them. The transformations of data, the addition of constructed new fields, and the removal of distracting fields is all done with the knowledge of how the representation model operates. This process is called **feature engineering**. Data fields are commonly referred to as **features** in ML. We will adopt that terminology for the rest of the chapter.

The goal of feature engineering is to make it as easy as possible for your ML model to have good performance. Different representations have different requirements for what works well, so you will find yourself creating different versions of the same raw dataset geared specifically to the ML representation. Get to know each ML representation you are using to make sure you are giving it the best possible chance to perform.

Feature engineering is an art and it is hard. But, it can add a lot of value and greatly increase your probability of success. We will introduce a few key concepts, but there is much, much more to learn.

Dealing with missing values

IoT data is notoriously messy (just in case the message has not been driven home yet) and missing values are a common occurrence. There are some options to deal with this problem in order to enhance the quality of your ML models. This is where the art comes into play and judgment is important.

The following are some methods for handling missing values:

- **Remove data rows with missing values**: This is crude, but if only a small percentage is lost, and this percentage appears to be random, then it will have minimal effect on the results. Use a tool such as Tableau to analyze the data with missing values and compare it to the data without missing values to judge the impact of removing the rows. R and Python work well for this task also.
- **Do not use features with a high number of missing values**: Just take them out. The effectiveness of a resulting model built with a feature that has a high percentage of imputed values will work about as well as a bicycle held together by bubble gum and toothpicks. The results will be questionable.
- **You can impute the values using the mean, median, or mode of the valid values for the feature**: This is somewhat unrefined but can work well in some situations. Always analyze the data using techniques, such as what was introduced in Chapter 6, *Getting to Know Your Data - Exploring IoT Data,* to determine what makes sense.
- **Create an ML model to impute the values based on the other features, then use the results in the ML model that predicts the target variable**: (what you want to predict, which is the purpose of building the model). Nested modeling. Now, we are cooking with gas!

The *mice* package in R is useful for identifying and handling missing values. The name *mice* is short for Multivariate Imputation by Chained Equations. It has multiple functions to do some advanced imputation to fill in missing values. It can use ML techniques, such as random forests and logistic regression, to impute values.

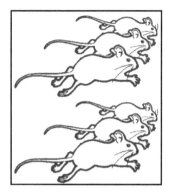

The R mice package. These guys impute missing values and live off residual keyboard cheese

The following code demonstrates a very simple example of using *mice* to impute values. We will start by loading in a sample dataset, *airquality*, which comes with the R installation. It represents data similar to what may be obtained with IoT devices:

```
#make sure all needed packages are installed
if(!require(mice)){
  install.packages("mice")
}
if(!require(VIM)){
  install.packages("VIM")
}
if(!require(lattice)){
  install.packages("lattice")
}

library(mice)
library(VIM)
library(lattice)

#load the airquality dataset (comes with R)
mice_example_data <- airquality
```

Next, we will summarize the data to view statistics and have an idea of where the missing values are:

```
#summarize original data.  Note NAs in Temp
summary(airquality)
```

The summary show the following results. Note the pattern of missing values (NAs):

```
     Ozone             Solar.R            Wind             Temp            Month            Day
 Min.   :  1.00    Min.   :  7.0    Min.   : 1.700    Min.   :56.00    Min.   :5.000    Min.   : 1.0
 1st Qu.: 18.00    1st Qu.:115.8    1st Qu.: 7.400    1st Qu.:72.00    1st Qu.:6.000    1st Qu.: 8.0
 Median : 31.50    Median :205.0    Median : 9.700    Median :79.00    Median :7.000    Median :16.0
 Mean   : 42.13    Mean   :185.9    Mean   : 9.958    Mean   :77.88    Mean   :6.993    Mean   :15.8
 3rd Qu.: 63.25    3rd Qu.:258.8    3rd Qu.:11.500    3rd Qu.:85.00    3rd Qu.:8.000    3rd Qu.:23.0
 Max.   :168.00    Max.   :334.0    Max.   :20.700    Max.   :97.00    Max.   :9.000    Max.   :31.0
 NA's   :37        NA's   :7
```

We will remove some more values to demonstrate how *mice* can impute missing data:

```
#remove some data from the Temp field
mice_example_data[1:5,4] <- NA
#removed some data from the Wind field
mice_example_data[6:10,3] <-NA

#show summary, note the NA count for Temp
summary(mice_example_data)
```

The summary now looks like the following:

```
     Ozone             Solar.R            Wind             Temp            Month            Day
 Min.   :  1.00    Min.   :  7.0    Min.   : 1.700    Min.   :57.00    Min.   :5.000    Min.   : 1.0
 1st Qu.: 18.00    1st Qu.:115.8    1st Qu.: 7.400    1st Qu.:73.00    1st Qu.:6.000    1st Qu.: 8.0
 Median : 31.50    Median :205.0    Median : 9.700    Median :79.00    Median :7.000    Median :16.0
 Mean   : 42.13    Mean   :185.9    Mean   : 9.848    Mean   :78.28    Mean   :6.993    Mean   :15.8
 3rd Qu.: 63.25    3rd Qu.:258.8    3rd Qu.:11.500    3rd Qu.:85.00    3rd Qu.:8.000    3rd Qu.:23.0
 Max.   :168.00    Max.   :334.0    Max.   :20.700    Max.   :97.00    Max.   :9.000    Max.   :31.0
 NA's   :37        NA's   :7        NA's   :5         NA's   :5
```

We can use *mice* to have a more sophisticated look at the patterns in missing data. The `md.pattern()` function will show the frequency of missing values by features in combinations:

```
#use mice to look at pattern of missing data. The first unnamed column
shows the count of rows
#with the complete or missing pattern as indicated by a 1 or 0 (missing) in
the named columns
#The result shows 107 rows with complete data in all rows. 35 rows with
only Ozone missing, 4 rows with only Solar.R missing, etc.
md.pattern(mice_example_data)
```

The output window will show the missing value pattern:

	Month	Day	Wind	Temp	Solar.R	Ozone	
104	1	1	1	1	1	1	0
34	1	1	1	1	1	0	1
4	1	1	1	1	0	1	1
3	1	1	0	1	1	1	1
4	1	1	1	0	1	1	1
1	1	1	1	1	0	0	2
1	1	1	0	1	1	0	2
1	1	1	0	1	0	1	2
1	1	1	1	0	0	0	3
	0	0	5	5	7	37	54

A more visual way to look at patterns is using an aggregation plot with the *VIM* package. The code and the following graph show where values are missing (red). The percentage numbers to the right also show how much of that feature is missing values. Watch out for any feature with over 5% missing. This gets tricky to impute appropriately and may be better left out of the dataset when building ML models. Use your best judgment. **Ozone** would be the only feature in this dataset over 5%:

```
#Let's view it visually using the VIM package
aggr_plot <- aggr(mice_example_data, col=c('gray','red'), numbers=TRUE,
sortVars=TRUE, labels=names(data), cex.axis=.7, gap=3, ylab=c("Histogram -
missing data","Pattern"))
```

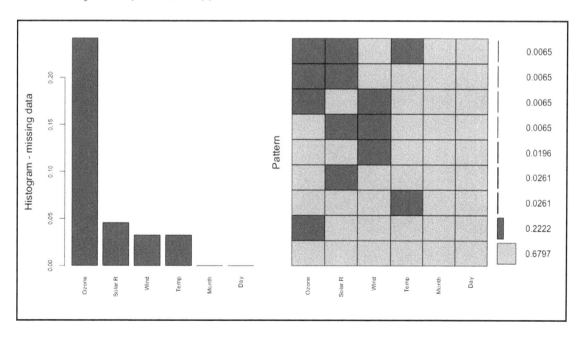

Aggregate plot of air quality data with added missing values

Now, we can use *mice* to impute the values. We will use the default of five sets of imputations:

```
#Remove the categorical variables for Month and Day before imputing.
#The mice() function is a Markov Chain Monte Carlo (MCMC) method that uses
correlation of the data and
#imputes missing values for each feature m times (default is 5) by using
regression of incomplete variables
#on the other variables iteratively with the maximum iterations set by
maxit.
imputed_example_data = mice(mice_example_data[-c(5,6)], m=5,
printFlag=FALSE, maxit = 50, seed=250)
```

We can view how the imputed values compare against the actual known values using a density plot. The known values are shown in blue and the imputed values are in light red. Remember that we set it to impute five iterations of values, so there are five light red lines:

```
#view density plot of results. Blue line is the observed actual data, the
red lines are from the imputed data
densityplot(imputed_example_data)
```

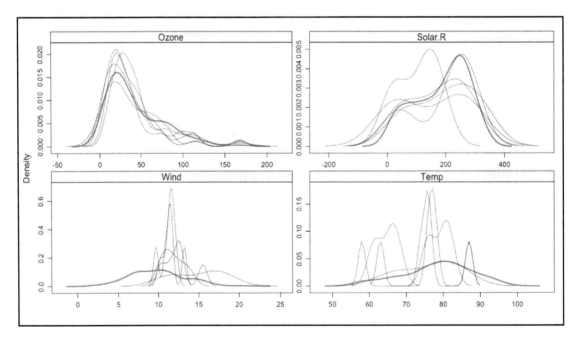

Density plot showing actual values against the imputed datasets

Finally, we can review the summary of the completed dataset including imputed values:

```
#use the complete function to get the dataset with imputed values filled in
completed_example_data <- complete(imputed_example_data,1)
#now let's look at the summary
summary(completed_example_data)
```

```
    Ozone            Solar.R          Wind            Temp
 Min.   :  1.0   Min.   :  7.0   Min.   : 1.70   Min.   :57.00
 1st Qu.: 18.0   1st Qu.:115.0   1st Qu.: 7.40   1st Qu.:72.00
 Median : 31.0   Median :212.0   Median : 9.70   Median :79.00
 Mean   : 42.6   Mean   :186.2   Mean   :10.01   Mean   :77.83
 3rd Qu.: 63.0   3rd Qu.:259.0   3rd Qu.:11.50   3rd Qu.:85.00
 Max.   :168.0   Max.   :334.0   Max.   :20.70   Max.   :97.00
```

There are many imputation methods in *mice*; using the following code, you can get the full list of options on the menu:

```
methods(mice)
```

```
 [1] mice.impute.2l.norm       mice.impute.2l.pan        mice.impute.2lonly.mean   mice.impute.2lonly.norm
 [5] mice.impute.2lonly.pmm    mice.impute.cart          mice.impute.fastpmm       mice.impute.lda
 [9] mice.impute.logreg        mice.impute.logreg.boot   mice.impute.mean          mice.impute.midastouch
[13] mice.impute.norm          mice.impute.norm.boot     mice.impute.norm.nob      mice.impute.norm.predict
[17] mice.impute.passive       mice.impute.pmm           mice.impute.polr          mice.impute.polyreg
[21] mice.impute.quadratic     mice.impute.rf            mice.impute.ri            mice.impute.sample
[25] mice.mids                 mice.theme
see '?methods' for accessing help and source code
```

Centering and scaling

Measurement values can be from vastly different ranges. Barometric pressure is typically measured in millibars with an average sea level at 1013 mbar while atmospheric temperatures normally range from -30 to 40 celsius. A method to adjust for these differences is called **centering**. You can center a feature by calculating the average of all the values in the feature, and then subtract it from each individual value. The resulting transformed feature has a mean of zero.

Imaging drawing a right triangle where the first side is 100 m long, the second is 1 m, and the third is 100.03 m long. It would be barely distinguishable from a 100 m long line. Now, imagine that the first side grows to 10,000 m long with the second side remaining the same. It would be impossible to tell that it is even a triangle at all. This is a similar problem for many ML models where the feature values are on vastly different scales.

Some examples of where this can be a problem: precipitation amount versus elevation or the price of a house versus the number of bedrooms. A solution to this is a method called **scaling**. Scaling divides each value of a feature by its standard deviation (calculated over all values in the feature). This forces the values to have a standard deviation of one.

Combine centering and scaling, and now all the (continuous value) features are comparable to each other. You just made it easier for ML models to tease out the signal from the noise.

The following sample code shows how this can be applied in R. This is a continuation of the *mice* example code from the previous section:

```
#center and scale the completed example data
if(!require(caret)){
  install.packages("caret")
}
library(caret)
#create the object defining the pre-processing
cs_example_prepocessObj <- preProcess(completed_example_data, method =
(c("center","scale")))
#apply the transformation
cs_example_data <- predict(cs_example_prepocessObj, completed_example_data)

#view summary of centered and scaled data
summary(cs_example_data)
```

The resulting dataset will be centered and scaled. The summary statistics will now look like the following:

```
      Ozone              Solar.R              Wind               Temp
 Min.   :-1.2217    Min.   :-1.9818    Min.   :-2.34863    Min.   :-2.1993
 1st Qu.:-0.7225    1st Qu.:-0.7877    1st Qu.:-0.73838    1st Qu.:-0.6155
 Median :-0.3407    Median : 0.2847    Median :-0.08863    Median : 0.1235
 Mean   : 0.0000    Mean   : 0.0000    Mean   : 0.00000    Mean   : 0.0000
 3rd Qu.: 0.5990    3rd Qu.: 0.8044    3rd Qu.: 0.41987    3rd Qu.: 0.7570
 Max.   : 3.6825    Max.   : 1.6336    Max.   : 3.01888    Max.   : 2.0240
```

Time series handling

IoT data is commonly captured at regular intervals, and the position of the value in the series can have a meaning. A dataset captured at regular intervals is called a **time series**. Time series present their own complications for ML.

As mentioned, the position of the value in the series can have meaning beyond just the value itself. Saying something has meaning in ML is basically saying it has predictive value. It should be captured as a feature in the model input so that a model can incorporate it into the learning process.

This can be done by transforming the data so that meaningful elements of the time series are captured as additional features in the dataset. The following are some examples:

- **Add the day of the week as a feature**
- **Add the month of the year as a feature**

- **The frequency of occurrences over a fixed period of prior data**: This can be done using multiple period lengths and creating a feature for each.

- **Average values over a series of prior values**: Be careful not to *peek* into the future and include values after the date. This data would be unknown when applied to new data when the trained model is released to the real world. Unless you are a time traveler... in which case you already knew that.

Validation methods

ML is a highly iterative process. Typically hundreds, thousands, and sometimes millions of variations are generated in the process. At this amount, even with a low probability of false positive results, you are essentially guaranteed to have not just one, but several false positives. The traditional application of statistics with a 95% confidence level breaks down at this amount of iterations. Most statistical tests assume that only one hypothesis is being tested. With ML, you are trying out thousands to millions of hypotheses in the search for the optimal model. You will certainly have models that pass all the statistical tests, just by sheer odds.

Following the principle of mistrust, no model is considered acceptable until it has been tested against data it has not seen before. This process is called **validation**.

Cross-validation

A popular method of validation is called **cross-validation**. It involves randomly dividing up the training set into a number of equal subsets of data rows. A subset is referred to as a **fold**. A model is then trained on all but one of the subsets. The set that it was not trained on is held out as a validation set to check on the error rate for the trained model.

Another model is then trained on all but one of the subsets, but a different one this time. The fold that is held out is used to check on prediction error for the model trained on the other folds. This continues so that each fold is held out exactly once, and all the data is used in both training and validation. The resulting set of models will each run its own prediction and the average of the results will be given as the output.

10 folds is the most commonly used amount, but the number is set more by convention than by anything special about the exact number of 10. **10-fold cross-validation** is the typical terminology used to describe this. The advantage of using cross validation is that you simulate a variety of datasets using the same set of training data. This increases the chance that the resulting model will generalize well. It also allows you to have a robust validation process, even if your training data is limited:

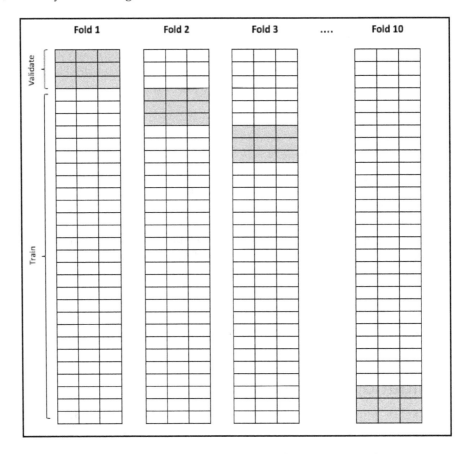

10-fold cross-validation. Validation set shown in blue for each fold, training set shown in white

The *caret* package in R makes it easy to incorporate cross-validation into your ML process. The ML process is commonly referred to as a **pipeline**.

The following code example sets up the training process that will be used later on in the code, when the model is actually trained. We will use this again later in the chapter:

```
#Create train control object that defines how training will be done.
#This example uses 10 fold cross validation which is repeated 5 time.
library(caret)
ctrl <- trainControl(method = "repeatedcv",number = 10,repeats = 5)
```

Test set

It is best practice to keep a percentage of your training data aside, until you have found what you believe to be the optimal performing model or set of optimized models (from different techniques).

This percentage of data held out, usually called the **test set**, will serve as your final test of the models that have been optimized through the validation process. If you are hiring a consulting company to perform the modeling, keep a test set to yourself and do not provide it to them. Use it to confirm the accuracy of their resulting optimized model. You should get similar results to what they reported. If not, you have something to discuss with them before you pay their fees.

Precision, recall, and specificity

The results of testing the effectiveness of an ML model against test data can be summed up into four categories (assuming the model is predicting between two classes, such as **yes/no** or **broken/not broken**). We will use the example of a wearable IoT sensor where the sensor data is being used to predict if someone is **walking** or **not walking**:

1. The ML model said the person was **walking**, but he was actually sitting on the couch watching *Dancing with the Stars* drinking a super-sized Sprite. This is a **False Positive (FP)**, also called a Type I error.
2. The ML model said he was **not walking** when he, in fact, was **walking** quite quickly to the restroom due to the super-sized Sprite he just drank. This is a **False Negative (FN)** or a Type II error.
3. The ML model said he was **walking**, and he was actually **walking**. This is called a **True Positive (TP)**.
4. The ML model said he was **not walking** and he was, in fact, snoring up a storm in his bed at the time–so **not walking**. This is called a **True Negative (TN)**.

Taken together, these can be placed into a 2x2 matrix with the number of occurrences of each type shown. This is called a **confusion matrix,** and all sorts of useful diagnostic information about the performance of an ML model can be generated from it.

The following table shows a generic example of a confusion matrix:

Confusion Matrix Example

Prediction	Actual (Reference)	
	Class1	Class2
Class1	True Positive (TP)	False Postive (FP)
Class2	False Negative (FN)	True Negative (TN)

Class1 is considered the target class for prediction in this example

Confusion matrix example

When generated in R, the confusion matrix will look like the following table. The `confusionMatrix` function in the *caret* package can be used to create it from the predictions of a trained model:

```
confusionMatrix(data = testPredictions, reference = classFactors, positive =
"Class1")
```

	Reference	
Prediction	Class1	Class2
Class1	380	57
Class2	79	484

Confusion matrix example in R.

If you take all the instances that the ML model predicted positive and actually were positive (as intended), and compare it against the total times it predicted positive whether as intended or not, you can get a measure for how much you can trust the positive predictions of a model. This is called **Precision**. It is also called **Positive Predictive Value** (**PPV**), but is usually referred to as Precision:

Precision = True Positives/(True Positives + False Positives)

If you take all the instances that the ML model predicted positive and actually were positive and compare that against the total number of actual positives–predicted or not, you can get a measure for how well the model can capture all the positive occurrences. It knows a thing when it sees a thing. This is called **Recall.** And also **Sensitivity**. And also **True Positive Rate** (**TPR**). And also **hit rate**. And also **probability of detection**. But mostly Recall and Sensitivity:

Recall = True Positives/(True Positives + False Negatives)

If you would like to judge your ML model's capability as a critic, you can take all the predicted negative which actually were negative instances, and compare this against all the total negative instances, predicted or not. This will give you a measure of how well a model knows something isn't a thing when it sees it. This is called **Specificity** or **True Negative Rate** (**TNR**):

Specificity = True Negatives/(True Negatives + False Positives)

Each of these measures alone can be misleading. For example, if a negative instance is rare, say 1% probability, then a model could show excellent Recall by simply always assuming an instance is positive. The Specificity in this case would be terrible even though the recall was good. It is always best to check multiple measures to verify your model performs well.

Understanding the bias–variance tradeoff

A core concept in ML is the bias–variance tradeoff. It fits in the category of no free lunches. The reduction of one often increases the other. The concept is tightly linked with one of the big dangers of ML, **overfitting**.

Overfitting is when a model contorts itself to fit the training data just right, but in doing so, it does a terrible job generalizing to new data examples. The resulting error on the training set will be low while the error on the test set will be high.

If you are not aware of this danger, you can easily fool yourself into thinking you have grown a highly accurate model, only to be embarrassed when it fails miserably out in the real world.

Bias

Bias is the propensity of an ML model to consistently learn the same thing. Consistency refers to the results of repeated iterations on variations on the same dataset. The higher the bias, the more off target the resulting learned model tends to be. If the bias is lower, the resulting trained models will consistently be more on target.

A high bias model will have a large error rate on both the training data and the test data. This is referred to as **underfitting**. In other words, a more complex model could fit the data better in both situations (training and testing).

The following example compares a linear model with low bias in regards to the dataset, and a high bias linear model in regards to a different dataset. We use the same simple model to show that the level of bias is not necessarily related to the choice of ML model. Although some models have a higher propensity to bias, it is the combination of the model and the data that matters:

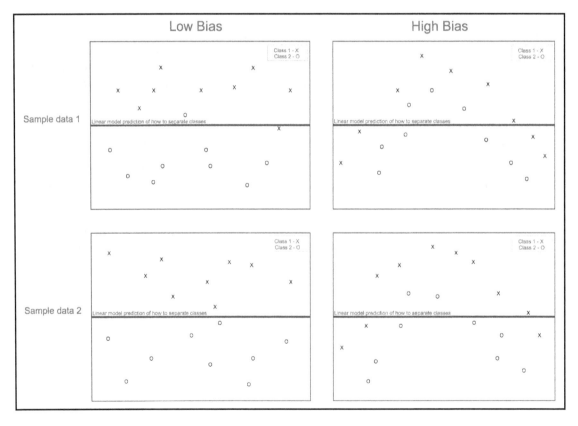

High and low bias models

Variance

Variance is associated with more complex models and refers to the ability of an ML model to contort itself to fit the training data too well. The resulting learned model will be very different depending on which variation of the dataset it is trained on. High variance models have the problem of **overfitting**.

A high variance model will have a low error rate on training data and a high error rate on test data. The high variance model fits itself too well to the precise composition of the training data. It learned all the random noise as well as the underlying signal in the data.

Variance is a big problem with more advanced ML models if they are left unchecked during the learning process. This is because of the incredible flexibility in the methods, which can effectively *memorize* almost any combination of data in the training set.

Trade-off and complexity

In a perfect world, you would have ML models that, after the learning process, have both low bias and low variance. However, as you may be aware, we live in a far from perfect world. So, as in most things, there is a trade-off needed to get the optimal result.

The goal of ML research efforts is to not only find the optimal trade-off combination but to also develop new ML techniques that sacrifice a little on one in exchange for a significant reduction in the other. For any given ML model, there is a trade-off to be made between bias and variance in order to find the optimal *configuration* that will generalize the best. Unfortunately, this optimal position is unknown and has to be inferred based on error calculations from the training and validation process.

More complex models can fit the data better and reduce error in the training process. However, they are prone to overfitting, which will increase the error on test data, and later on new real world data. The following image represents a range of complexity *settings* for a model. The goal is to find the optimal place where both training and test error is minimized. This represents a best compromise, which you would expect to generalize well to future datasets when the trained model is put into production:

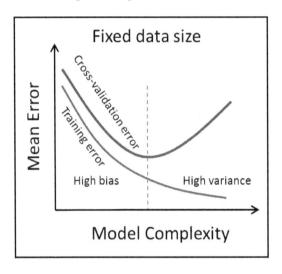

Bias - Variance tradeoff as model complexity increases. Source: http://horicky.blogspot.com/2012/06/

Fortunately, there are methods, such as **regularization**, designed to help prevent overfitting in order to increase the likelihood that the resulting trained model will be in the optimal trade-off area. These methods are incorporated into the R packages that you will be using to grow your ML models.

Comparing different models to find the best fit using R

It is best practice to not only find the optimal version of a trained ML model but to compare multiple trained optimized ML algorithms. Each ML algorithm has its strengths and weaknesses. Choosing only one is limiting yourself. Select several ones that are likely to grow into good trained models given the particular problem you are solving. Then, compare them against each other, and let the best model win.

There are several ways to compare ML models against each other. ROC charts and AUC measures are two of the more popular methods. We will introduce each next.

ROC curves

Originating from World War II radar engineering, the **receiver operating characteristics (ROC) curve** is a common way to compare the effectiveness of ML models against each other. It measures the Recall rate against the **fall-out rate** (calculated as [*1-specificity*]) along a threshold measure. The fall-out rate is also known as the **False Positive Rate (FPR)** or the **probability of false alarm**.

You may have noticed a trend in that a lot of the measures have several different names. It can get confusing but it is important to know the pseudonyms of the measures since different articles, blogs, and research papers will use different names for them.

In most cases, the ROC curve will be used with binary classification problems. Some examples of binary classification questions include **failure/no failure**, **operating/not operating**, **raining/not raining**, and **purchase/no purchase**. An ROC curve shows the change in trade-off between the benefits of correct classifications (true positives) and the costs of incorrect classifications (false positives), along intervals of a threshold parameter.

It can help to think of the true positive rate as follows:

True positive rate = Correctly classified positives / All positives in the training set

And think of the false positive rate as follows:

False positive rate = Incorrectly classified negatives / All negatives in the training set

The following graph is an example of an ROC curve for a single model. True positive rate (also called Recall or Sensitivity) is shown on the vertical *y* axis, and the false negative rate (false alarm rate) is shown on the horizontal *x* axis. The diagonal dotted line represents what a model made of random guesses would look like. The closer a model's ROC curve is to the line, the less distinguishable it is from using random guesses. A curve below the dotted line is worse than random guessing; but it can still have some useful value just by taking the opposite of what it predicts. The curved blue line represents the ML model being graphed:

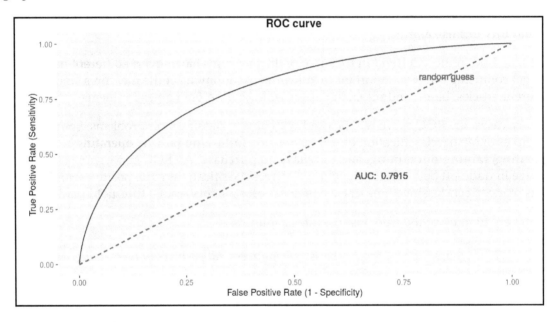

The ROC example chart. All ROC images generated using the demonstration tool at `https://kennis-research.shinyapps.io/ROC-Curves/`.

Normally, you would be comparing multiple ML models on the same graph, each with its own curve. However, it is easier to grasp the intuition of the method by using only one ML curve. Read the chart by following the curve from left to right. The left side of the chart represents more conservative threshold settings for the ML model while moving to the right represents more and more liberal settings.

A perfect model would perfectly discriminate between positive and negative instances along all threshold settings until you get to the most liberal setting, which would consider all examples as positives. It would *hug* the upper left corner of the chart. An example of an extremely good model shown on an ROC chart is shown in the following figure:

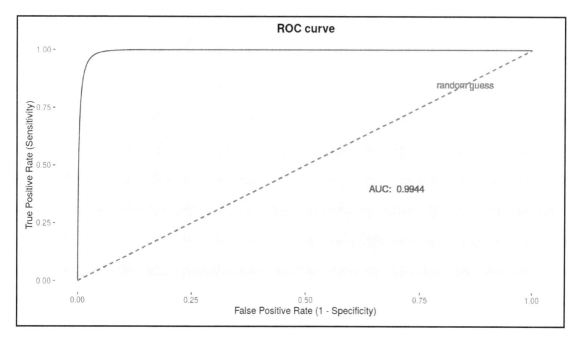

A near perfect ML model. Don't believe it, this is about as rare in the real world as leprechauns playing polo while riding unicorns

ROC curves are generated by running the training data through the trained model to generate the predicted score (or probability) of the likelihood of a positive classification for each instance. The results are sorted in order with the most likely first. Each prediction is compared to the actual classification of the instance and a running score of the true positive rate and the false positive rate is kept as you move down the list.

Each true positive rate and false positive rate combination is graphed on the chart with a line connecting the points. In reality, an ROC curve is a step function that approaches a true curve, as the size of your training set grows.

As you move down the list into less and less likely positives (based on the model's prediction), this effectively shifts through a range of thresholds from most conservative (your top scoring instance) to the most liberal (your lowest scoring instance). The resulting curve shows the performance of your ML model along a wide range of threshold scenarios. When you are comparing ML models using ROC curves, you are comparing their performance under many difference threshold conditions. This gives you a fuller picture of performance.

ROC curve charts can be generated easily in R. Using the *pROC* package, you can generate chart images just using the `roc` and `plot` functions. Here is a simple example:

```
#load pROC library
library(pROC)
#create ROC object based on the model and its class lables
rocCurve <- roc(response = classFactors,
 predictor = testPredictionsProb,
 levels = rev(levels(classFactors))) #roc function assumes the second class
is the target, so we will reverse labels

#plot curve
plot(rocCurve, legacy.axes = TRUE, identity = TRUE, col = "blue", add =
FALSE)
#you can also add another model curve to the chart by calling this function
again with the 'add = TRUE' option
```

The code will produce an ROC curve plot similar to the following example:

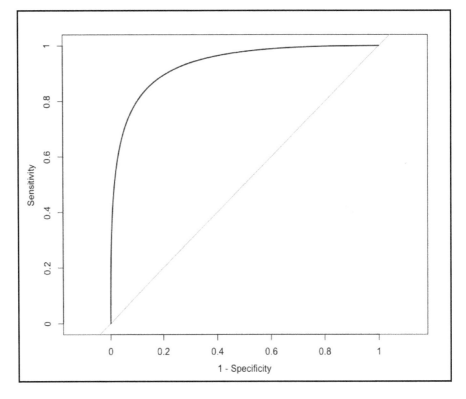

Example of an ROC curve plot in R.

The following are some benefits of using ROC curves:

- **Not sensitive to changes in class distributions**: Shifts in the numbers of positive and negative examples will not affect the ML model's ROC curve, assuming the model remains as effective in discriminating between them.
- **Useful even if classification error costs are unequal**: When the costs of false positives or benefits of the correct classification of positives change, the ROC curve is unaffected. Only the region of interest along the curve changes. In other words, the optimal threshold setting will shift but the shape of the curve will not.
- **Allows the comparison of the performance of different ML models along various threshold settings**: Some models will perform best at conservative settings while others may be the best at more liberal settings. The best model, therefore, depends on the underlying business case.

The following are things to keep in mind with ROC curve analysis:

- **Difficult to use intuitively for multi-class models**: It is hard to visualize beyond 2-dimensional space and the dimensions grow quickly with multi-class prediction models. There are methods to do this, but they are still not easy to interpret.
- **Hard to explain to non-analytical audiences**: There is a learning curve to ROC curves (it is fun to use the word curve). However, non-specialist people can certainly learn how to understand it with repeated exposure. The author recommends educating them if possible. Organizations that understand these charts can use them when making cost/benefit business decisions. Once they get over the hump of learning to interpret the charts, they will find them very useful.

Area Under the Curve (AUC)

AUC is simply the portion of the ROC chart "square" that is underneath the ROC curve of the ML. Since it is a proportion, it will always range from 0 to 1. An AUC of 1 represents a curve that covers the entire graph, and therefore it is perfectly aligned to the upper-left corner. This would be the aforementioned rarely observed, yeti-like *perfect model*.

The random model represented by the dashed line in the ROC chart has an AUC of 0.5. So, in real world situations, you will be looking at AUC numbers from 0.5 to 1.0. How to interpret an AUC number depends a lot on the industry and business situation. An AUC of 0.6, indicating better than random, may be a fantastic model for stock picking in the finance industry; while the same AUC measure would be an utter failure for cancer detection in the medical industry.

AUC numbers are a useful way to compare models using a single number instead of chart. This comparison could be between different models, or on a model against itself after it has been tweaked or retrained. However, there is a danger when only looking at the AUC value as you are losing some valuable information.

An AUC number gives you a rough idea of performance but tells you little about the actual shape of the curve. You lose the ability to determine the performance of a model at different threshold settings. At more conservative settings, an ML model with a lower AUC value may actually perform better than another model with a higher AUC.

AUC values are useful shorthand for doing quick comparisons and for boiling down an ROC curve to one number. But you should always review the full ROC curve before making any business decisions, especially if the AUC values are close.

AUC values can be quickly generated in R using the *pROC* package also. Building on the prior ROC code example, the AUC values can be obtained by using the `auc` function:

```
auc(rocCurve)
```

Random forest models using R

Most ML textbooks start you off with a simple model like a Perceptron. But if you have made it this far in the book, you are a rock star and deserve to be introduced to the big guns. Since they usually provide better results, you will run into these modes far more frequently than perceptrons anyway.

We will start with Random Forest models. Besides having a cool sounding name, they are flexible and tend to generalize well. They also have value in explaining the usefulness of input features using a method called **variable importance**.

Random forest key concepts

Random forest is a decision tree-based ML modelling process. Decision trees predict target variables by growing a hierarchy of successive splits across input features, based on the information gain of each split. If this sounds confusing, just think of it as a series of decision rules that result in a prediction at the end. The following diagram may help explain the idea:

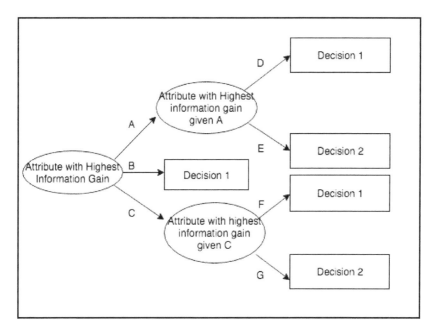

Decision tree ID3 algorithm simple diagram. Source: Wikimedia commons

Random forests take this concept a step further by introducing randomness and repetition. From the original training set, a random variation of the training set is created by taking a random split and **bootstrapping** a dataset to train a tree. Bootstrapping uses random draws from a dataset to create a (usually) larger dataset as a way to simulate different datasets from the same population of data records.

A popular form of random forest also adds some randomness to growing the tree. A random feature is selected from a subset of features to split on at each branch. This whole process is repeated over and over as a forest of decision trees is created. There are typically over 1,000 trees in one model. The model then averages the decisions of all the trees to arrive at the predicted value:

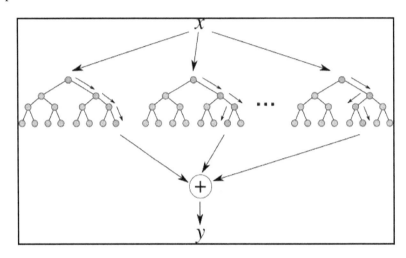

Random forest visual. All tree variations vote to arrive at the consolidated answer *y*.

This is an overly simplified explanation as there is much more to it. There are also several tuning parameters depending on the problem being investigated. This is where the art in data science comes into play. This process reduces variation by a *wisdom of crowds* effect. The cost is a little increase in bias.

Random forest R examples

Again, this is where R shines (and also is dangerous), as it can do a lot of the tuning for you. We will show some example code to demonstrate what a few lines of R code can do. But the author recommends careful testing and data exploration before settling on the parameters and methods.

This code takes the imputed values from the *mice* section and predicts if the temperature is warmer than the average (which we categorize as **hot**) or cooler than the average (**cold**), based on the values for **Wind**, **Ozone**, and **Solar radiation**:

```
#Add classes to the imputed data based on Temperature.
#This is what will be the target variable for the random forest model
cs_example_data$tempClass <- ifelse(cs_example_data$Temp > 0,"hot","cold")
```

```
#make sure needed packages are installed, then load them
if(!require(randomForest)){
 install.packages("randomForest")
}

library(randomForest)
library(caret)

#define how we are going to train the model
ctrlCV <- trainControl(method = "repeatedcv", number =10, repeats=5,
returnResamp='none')

#define the target variable
target <- "tempClass"

#define the predictor features
predictors <- c("Ozone","Solar.R","Wind")

#split data into training and test
training <- createDataPartition(cs_example_data$tempClass, p=0.7,
list=FALSE)
trainData <- cs_example_data[training,]
testData <- cs_example_data[-training,]

#train the random forest model and specify the number of trees. Use caret
to control cross-validation
rfModel <- train (trainData[,predictors],
 trainData[,target],
 method = "rf",
 trControl = ctrlCV)

#run prediction on test data to get class probabilities
testPredRFProb <- predict(rfModel, testData, type = "prob")
#run prediction again to get predicted class
testData$RFclass <- predict(rfModel, testData)

#grab the positive class probability (hot) and the predicted classes
testData$RFProb <- testPredRFProb[,"hot"]

#Show confusion matrix for results
confusionMatrix(data = testData$RFclass, reference = testData$tempClass,
positive = "hot")
```

The resulting confusion matrix is shown next. This is a much smaller sample size than we would like, and the model performance is not all that great. But it does have some predictive value. It is not half bad for a simple example:

```
Confusion Matrix and Statistics

          Reference
Prediction cold hot
      cold  14   5
      hot    6  20

               Accuracy : 0.7556
                 95% CI : (0.6046, 0.8712)
    No Information Rate : 0.5556
    P-Value [Acc > NIR] : 0.004499

                  Kappa : 0.5025
 Mcnemar's Test P-Value : 1.000000

            Sensitivity : 0.8000
            Specificity : 0.7000
         Pos Pred Value : 0.7692
         Neg Pred Value : 0.7368
             Prevalence : 0.5556
         Detection Rate : 0.4444
   Detection Prevalence : 0.5778
      Balanced Accuracy : 0.7500

       'Positive' Class : hot
```

Resulting confusion matrix summary from random forest modeling.

Gradient Boosting Machines (GBM) using R

Similar to random forest, GBM is a decision tree-based model that combines predictions from multiple trees to arrive at an aggregated response. However, instead of thousands of independently grown trees that vote for an answer, GBMs are a series of shallow trees linked together in succession.

Gradient Boosting Machines are a popular and powerful ML technique. A variant of GBMs, called **XGBoost**, has won several recent Kaggle competitions.

GBM key concepts

The depth or shallowness of a decision tree refers to how many levels of hierarchies it has. The smaller the number of hierarchies, the more shallow the tree. GBM uses successive weak learners, which are trained on a measure of error from the previous model. A weak learner means it has some predictive power but not much. A shallow tree is typically weak, as it is only using one or a small number of features to split the training data.

The resulting predictions are added together to arrive at a final prediction. There are several variants that use different methods of estimating error and determining how shallow to make each tree.

GBMs work by successively dialing in on higher error areas using the error of the previous model to fit the next model, and so on and so forth. This addresses a problem when using a single decision tree. A single tree splits the data into smaller and smaller groups at each branch. This leads to overfitting as it begins to fit noise, especially when it gets into small sample sizes at the ends of the branches. GBMs avoid this by reusing the entire dataset at each successive learned tree:

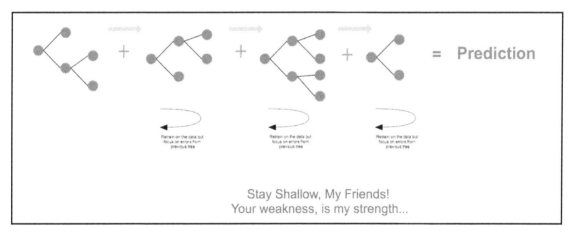

GBM concept diagram

The Gradient Boosting Machines R example

In R, the *gbm* package can be used to train a GBM. GBMs have the tuning parameters of tree depth and shrinkage. As always, the beauty and danger of R is that it can tune these parameters for you. The following code uses the *caret* package to fit a GBM model and optimize the tuning parameters:

```
#make sure needed packages are installed, then load them
if(!require(gbm)){
 install.packages("gbm")
}

library(gbm)

#reuse train control and training data from random forest example

#train the random forest model and specify the number of trees. Use caret
to control cross-validation
 gbmModel <- train (trainData[,predictors],
 trainData[,target],
 method = "gbm",
 trControl = ctrlCV,
 verbose = FALSE)

#run prediction on test data to get class probabilities
testPredGBMProb <- predict(gbmModel, testData, type = "prob")
#run prediction again to get predicted class
testData$GBMclass <- predict(gbmModel, testData)

#grab the positive class probability (hot) and the predicted classes
testData$GBMProb <- testPredGBMProb[,"hot"]

#Show confusion matrix for results
confusionMatrix(data = testData$GBMclass, reference = testData$tempClass,
positive = "hot")
```

The confusion matrix will look similar to the following table. In our small sample, GBM is not doing so shabby:

```
Confusion Matrix and Statistics

              Reference
Prediction cold hot
      cold    16    5
      hot      4   20

                  Accuracy : 0.8
                    95% CI : (0.654, 0.9042)
       No Information Rate : 0.5556
       P-Value [Acc > NIR] : 0.0005445

                     Kappa : 0.597
   Mcnemar's Test P-Value : 1.0000000

               Sensitivity : 0.8000
               Specificity : 0.8000
            Pos Pred Value : 0.8333
            Neg Pred Value : 0.7619
                Prevalence : 0.5556
            Detection Rate : 0.4444
      Detection Prevalence : 0.5333
         Balanced Accuracy : 0.8000

          'Positive' Class : hot
```

Resulting confusion matrix summary from gradient boosting machines.

Ensemble

Ensemble methods are a way to combine ML models together to generate a prediction. Think of it as an ML model committee where each ML model casts its vote and the tallied result is the prediction.

There are various methods to *tally the votes*, and you will want to experiment with them to see if you can increase the performance of your ensemble model. However, this is outside the scope of this book.

Research and real world usages have shown that ensemble methods often perform better than any of the incorporated models alone. Ensemble methods are a way to improve real-world performance by reducing the prediction variation of any one model. They should be in your data science toolkit for IoT analytics.

Anomaly detection using R

Anomaly detection is a way to use historical data to identify unusual observations without requiring a labeled training set. Modern anomaly detection methods take into account long-term trends and cyclical variation in the data while determining which observations to flag as anomalies.

Twitter has recently released an advanced open source anomaly detection package for R called *AnomalyDetection*. It is geared toward detecting anomalies in single value high frequency (less than a day) time series data; however, it is possible to set an option to handle datasets longer than a month. It can also be used on a vector of non-time series data.

It is good at handling the effects of trends and seasonality - although seasonality, in this case, is at the minutes to days level not yearly. The GitHub page is located here (`https://g ithub.com/twitter/AnomalyDetection`), and it can be installed easily as an R package using the following R code. Make sure to spell Anomaly with a capital A. *anomalyDetection* is a different package (welcome to the world of R):

```
install.packages("devtools")
devtools::install_github("twitter/AnomalyDetection")
```

The following example shows how anomaly detection can be used on sensor data. Anomaly detection is useful in itself, but the frequency of anomalies detected in a time window (hourly or daily) can have good predictive value when used as an input into other models. For example, the frequency of pressure sensor anomalies in the last hour combined, with an average temperature sensor reading, could be highly predictive of a future generator failure.

The following example code takes the **Wind** values from the imputed dataset and looks for anomalies. The search can be either forward or backward, or both:

```
#load library
library(AnomalyDetection)

#This uses the vector method since no timestamp is present. If timestamp is
present, use AnomalyDetectionTs
res = AnomalyDetectionVec(cs_example_data$Wind, max_anoms=0.05, period=60,
direction='both', only_last=FALSE, plot=TRUE)
res$plot
```

The code creates a plot, which is shown in the following figure. The points that it determines are possible anomalies are circled in blue:

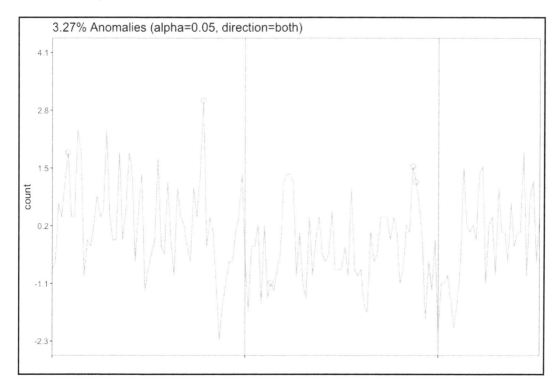

Anomaly detection on Wind values in our example dataset

Forecasting using ARIMA

Sometimes, you will have the need to forecast future values of a time series. For example, this could be a requirement to estimate the next several months of active IoT devices; or, it could be a need to project the usage hours of remote oil well pumps. One of the most popular methods to forecast time series is **AutoRegressive Integrated Moving Average (ARIMA)**.

ARIMA is not one model but a collection of related methods that attempt to describe autocorrelations in the data in order to forecast future values. ARIMA is a combination of moving average and autoregressive techniques. **Autoregressive** means that the forecasting of future values of a variable is based on the linear combination of the past values of variables.

ARIMA incorporates both trend and seasonality effects into future forecasts. It can model both seasonal and nonseasonal data with a range of methods.

Using R to forecast time series IoT data

The *forecast* package contains ARIMA functions in R. You can install it with the following code:

```
install.packages("forecast")
```

The `Arima` function has settings for the nonseasonal component of a forecast and the seasonal component (if needed). Each is composed of three numbers that represent the order of the autoregressive part, the degree of differencing to be used, and the order of the moving average part. This is commonly notated as (p,d,q) in R documentation. As with all things in data science, the right place to start is to look at your data, note any unusual trends, and perform some diagnostic statistical analysis to understand what are the appropriate values to use for (p,d,q) for both the nonseasonal and seasonal components.

Fortunately, and also dangerously (has that been mentioned before?), R can handle a lot of this for you and automatically determine the appropriate values based on a series of tests. This is done using the `auto.arima()` function. You should also analyze the results and the residual values to determine if your forecast model is viable.

The following example code takes the **Wind** values from the New York air quality dataset that we have been using in this chapter and fits an ARIMA model:

```
#load forecast library
library(forecast)

#create a time series on the Solar radiation data. The air quality data was
captured from May 1, 1973 to September 30, 1973
windTS <- ts(completed_example_data$Wind, start = c(1973,5,1), frequency =
365.25)

#show values over time
plot.ts(windTS)

#fit an arima model
```

```
fit <- auto.arima(windTS)

#plot forecast for the next month
plot(forecast(fit, h=30))
```

The resulting forecast plot shows some wide variation in projected **Wind** values. You should not quit your job to be a weatherman based on this simple R code ARIMA example:

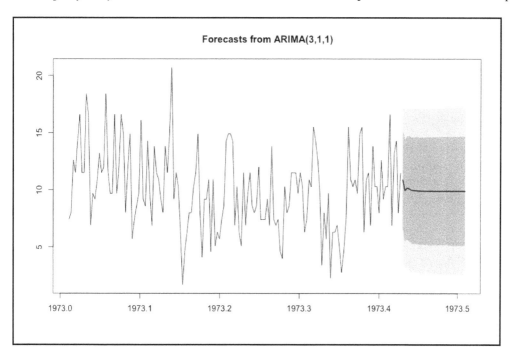

ARIMA forecast of Wind values. Note the auto.arima function chose a 3,1,1 model (p,d,q notation).

Deep learning

Deep learning is an area of data science that is experiencing rapid advancement and generating a lot of excitement. Some deep learning models are better at certain types of image recognition than humans. When stories in the media mention artificial intelligence, they are usually referring to deep learning models.

Deep learning models are very complex although several of the concepts are similar to the ML concepts we have discussed so far in this chapter (such as the bias-variance tradeoff). Deep learning models can have millions of features and can take days or weeks to train.

Use cases for deep learning with IoT data

Deep learning can do wonders for complex data, with thousands to millions of features and a large history of labeled examples to use as training sets. The rapid advancements in image recognition has as much to do with the vast trove of identified images that Google and others have collected over the years, as to the advances in the deep learning algorithms used.

For IoT data, this can limit the usefulness of deep learning techniques. Most IoT data is relatively new without a long history of labeled examples. Many IoT devices have only a few sensors, so the feature set is not as complex. In these situations, many of the ML techniques discussed previously can do as good, if not better, job of prediction than deep learning techniques. Deep learning is also more computationally expensive in both time and compute power (that is, higher cost).

However, if the IoT data flow includes a large number of features and hundreds of thousands to millions of labeled training data is available, deep learning techniques may be able to provide a significant boost in predictive power. This is clearly the case in autonomous vehicle development. It could also do wonders where images are captured as part of the device functionality (static or video).

Deep learning packages tend to be interacted with best by Python as opposed to R. They are also relatively new, so expect documentation and tutorials to be limited. This makes them a little more finicky to work with than the prior examples in this chapter. You will need more time and expertise to develop deep learning models than for more well-trodden ML models, such as random forest.

Use what method makes the most sense for the individual use case and available training data. Consider the effectiveness requirements and see whether using a deep learning modeling technique is likely to provide enough boost in accuracy to warrant the expense.

A Nickel Tour of deep learning

Deep learning is a big umbrella that covers many projects and neural network configurations using a variety of methods. The following chart can give you an idea of the variety of architectures available. There is typically a trade-off between the accuracy obtainable and required computing time to train the models that has to be considered. The right trade-off depends on the use case. The y axis represents accuracy and the x axis represents compute requirements:

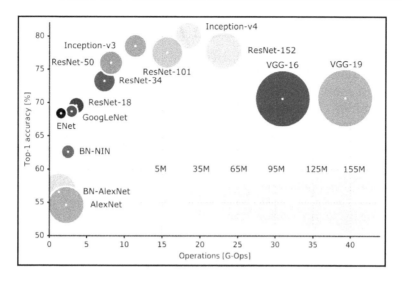

The comparison of deep learning network architectures. Source: medium.com

This is a big field and there are many areas to explore. There are methods that specialize in feature extraction from images, sound, and text. There are methods for classifying thousands to millions of images. There are methods for word translation that remember some previous words already translated in a sentence to improve accuracy on the current word being translated.

Some use cases combine network architecture types. The following is an example of a use case that extracts features from an image, then uses a **Convolutional Neural Net (CNN)** to classify elements in the image, and uses a **Recurrent Neural Net (RNN)** to match the extracted features to word choice to create a text caption for the original image:

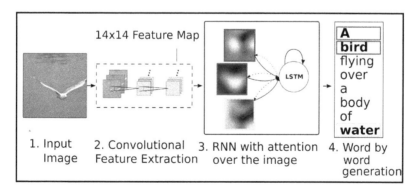

Deep learning use case. Source: medium.com

Setting up TensorFlow on AWS

In November 2015, Google released an open source software platform for deep learning called **TensorFlow**. TensorFlow has a flexible architecture, which allows it to spread computations across multiple CPUs or use a **Graphical Processing Unit (GPU)**. GPUs have thousands of computing cores, which facilitate massive parallel processing and align well with deep learning training needs. The most common way to interact with it is with Python code.

The Python *keras* package acts as an interface layer to TensorFlow, making programming simpler. The author recommends using *keras* instead of programming TensorFlow directly.

So, how can you easily set up TensorFlow with the *keras* interface all on top of a GPU unit to accelerate training times? Fortunately, AWS provides AMI instances with all of this, and more, already included. You can easily launch one onto an EC2 instance with GPU support (make sure to check pricing first - GPUs are in high demand). These are called **AWS Deep Learning AMIs,** and information about how to get started can be found at `https://aws.am azon.com/amazon-ai/amis/`.

Summary

This chapter was a whirlwind tour of various areas in data science. It was covered with an eye on how to use each for the IoT analytics. Believe it or not, we covered only a small amount of topics in a very big space. Hope your head does not hurt too much.

11
Strategies to Organize Data for Analytics

You survey your team as they tap away diligently on their MacBooks scattered around their cubicle. You have been promoted to the position your old boss held and now have a small team of data scientists. Some are at standing desks, some are at minipods, and some are huddled around a small conference table in the middle of your area.

Your boss, the VP of Connected Services, approaches down the hallway with a pleasant smile. He makes eye contact as soon as you see him.

"How is the team settling in?" he asks. You give him positive status updates, and he nods and murmurs his approval.

"I had a thought," he says, "Your team does great work. But the speed that they deliver analytics is the same now as it was a few months ago. Is there anything we can do that would help them iterate faster?"

You smile with an *what an interesting thought* expression. You have been thinking the same thing for weeks.

"Most of the time spent for any analysis that we do is on collecting, cleaning, and massaging the data," you say, "It can be 80% or higher. I'll get the team together with our database experts to brainstorm ways to reduce that. I think that will have the highest impact."

He smiles and gives a quick nod. Then, he walks off to his next meeting. You know that means you had better deliver the time savings in order to meet his expectations. You are just not sure how to do it.

This chapter is focused on how to organize data in a way that makes it much easier for data scientists to extract value. We will introduce the concept of **linked analytical datasets (LAD)** as a way to dramatically improve the speed of **machine learning** (**ML**) modeling development. You will learn how to balance maintainability with data scientist productivity.

We will also discuss how to keep your data lake from turning into a data swamp. IoT data will not produce much value if it is difficult to work with. And it will produce even less value if no one is allowed to get to it.

This chapter will also discuss developing a data retention strategy for IoT data. This will focus on retaining value for analytics while reducing the cost to maintain the large volumes of historical data.

This chapter covers the following topics:

- Introduction to the concept of LAD
- The process to build LADs
- Managing data lakes
- Data retention strategies

Linked Analytical Datasets

The concept of LAD ties together the well-established ideas of analytical datasets and relational databases. Combining them together accelerates how quickly data scientists can get to the part both you and they care about most—the analytics.

The term LAD is being introduced in this book, although the general concepts are not new. However, there does not appear to be a common name for this arrangement, so the intent is to give it one. So, now that we have LAD, let's see if it takes off.

Analytical datasets

The process of creating analytical datasets is simple in concept but hard in execution. You have probably created one already, whether you know it or not. Analytical datasets combine a bunch of useful features together into each record instance.

This is done for both data understanding purposes (think about `Chapter 6`, *Getting to Know Your Data - Exploring IoT Data*) and for ML purposes (think about `Chapter 10`, *Data Science for IoT Analytics*). The goal is to combine at least 80% of what an IoT analyst would need to answer questions for a particular subject into one table. The table is also constantly and automatically created for them. It is as simple as that.

Building analytic datasets

Analytical datasets are semi-denormalized tables. By semi-denormalized, this means including not just the ID code of a field but the description for it as well. You may also decide to create categories based on value ranges and include these as separate features.

The goal is to make life easy for your analysts more than a focus on efficiently storing values, as it would be with purely relational database design. You are, essentially, prebuilding the transformed datasets that an analyst would be building using SQL to preprocess a dataset in preparation to train an ML model anyway.

As data wrangling takes 80-95% of a typical analysts time, having most of this already built, tested, and the business logic incorporated saves a tremendous amount of time. And this happens not just once for one person, but many times, for many people. This compounding effect dramatically increases the value of prebuilding the analytical datasets.

The mission should be to include features in the table that would be used for several different projects and subject matters. It requires some educated balancing to pick the optimal features. You will never get 100% of what analysts need into one table, but a goal of 80% can do a tremendous amount of good.

The following process will help in deciding how to build an analytic dataset for a particular topic. We use an example of GPS positional data from an IoT device. Each instance in the dataset will be a combination of time and location:

1. **Determine the resolution of the data**: What level of aggregation is needed? Will an individual record be at a device level, a reported instance level, or a time period level? This should be determined by what makes the most sense based on the incoming data resolution, and how it will probably be used for business purposes. In our example, the resolution is at a GPS position reporting frequency, which is every 10 seconds.

2. **List out all the variations, categories, calculations, and descriptions that are added or transformed from the data**: This should be what your team finds useful for modeling. This can also result from discussions with business experts on what could be useful to them. In our GPS position example, it is as follows:
   - Latitude
   - Longitude
   - The day of the week
   - Time since previous GPS position record
   - Speed (calculated from previous rolling set of records)
   - The current time zone offset
   - Daytime or nighttime
   - GPS grid identifier (refer to `Chapter 9`, *Applying Geospatial Analytics to IoT Data*)
   - The exact time at UTC
   - The exact local time
   - The current state of the device (driving, idling, or parked)

3. **Review each item for how often they are likely to be used in analysis, ML modeling, or reporting**: Decide if the cost of creating and storing the information is worth it for how often it is used. In our example, the exact local time and the day of the week were eliminated. This is based on the expected frequency of use versus the storage and computational costs of keeping the information. This is a balancing act and your decision may shift over time as different fields become more or less valuable to your business.

4. **Create data transformation code that automatically creates and maintains the information in one table**: The goal is to do this in an automated fashion so that the data scientists do not have to recreate it each time they need it.

5. **Create a unique identifier for each record, if it does not already exist**: In this case, it would be the exact UTC time combined with the unique device identifier, so there is a need to create a separate ID field for the combination. This is done to make life easy for the data scientist, who should not have to worry about complicating their analytics by connecting datasets using two different fields. Combine it into one to simplify things for them:

UTC|DeviceID	DeviceID	UTC Time	Latitude	Longitude	Time since previous (sec)	Speed (km)	Current time zone offset	Day/Night	GPS grid Identifier	Current State
20170619031504|0678991B1	0678991B1	6/19/2017 3:15:04	41.881832	-87.623177	15	0	-5	N	U2345	Parked
20170619031524|0678991B1	0678991B1	6/19/2017 3:15:24	41.881834	-87.623181	20	5	-5	N	U2345	Driving
20170619031544|0678991B1	0678991B1	6/19/2017 3:15:44	41.881828	-87.623182	20	20	-5	N	U2345	Driving
20170819031604|0678991B1	0678991B1	6/19/2017 3:16:04	41.881841	-87.623187	20	25	-5	N	U2344	Driving

Analytical dataset example in table form

Linking together datasets

When building each analytical dataset, you should ask yourself *how you can link them to other analytical datasets? Which fields are natural bridges to related key datasets?* Then, intentionally build the analytical dataset in a way that makes it easy to connect to others. This is typically done by creating a new or using an existing identifier key. The identify key would be the same in both datasets.

If this sounds familiar it is the exact same concept as with relational database design. It is also closely related to the star schema design in Online Analytical Processing (OLAP) data warehousing. The goal is, however, somewhat different.

With relational database design, the goal is to minimize or even eliminate data duplication by denormalizing the data into multiple linked tables. Denormalizing separates the identifier from its description in different tables, so that the description is only stored once.

With star schema design, the goal is to make drill down, drill through, and predefined metric calculations easy and fast. Datasets are stored and linked along dimensions such as time, category, fiscal year, and company divisions.

However, with LAD design, the goal is to minimize joins while still allowing easy creation of hybrid datasets, not previously conceived. The goal is to minimize data transformation work for the IoT analyst, who is building training sets for ML modeling. The tradeoff is in data size, the initial ETL complexity when developing the analytical datasets, and the duplication of data.

The following diagram shows a simple example:

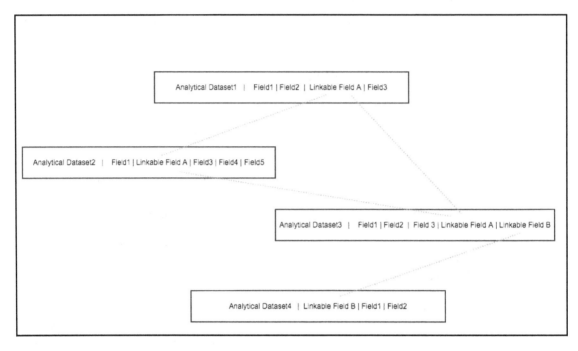

Linked Analytic Dataset design

The cost of storing large datasets has dropped dramatically when using big data system, such as HDFS or S3. The cost of missing an IoT analytics business opportunity due to your data scientists being tied up with data munging can be very high. It is a worthy tradeoff and can greatly accelerate the iteration time for new ML model development.

Follow these steps to identify and build links between analytical datasets:

1. **Identify fields that can create a bridge to other analytical datasets:** These datasets may either be already created or are being considered for creation. In our GPS data example, the combination of latitude and longitude identifies a location. Certain locations, such as rest stops, distribution centers, and fueling stations, have useful and possibly predictive data tied to them.

2. **If necessary, combine multiple fields to create a single field that identifies the linkage**: Big data systems handle single field joins much better than multiple field joins. It also makes it much simpler for the data scientist to use and therefore less likely to make a mistake in combining datasets. Following our example, you can combine a slightly rounded latitude and longitude value into a single identification field and store it in a separate field in your dataset. The rounding is to adjust for extremely precise GPS values that are at the location, but just in different areas of the parking lot.

3. **Repeat for all linkable fields in the dataset**: The GPS grid identifier is another candidate.

4. **Add the dataset and its links to a master diagram to use as reference.**

The following diagram shows how our simple GPS example can link to other analytical datasets:

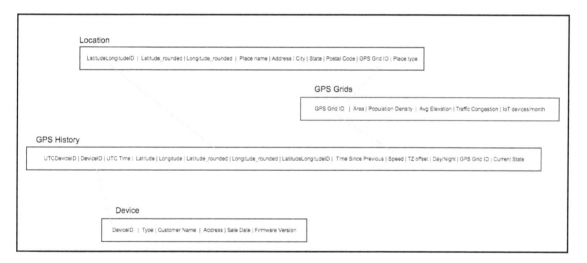

Simple LAD example

Managing data lakes

Data lakes are places used to dump tons of potentially valuable data from multiple sources. Some sources will be IoT devices, while some sources will be internal company data such as production, purchasing, or customer service records. The concept is to put all of this variety of data in one place so it can be accessible through a unified interface. In the case of Hadoop, the data lake would be stored in HDFS and probably accessed through Hive or Spark.

When data lakes turn into data swamps

Swamps are formed when water flows into an area where it collects and stagnates. Algae covers over the water. When a data lake has a mass of raw data flowing in but no organization and little usage of it to mix up the waters, it becomes what is facetiously referred to as a data swamp.

This often happens when the decision is made to copy data from many systems into one area, such as HDFS, without any changes to it. Analysts can find it difficult to access due to security restrictions. Even when they do have access it, they find it difficult to make sense of the plethora of (typically) relational tables, with no instruction key on what the ID field codes mean or what business logic should be used when working with the data.

They often give up in frustration. In such a case, a huge amount of potentially valuable data festers, unused, eating up storage space and money.

Data refineries

Well functioning data lakes are not actually uniform pools of data water. They are more like a system of petroleum refineries. In a petroleum refinery system, the raw West Texas Intermediate crude flows in by pipeline or supertanker into several different refineries. The refineries then process it into several different refined petroleum-based products, from gasoline to petroleum jelly and even animal feed.

Sometimes, the results of one refinery are an input into another refinery, which further processes and combines it with other refined products. Not to take the analogy too far, but nobody takes the crude oil out of the ground and puts it in their gas tank.

A very similar process happens with data refineries. Nobody uses the raw crude data; they use the high-value processed and finished products. The following diagram demonstrates the concept:

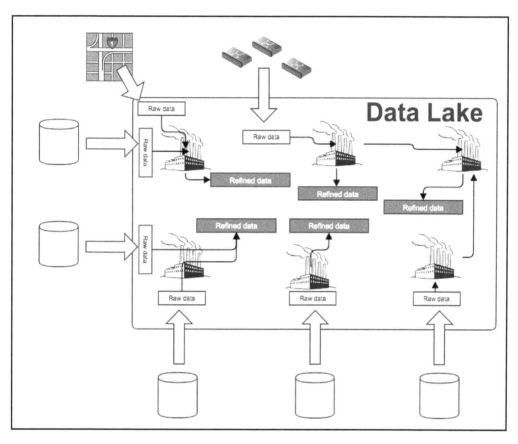

Data refineries operating inside your data lake

Developing a progression process

Data science is all about experimentation. IoT analytics has great potential. However, no one is certain of how it will develop. Put them both together and an enormous amount of experimentation should be expected. To keep this from becoming an impossible-to-manage mess, there needs to be a way to progress ad hoc datasets from early development into repeatable and stable data products.

Setting up a progression process will help manage this. Data science is highly iterative, which makes it difficult to find a clear point that signals a change in state, as with normal database development projects.

A way to handle this is by setting up regular review periods where a team determines which datasets are ready to progress to the next stage of development. Decide how often this should happen, define the stages and the corresponding requirements for each, all based on your unique situation.

We will review a suggested progression path that you can tailor to the needs of your unique IoT analytics environment.

Segment your data lake into three general areas:

- **Sandbox**: A data scientist has full access to read and write in this area. They may have a sandbox to themselves in addition to one for the team. This is for initial experimentation and model development.
- **Mature**: A data scientist has full access to this area but does not have their own mature environment, the team shares it. All code and scripts used to generate datasets kept in this area should be under source code control.
- **Production**: A data scientist has full read access but no write capability. Datasets in this area have been fully tested, code and scripts used to generate datasets are under source code control, and a change control process is in place.

The suggested progression process to move datasets between areas is here:

- **Establish a regular recurring review of your datasets**: This could be every month, every quarter, or semi-annually. Use whichever makes the most sense for how quickly your IoT analytics is developing. But the review should be regular and enforced. It is too easy to delay due to the small iterations that occur with analytics. Avoid this trap and force your team to do it.
- **Review the datasets in all three areas for any that should be deleted**: These could be development datasets that never made it far, or old versions of ones that are now in production. Take a cue from Java and have a regular garbage collection event to keep your data lake optimized.
- **Review Sandbox datasets that are ready to move to the Mature area**: These are the ones that are either project specific and ready for team testing, or are useful to the team for their general work. The latter should be set up as regularly recurring and scheduled jobs to build the datasets. This type of datasets will help accelerate many projects in the future.

- **Review Mature datasets for ones that are ready to move to Production**: These are typically more project-specific and have passed all the testing. Once it is moved into production, future changes should be minimal. At this point, control of the dataset should be handed over to a separate group to maintain and provide service-level support.

The data retention strategy

Even big data eventually gets too big and costly to maintain. Remembering the goal of minimizing costs while still maximizing value, make sure to develop a retention strategy for IoT data. Data could be simply deleted after it is retained for a certain amount of time. However, by doing this, you could miss out on building a future profitable analytics service that was not thought of before the data was thrown away.

There are other options that allow you to retain value of the data while minimizing the costs. We will discuss some of these next.

Goals

The goals of a retention strategy for IoT analytics are twofold:

- **Maintain Value**: Advanced modeling techniques, such as deep learning, need lots of history to maximize prediction effectiveness. It is also difficult to know ahead of time which fields will be valuable for a future unknown project. The traditional data retention strategies of storing records for a fixed period of time and then deleting the full dataset could result in lost profitable opportunities. A different mindset is needed.
- **Minimize Costs**: IoT data can get big quickly. Even with cloud-based HDFS storage, costs can get large. Keeping everything forever could easily cost more than the value it provides. The more accessible data is, the more costly it becomes. There should be some compromises to keep your costs low.

Retention strategies for IoT data

We will cover three strategies to reduce the storage size of data. These can be used individually or in combination. We will discuss the pros and cons of each and walk through an example retention plan that takes advantage of all three.

Reducing accessibility

You can reduce costs significantly without deleting any data by reducing the relative accessibility of the data. We will cover some ways to do this next:

- **Compression**: Compression is your friend. Compressing data leaves you with all the information at the (typically) slight penalty of increased time to access it. Using compression formats such as Avro and Parquet can significantly reduce storage size (and therefore costs) in Hadoop clusters and S3 folders, while often improving performance. The performance improvements require some thoughtful design of the file format, but are a best practice anyway. HDFS supports other compression formats such as GZIP and Snappy as well. This should be the first thing you do to reduce the file size. Even better, plan for it as part of the initial storage design.
- **Changing the storage technology to lower-cost options**: Keep the data, but move to lower-cost methods. There is usually a performance penalty, but this can easily be worth it if the data moved is not accessed often. This could be a change from SSD-backed storage to hard disk-backed storage. The final step could be from hard disk to tape.
- **Changing accessibility service levels**: This method is more geared toward cloud storage services and is analogous to changing storage technology (although you can do that also in the cloud). For Amazon S3, this could be a change to Standard–Infrequent Access level service or to Amazon Glacier for very infrequently accessed data. S3 allows automated scheduling of when files should be moved into lower service levels based on rules, such as the age of the file.
- **Changing redundancy levels**: HDFS keeps multiple copies of files for durability. The standard setting is three copies, but this is configurable. You could change the redundancy level for less valuable files and save some costs. Amazon S3 also has a reduced redundancy option.

Reducing the number of fields

As you get to know your IoT data, you will find some fields are more valuable than others. Through your discoveries using techniques from Chapter 6, *Getting to Know Your Data - Exploring IoT Data*, and Chapter 10, *Data Science for IoT Analytics*, you will find fields (features) that keep coming up as statistically significant, and some that just never seem to matter.

For older files, you can follow some methods to keep the useful fields, while getting rid of the ones that do not seem to have an impact:

- **Transform older data to only keep useful fields**: Move older data to either a new file or table but only keep those useful fields. Then, delete the old records.
- **Split out useful fields and treat them differently**: For older records, you could keep the useful fields in *hot* areas that are easily accessible, while shipping the less useful fields off into cold storage
- **Summarize and remove large data fields such as text or binary files** (such as image or sound): As an example, you could reduce a lengthy free-form text field to the count of key word occurrences.

Reduce the number of records

Now, finally, you could simply just delete old records. But wait, there are some other options where you can at least retain some possibly useful information. Once you delete the history, it is gone for good. The fear should be that you will find out later that if you had just kept that data, it could have been used to create a more valuable ML model and generated some additional revenue. Some other options are listed next:

- **Deleting raw data but keeping the refined versions of it**: After a certain amount of time, having both the raw data and the refined version probably does not add much value. You can delete older raw data files without losing much value.
- **Summarizing old data**: Instead of deleting the data completely, summarize individual records into weekly or monthly summary values. The appropriate summary statistic may be an average or a sum, or preferably, an entire set of summary statistics. For example, you may want to save the mean, the standard deviation, the maximum, the minimum, and the record count. This can reduce thousands of rows into one, so it is perfectly fine to have a much wider resulting dataset. You will be losing some value in the data, as you will not have full resolution. But you are still retaining some informational value in the summary statistics. You could even use the statistics to simulate individual records later if you had to.
- **Deleting old data**: This should be the final and last option. Remember, analytics is built from the data and once that data is gone, the analytics you could have done goes with it.

The retention strategy example

We will return to the GPS position data example to set up a retention policy. The raw data is landed into an HDFS table and kept uncompressed. A series of data refineries transforms the data into cleaned and useful analytical datasets. All of the analytical datasets are compressed in Parquet format–still in HDFS.

Upon the review of the raw data, it was determined that any problems in the initial transformation are typically discovered within a week. No problems were found more than a month later. Due to this, the raw data was retained for the latest month, and then moved into S3 Standard. In S3, a ruleset was created to move the data into Standard-Infrequent Access after another month, and then into Amazon Glacier a month after it. After another three months, the data is scheduled to be deleted from Amazon Glacier.

After several months of statistical analysis and modeling, several key fields were identified in each analytical dataset. It was also discovered that data records from more than two years prior were rarely accessed. Records from more than three years prior were never accessed.

The data from two years prior was moved out of HDFS into S3 Standard. Data between two and three years old was transformed to only keep the key fields. The older data is moved to Amazon Glacier. After four years, the data is summarized at a daily aggregation with metrics on record counts, starting, ending, and average position for each device along with distance traveled and the travel time. This data is kept in S3 Standard as it is 10,000 times smaller in size. The full data is then removed.

Summary

In this chapter, we reviewed how to increase data scientist productivity by reducing time spent manipulating data. The concept of LAD was introduced, along with a process to build them.

Concepts to help prevent data lakes from turning into a data swamp was discussed. Changing perspectives from a data lake to a series of active refineries and production chains helps to plan for a useful data storage area.

Strategies for data retention were also reviewed. Consider the twin goals of maximizing value while minimizing costs when designing a retention strategy. In the next chapter, we will discuss the economics of IoT analytics. The chapter covers ways to look for business value in the data along with a detailed predictive maintenance example.

12
The Economics of IoT Analytics

You sit in your office staring out the window at the building across the street. You feel the tap, tap, tap of your pen against your forehead as you fiddle with it lost in thought. Your boss left your office twenty minutes ago.

"We need a predictive maintenance program," he had said, "But it can't lose money! We need more revenue coming in. But I don't want you wasting your time on analytics that won't make us money."

You agreed and nodded your head with a thoughtful smile firmly held on your face. You know how to think about analytics but not necessarily how to look at it from a revenue and cost perspective.

"And I want you to keep trying new things! Let's keep up the experimentation. You are doing great! Just don't lose money," he continued.

Okay, sure, you think. *How do I do that?*

This chapter will explain how to think about a business case for IoT analytics projects. It discusses ways to optimize the return on investment by minimizing costs and increasing the opportunity for revenue streams.

The costs and benefits of the business case can and should be worked directly into the IoT analytics process. By doing this, the methods can not only have good predictive value but can also be optimized for producing profitable services.

We will also review ways to apply analytics to maximize value with an example case of predictive maintenance. Predictive maintenance is a common application of IoT analytics and can lower costs if applied in such a way that the savings outweigh the costs.

In this chapter, we will cover the following topics:

- The economics of cloud computing and open source:
    - Variable versus fixed costs
    - The option to quit
    - Cloud costs can escalate
    - Open source software considerations
- Thinking about revenue opportunities:
    - The extensions of current business practices
    - New services
- The economics of predictive maintenance:
    - Valuation formula
    - The R code to calculate cost curve for the **machine learning** (**ML**) model implementation

The economics of cloud computing and open source

At first glance, it may seem like cloud computing should be valued in the same way as on-premises systems. It may also seem that open source solutions always make the most sense as there are no license fees. It is free, right?

We will walk through some ways to think about valuing cloud computing and open source software for IoT analytics. Like most things, it is more complicated than it seems at first.

Variable versus fixed costs

Variable costs expand and contract with the amount of usage. Examples are automotive production parts for assembling vehicles, fuel in transportation, and cloud services. Fixed costs are constant no matter the amount of usage needed. Examples are data centers, rack servers, and equipment (or cloud environment) management.

In a traditional business case, fixed costs are assumed to continue until they are able to be sold at some anticipated amount. This rarely occurs in a short period of time. Variable costs are assumed to be tied to the usage required. Even variable costs in this scenario often take time to wind down after a decision is made to stop a project. The following conceptual chart demonstrates how to think about this situation:

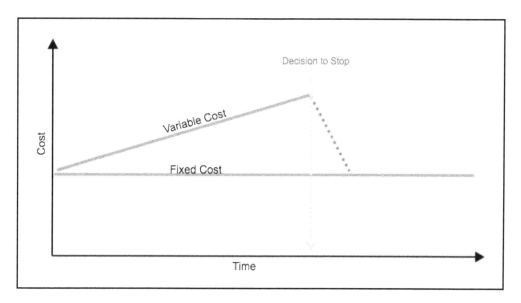

Traditional fixed and variable costs

The option to quit

With cloud computing and IoT analytics, almost all costs are variable. Some fixed costs exist due to environment maintenance (labor). These should be included in the business case, but it is minimal versus the variable costs. If a decision is made to stop a project in this scenario, all costs can be immediately eliminated. We will call this an option to quit.

An option to quit has value and should be included when making a business case for IoT analytics. At the point an IoT analytics project is determined not to be viable, all costs can be terminated immediately. The following diagram illustrates this situation:

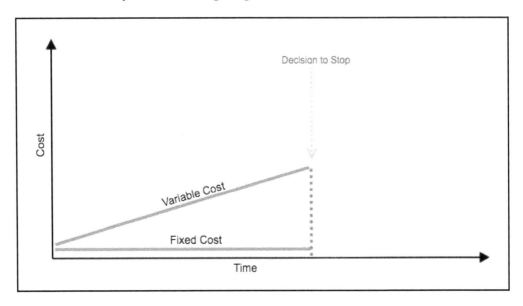

Cloud IoT analytics variable costs with option to quit

Cloud costs can escalate quickly

This is not all sunshine and roses though, as cloud services costs can escalate quickly if not well designed and closely monitored. If an IoT analytics project is designed with cloud services that call other cloud services more frequently than needed, the effect can be dramatic.

For example, consider an AWS Lambda function that checks the stored status of all IoT devices on Amazon IoT Hub using a message queue service. A web developer creates a user interface that calls this function every time a page loads or is refreshed. All three of the services will generate charges each time the function is called. Costs can escalate quicker than anticipated. A better design would be to set up a schedule for the AWS Lambda function to run every few minutes and store the results in a cached reference for the web interface to use.

If an IoT analytics application is created that does not scale both up and down, this can get expensive too. If the compute requirements are designed to meet maximum expected need instead of scaling as needed, you will be paying for unneeded capacity.

Monitoring cloud billing closely

Most cloud infrastructure services, including AWS, provide a way to set up rules to alert you if costs are over a certain threshold. The rules can be set for hourly, daily, or monthly basis. These should be set up right away so that you know immediately if costs are more than expected.

Open source economics

Open source software, such as R or Python, is low cost but not really free in practice. There are expenses that need to be considered for any IoT analytics business case where open source software components are used.

Intellectual property considerations

Not all open source code is licensed for commercial and profit use. You will need to check under what type of **Intellectual Property (IP)** license the open source code is being offered before you incorporate it into a revenue generating commercial project. This will involve some legal fees at minimum to make sure you are in compliance with IP requirements. The following diagram shows a subset of open source license types:

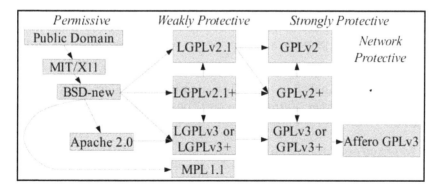

Open source license types examples. Source: Wikipedia Commons

Scale

Scaling IoT analytics on open source software can produce some challenges. You will probably be using R or Python to explore and productionalize your ML modeling and many other analytics. Both will scale to the size of a single compute instance. For example, R keeps everything in memory so the limitation is the size of memory on that instance.

Neither of the programming languages is natively distributed (not many are), so to scale beyond a single compute instance, you need to employ additional frameworks and design complications. This is one of the benefits of using Apache Spark. If you can do your analytics in a parallel fashion, you can use Spark to manage the distributed computations. This is the same map and reduce concept introduced in `Chapter 5`, *Collecting All That Data - Strategies and Techniques*.

With Spark, the Python code can be passed as a distributed job with results collected into a data frame. All library packages required for the code must be present on each node in the cluster however. To do this efficiently, you will need a package manager. The company Continuum offers a package manager called Anaconda Scale (`https://docs.continuum.io /anaconda-scale/`) for example. Package management software adds some costs, which should be included in your business case.

The same concept can be achieved with R using the SparkR package. Again, a package manager should be used to install and manage libraries across the cluster.

Support

Open source software is free...and without warranty or support. If there is a problem, you will need to fix it. Most likely, you will not have the skill set on your team to correct complicated problems. There are several companies that offer technical support for open source software. Some even provide a supported version of open software, but for a fee, of course.

An example is Revolution Analytics, which is now owned by Microsoft. It offers a supported version of the R open source software. There is a support and licensing fee associated with it.

In general, if you have open source code that you are dependent on to run revenue generating business, you will need support for when things go wrong. Either you will need to hire the skill set, or you should contract with a company that specializes in this support. These costs should be considered for any business case.

Cost considerations for IoT analytics

There are some cost considerations associated with IoT analytics specifically. They are not unique to IoT but become more pronounced with the scale and processing needs associated with it.

Cloud services costs

IoT analytics requires multiple layers of cloud services. There is often an IoT hub, message queue, load balancing, compute, storage, ML service, data warehouse, and security services included in an IoT analytics solution.

As mentioned previously, these costs can add up quickly if not designed carefully and monitored closely. Make sure to include all services in a business case and use cloud flexibility to minimize costs.

Expected usage considerations

Model your expected IoT analytics usage requirements carefully. A business case should not include only the services used for analytics during data processing and storage. It should also include costs for both ad hoc analytics and data science modeling on the stored historical data.

Thinking about revenue opportunities

Once you have an IoT analytics platform set up, have cleaned and refined the data, used exploratory analysis and visualizations to understand it, enhanced IoT data with external datasets, applied geospatial analytics where appropriate, used data science to understand and predict, and organized your data lake for analytics efficiency; you can take a step back and think about additional revenue opportunities.

These are ones that you may not have considered before you had a deep understanding of the data. Opportunities may also simply not have been previously possible until an IoT analytics infrastructure was built.

Here are some revenue possibilities to consider:

- **Extensions to your current business processes**: These ideas closely align with what you are already doing and can add additional value to your customers. It is always beneficial to think of services from the perspective of the end customer. Put yourself in their shoes and think what would save you costs and help you run your business better. Even better, ask them for their input. Some areas to think about are as follows:
    - **The monitoring of field operations**: Getting data instantly on the status of field equipment is often the reason for adding an IoT device in the first place. But you can add value to your customers by providing monitoring and alert services to them so they do not have to create it for themselves. You are in a position to have a greater economy of scale since your costs can be spread out among many customers.
    - **The tracking of field equipment location and status**: Again, you are in the position to spread your costs over many customers, so you can add this as a service to them inexpensively. It will be less costly for them than creating it on their own.
    - **Improved field repair services:** If your company also services the equipment connected to an IoT device, you have the opportunity to have faster and better field service levels. If you are also monitoring the equipment and tracking location and status, this is a natural next step. Not only do you know right away if there is a problem, you know exactly where it is located and which parts to bring to correct it. Even if you do not provide field service of the equipment, you can serve as an intermediary to companies that do provide that service. Since you are making the entire process more efficient, this has value to both the end customer and the field service company. There is a revenue stream from both sides that could be going into your pocket.
- **New revenue opportunities**: These ideas are additional services not directly related to current business processes. Think about it; you have new information about location and operation of IoT devices flowing into a centralized location. This is information you did not have before. Take a minute to look at it differently, and think how your business would have generated revenue from it if the information had always been available. Try to get out of the mental context of how things have always been. Some things to think about are as follows:

- **Value from the pool of IoT data itself**: Think which other business and industries would find the data you have valuable. Package it up in a way that protects your customers and provides the information these other companies need. Then, charge them to get it. We discussed an example earlier in the book about IoT thermostat data, which was being aggregated and sold to power generating companies. Cellular network companies package up cell phone location data in a way that indicates current traffic congestion along highways. Some cell phone app companies collect GPS position and package that up to sell to retailers as an indicator of foot traffic at their stores. Financial and insurance companies certainly find value in indicators of business segment activity available earlier than official statistics.

- **New business services**: Think about where having the IoT data and the analytics power you have created could put your company in a better position to provide a service than anyone else. It may even be in a currently unrelated business. Back to the IoT thermostat example. Since the company can both detect HVAC problems and know the location of the unit, it is in a position to efficiently schedule the correct repair procedure. This concept was mentioned earlier in the *extension of current business processes* section of this chapter. However, in this case, the IoT thermostat company currently has no service function. They may want to start one, however, as they are well positioned to do so. Imagine if the thermostat sends an email to the customer that it detected a problem and can have a repair person there to fix it in two hours at a predefined reasonable price. And all the customer has to do is click on **Ok,** as shown in the following image:

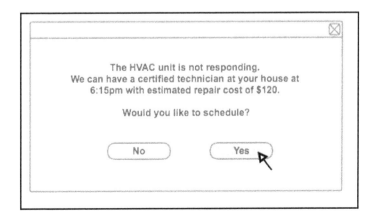

- **Services that would be very valuable to the customer that you could not have provided before**: Think about how a customer can use the data you now have to improve their business. They may already be doing some of these things, so again, it is very valuable to connect with them and ask them. Package up that service and sell to all the customers. An example, if you provide a GPS tracking device for logistic companies attached to on-road trailer units, think how customers could find that data valuable to them. You could provide bench marking services to customers to compare miles traveled for their units to similar companies. You could aggregate their position data over time to show them a route concentration map. You could compare their map to the industry, which may be very valuable to them when considering expansion planning.

The economics of predictive maintenance example

Predictive maintenance is a common value proposition cited for IoT analytics. We will walk through an example as a way to highlight how to think financially about when it makes sense and when it does not.

Situation

The economics of predictive maintenance may not be entirely obvious. Believe it or not, it does not always make sense, even if you can predict early failures accurately. It many cases, you will actually lose money by doing it. Even when it can save you money, there is an optimal point for when it should be used. The optimal point depends on the costs and the accuracy of the predictive model.

The value formula

A formula to guide decision making compares the cost of allowing a failure to occur versus the cost to proactively repair the component while considering the probability of predicting the failure:

Net Savings = (Cost of Failure * (Expected Number of Failures - Expected True Positive Predictions)) -
(Proactive Repair Cost * (Expected True Positives + Expected False Positives))

If the cost of failure is the same as the proactive repair cost, even with a perfect prediction model, which we know from `Chapter 10`, *Data Science for IoT Analytics* is highly unlikely, then there will be no savings. Make sure to include intangible costs into the cost of failure. Some examples of intangible costs include legal expenses, loss of brand equity, and even the customer's expenses.

Predictive repair does makes sense when there is a large spread between the cost of failure and the cost of proactive replacement, combined with a well-performing prediction model. For example, if the cost of a failure is a locomotive engine replacement at $1 million USD and the cost of a proactive repair is $200 USD, then the accuracy of the model does not even have to be all that great before a proactive replacement program makes financial sense.

On the other hand, if the failure is a $400 USD automotive turbocharger replacement, and the proactive repair cost is $350 USD for a turbocharger actuator subcomponent replacement, the predictive model would need to be highly accurate for that to make financial sense.

An example of making a value decision

To illustrate the example, we will walk through a business situation and then some R code that simulates a cost benefit curve for that decision. The code will use a fitted predictive model to calculate the net savings (or lack thereof) to generate a cost curve. The cost curve can then be used in a business decision on what proportion of units with predicted failures should have a proactive replacement.

Imagine you work for a company that builds diesel-powered generators. There is a coolant control valve that normally lasts for 4,000 hours of operation until there is a planned replacement. From analysis, your company has realized that the generators built two years prior are experiencing an earlier than expected failure of the valve.

When the valve fails, the engine overheats and several other components are damaged. The cost of failure, including labor rates for repair personnel and the cost to the customer for downtime, is an average of $1,000 USD. The cost of a proactive replacement of the valve is $253 USD.

Should you replace all coolant valves in the population? It depends on how high a failure rate is expected. In this case, about 10% of the current non-failed units are expected to fail before the scheduled replacement. Also, importantly, it matters how well you can predict the failures.

The following R code simulates this situation and uses a simple predictive model (logistic regression) to estimate a cost curve. The model has an AUC of close to 0.75. This will vary as you run the code since the dataset is randomly simulated:

```
#make sure all needed packages are installed
if(!require(caret)){
  install.packages("caret")
}
if(!require(pROC)){
  install.packages("pROC")
}
if(!require(dplyr)){
  install.packages("dplyr")
}
if(!require(data.table)){
  install.packages("data.table")
}

#Load required libraries
library(caret)
library(pROC)
library(dplyr)
library(data.table)

#Generate sample data
simdata = function(N=1000) {

#simulate 4 features
 X = data.frame(replicate(4,rnorm(N)))
 #create a hidden data structure to learn
 hidden = X[,1]^2+sin(X[,2]) + rnorm(N)*1
 #10% TRUE, 90% FALSE
 rare.class.probability = 0.1
 #simulate the true classification values
 y.class = factor(hidden<quantile(hidden,c(rare.class.probability)))
 return(data.frame(X,Class=y.class))
}
```

```
#make some data structure
model_data = simdata(N=50000)

#train a logistic regression model on the simulated data
training <- createDataPartition(model_data$Class, p = 0.6, list=FALSE)
trainData <- model_data[training,]
testData <- model_data[-training,]
glmModel <- glm(Class~ . , data=trainData, family=binomial)
testData$predicted <- predict(glmModel, newdata=testData, type="response")

#calculate AUC
roc.glmModel <- pROC::roc(testData$Class, testData$predicted)
auc.glmModel <- pROC::auc(roc.glmModel)
print(auc.glmModel)

#Pull together test data and predictions
simModel <- data.frame(trueClass = testData$Class,
                       predictedClass = testData$predicted)

# Reorder rows and columns
simModel <- simModel[order(simModel$predictedClass, decreasing = TRUE), ]
simModel <- select(simModel, trueClass, predictedClass)
simModel$rank <- 1:nrow(simModel)

#Assign costs for failures and proactive repairs
proactive_repair_cost <- 253    # Cost of proactively repairing a part
failure_repair_cost  <- 1000    # Cost of a failure of the part (include all
costs such as lost production, etc not just the repair cost)

# Define each predicted/actual combination
fp.cost <- proactive_repair_cost # The part was predicted to fail but did
not (False Positive)
fn.cost <- failure_repair_cost  # The part was not predicted to fail and it
did (False Negative)
tp.cost <- (proactive_repair_cost - failure_repair_cost) # The part was
predicted to fail and it did (True Positive). This will be negative for a
savings.
tn.cost <- 0.0                          # The part was not predicted to fail and
it did not (True Negative)

#incorporate probability of future failure
simModel$future_failure_prob <- prob_failure

#Function to assign costs for each instance
assignCost <- function(pred, outcome, tn.cost, fn.cost, fp.cost, tp.cost,
prob){
 cost <- ifelse(pred == 0 & outcome == FALSE, tn.cost, # No cost since no
action was taken and no failure
```

```
                         ifelse(pred == 0 & outcome == TRUE, fn.cost, # The cost
of no action and a repair resulted
                              ifelse(pred == 1 & outcome == FALSE, fp.cost, #
The cost of proactive repair which was not needed
                                   ifelse(pred == 1 & outcome == TRUE,
tp.cost, 999999999))))   # The cost of proactive repair which avoided a
failure
 return(cost)
}

# Initialize list to hold final output
master <- vector(mode = "list", length = 100)

#use the simulated model. In practice, this code can be adapted to compare
multiple models
test_model <- simModel

# Create a loop to increment through dynamic threshold (starting at 1.0 [no
proactive repairs] to 0.0 [all proactive repairs])
threshold <- 1.00
for (i in 1:101) {
 #Add predicted class with percentile ranking
 test_model$prob_ntile <- ntile(test_model$predictedClass, 100) / 100
 # Dynamically determine if proactive repair would apply based on
incrementing threshold
 test_model$glm_failure <- ifelse(test_model$prob_ntile >= threshold, 1, 0)
 test_model$threshold <- threshold

 # Compare to actual outcome to assign costs
 test_model$glm_impact <- assignCost(test_model$glm_failure,
test_model$trueClass, tn.cost, fn.cost, fp.cost, tp.cost,
test_model$future_failure_prob)

 # Compute cost for not doing any proactive repairs
 test_model$nochange_impact <- ifelse(test_model$trueClass == TRUE,
fn.cost, tn.cost) # *test_model$future_failure_prob)

 # Running sum to produce the overall impact
 test_model$glm_cumul_impact <- cumsum(test_model$glm_impact) /
nrow(test_model)
 test_model$nochange_cumul_impact <- cumsum(test_model$nochange_impact) /
nrow(test_model)

 # Count the # of classified failures
 test_model$glm_failure_ct <- cumsum(test_model$glm_failure)

 # Create new object to house the one row per iteration output for the
final plot
```

```
master[[i]] <- test_model[nrow(test_model),]

# Reduce the threshold by 1% and repeat to calculate new value
threshold <- threshold - 0.01
}

finalOutput <- rbindlist(master)
finalOutput <- subset(finalOutput,
                    select = c(threshold,
                                glm_cumul_impact,
glm_failure_ct,                                nochange_cumul_impact)
)

# Set baseline to costs of not doing any proactive repairs
baseline <- finalOutput$nochange_cumul_impact

# Plot the cost curve
par(mfrow = c(2,1))
plot(row(finalOutput)[,1],
    finalOutput$glm_cumul_impact,
    type = "l",
    lwd = 3,
    main = paste("Net Costs: Proactive Repair Cost of $",
proactive_repair_cost, ", Failure cost $", failure_repair_cost, sep = ""),
    ylim = c(min(finalOutput$glm_cumul_impact) - 100,
            max(finalOutput$glm_cumul_impact) + 100),
    xlab = "Percent of Population",
    ylab = "Net Cost ($) / Unit")

# Plot the cost difference of proactive repair program and a 'do nothing'
approach
plot(row(finalOutput)[,1],
    baseline - finalOutput$glm_cumul_impact,
    type = "l",
    lwd = 3,
    col = "black",
    main = paste("Savings: Proactive Repair Cost of $",
proactive_repair_cost, ", Failure cost $", failure_repair_cost,sep = ""),
    ylim = c(min(baseline - finalOutput$glm_cumul_impact) - 100,
            max(baseline - finalOutput$glm_cumul_impact) + 100),
    xlab = "% of Population",
    ylab = "Savings ($) / Unit")
    abline(h=0,col="gray")
```

As can be seen in the resulting net cost and savings curves, based on the model's predictions, the optimal savings would be from a proactive repair program of the top 30 percentile units. The savings decreases after this, although you would still save money when replacing up to 75% of the population. After this point, you should expect to spend more than you save. The following set of charts is the output from the preceding code:

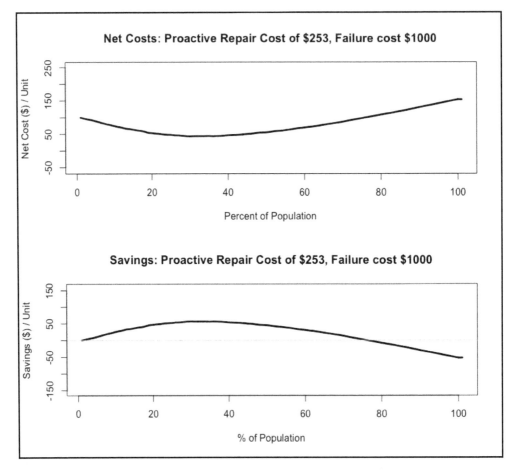

Cost and savings curves for the proactive repair $253 and failure cost at $1,000 scenario

Note how this changes in the following graph when the failure cost drops to $300 USD. At no point do you save money, as the proactive repair cost will always outweigh the reduced failure cost. This does not mean you should not do a proactive repair; you may still want to do so in order satisfy your customers. Even in such a case, this cost curve method can help in decisions on how much you are willing to spend to address the problem. You can rerun the code with **proactive_repair_cost** set to **253** and **failure_repair_cost** set to **300** to generate the following charts:

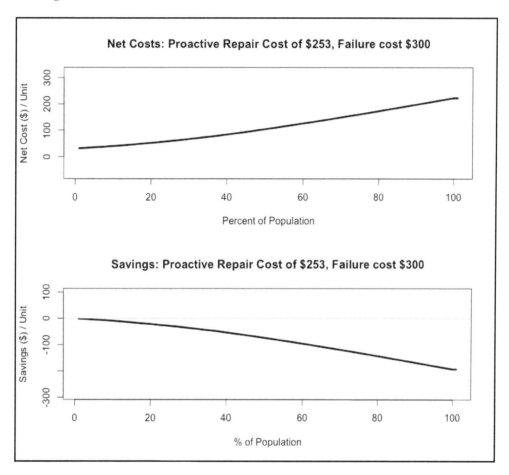

Cost and savings curves for the proactive repair $253 and failure cost at $300 scenario

And finally, notice how the savings curve changes when the failure cost moves to $5,000. You will notice that the spread between the proactive repair cost and the failure cost determines much of when doing a proactive repair makes business sense. You can rerun the code with **proactive_repair_cost** set to **253** and **failure_repair_cost** set to **5000** to generate the following charts:

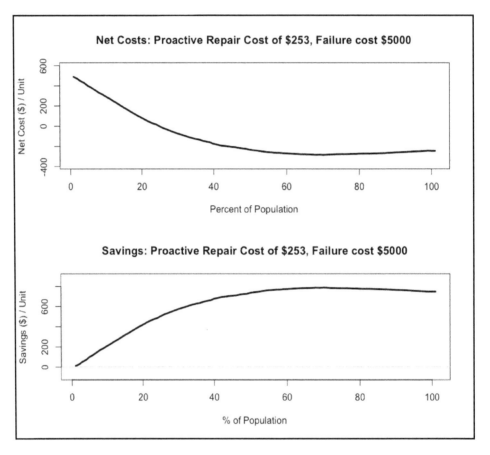

Cost and savings curves for the proactive repair $253 and failure cost at $5,000 scenario

Ultimately, the decision is a business case based on the expected costs and benefits. ML modeling can help optimize savings under the right conditions. Utilizing cost curves helps to determine the expected costs and savings of proactive replacements.

Summary

In this chapter, we discussed the economics of cloud computing and open source software. We reviewed cost considerations for IoT analytics and how to think about revenue opportunities. We also covered ways to think about an IoT analytics business case.

The economics of predictive maintenance was discussed as an example of how to view the costs and benefits of an applied IoT analytics ML model. An example framework for calculating the cost benefit was presented along with some R code, demonstrating how to generate a cost curve based on the ML model.

13
Bringing It All Together

The President of Operations at your company, previously the VP of Connected Services and your boss, smiles as he firmly shakes your hand.

"Revenues are up 10% and it is clearly attributable to the work of your team," he says. "The CEO and I have decided to create a new position, Vice President of Connected Analytics. I want you to lead it."

"Thank you and I hope to earn the confidence placed in me," you say, trying to hide your smile.

"Oh, you already have that," he winks, "You can tell your team. They stay with you and we're adding a data management team and a frontend prototyping team to your group. Did I tell you that we are doubling the number of IoT products in the next fiscal year?"

He nods and turns to stroll away still smiling.

"You start immediately," he says over his shoulder.

You think to yourself, *I finally made it. After all the work and stress, I made it*. You enjoy the thought for a few minutes. Until you come to the realization: *Wait, how am I going to manage double the products and a much larger team while still meeting the revenue expectations of the C...E...O?*

But that would be a different book...

This final chapter wraps up this book and reviews what you have learned. It includes some parting advice on how to get the most value out of Analytics for the Internet of Things. There is also a sample project included to challenge yourself and try on your own.

This chapter covers the following topics:

- A review of the key themes of this book:
    - IoT data flow
    - IoT exploratory analytics
    - IoT data science
    - Build revenue from IoT analytics
- Sample challenge projects
- So long, farewell, auf wiedersehen, goodbye:
    - Best wishes and happy hunting!

Review

The range of steps in the flow of IoT data from the device to the presentation of analytic results was covered in this book. This is a wide range of topics, but it does all fit together. The following diagram maps this out and shows how each chapter in the book relates:

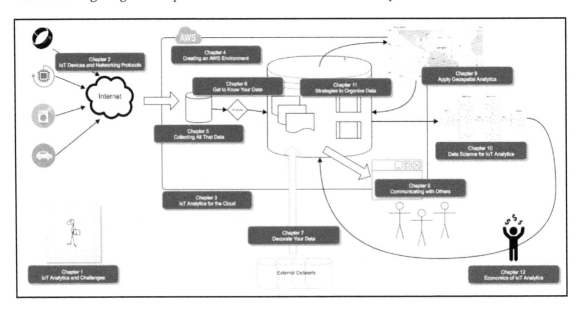

General IoT data and analytic flow as covered in this book.

The IoT data flow

In order to understand a complex system, such as the flow of data from IoT devices, or the flow of risk and money in a Collateralized Debt Obligation (CDO), as depicted by the IMF in the following diagram, you need to map out the process. Then, you need to understand how each stop along the way contributes to the end result. This can help avoid unprofitable projects - and worldwide recessions.

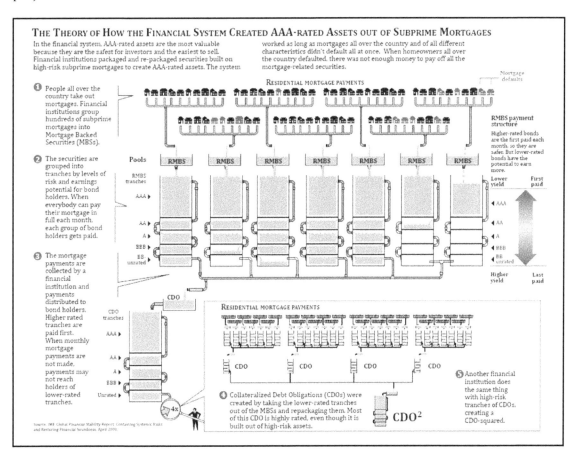

How AAA assets were created out of subprime mortgages - money flow diagram. Source: IMF

We discussed the many challenges with IoT data. It is notoriously messy, and will often have missing and incorrect values. In Chapter 1, *Defining IoT Analytics and Challenges*, we reviewed problems with data quality, problems related to time, problems related to spatial position, and analytic challenges that are more pronounced with IoT data.

Understanding the limitations of IoT devices and the various communication protocols associated with them will help you greatly when using the resulting data for analytics. In Chapter 2, *IoT Devices and Networking Protocols,* an introductory overview was provided along with some benefits and drawbacks for each communication architecture.

Collecting and processing IoT data is challenging due to the scale and the uncertainty of how it will be used. Even anticipating what business opportunities will be found through analysis of it is difficult. In Chapter 3, *IoT Analytics for the Cloud,* the benefits of using cloud architecture was introduced, along with some key cloud service provides for IoT-related analytics.

A walkthrough on how to create a secure cloud environment for analytics was covered in Chapter 4, *Creating an AWS Cloud Analytics Environment.* Big data technologies to store and process large volumes of IoT data were reviewed in Chapter 5, *Collecting All That Data - Strategies and Techniques.*

In short, we covered the following recommendations:

- IoT data is big and messy, expect it.
- Know your devices and know how the data is transported.
- Store and process IoT data in an environment that can grow and shrink as needed. Cloud services fit the bill.
- Use big data technology, so your solution on a small scale needs few changes to function on a large scale.

IoT exploratory analytics

Exploring your data, combining it with external data (such as maps), and using visualization to communicate your findings can have a dramatic impact. The following image was created by John Snow in the late 19th century to demonstrate his analysis of Cholera illness data, which found that the 1854 Cholera epidemic was linked to water sources. This led to a better understanding of the causes of the disease, saving hundreds of thousands of lives.

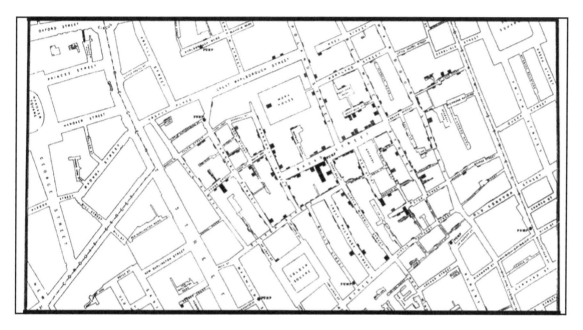

John Snow Cholera map. Source: Center for Disease Control

Once the IoT data has been collected in a centralized place, you need to explore it to understand the data and learn its patterns. In Chapter 6, *Getting to Know Your Data - Exploring IoT Data,* you learned how to use Tableau to quickly understand your data, find problems, and view it on a map. This also starts the hunt for features that could have predictive value to use in data science techniques.

Adding external data can greatly enhance the potential value of analytics. We discussed several sources for value-enhancing data including geographic, economic, and demographic datasets in Chapter 7, *Decorating Your Data - Adding External Datasets to Innovate.*

Communicating what you find through your exploratory analytics of IoT data is also very important. Others need to find useful patterns and trends in an easy-to-understand way. Dashboarding, alert concepts, and presentation styles were covered in `Chapter 8`, *Communicating with Others - Visualization and Dashboarding*.

In short, we covered the following recommendations:

- Know your data inside and out
- Add external data to add value
- Communicate your findings effectively
- Increase efficiency across your company through useful dashboards and alerts

IoT data science

Finding unexpected value from a complex set of data is one of the benefits of data science, although you will generally find it more useful to spread some intelligent decision making across a large scale or at a high velocity. But sometimes, you will find some unexpected and creative value from seemingly mundane data. A wild example is depicted in the following image, which was generated by a Google deep learning algorithm:

Deep learning model generated hallucinogenic image. Source: TheNewStack.io

After you understand what the IoT devices are reporting, combine it with external data, identify interesting patterns, and communicate the information to others, you can add additional value with geospatial analytics.

IoT devices are typically geographically distributed and can even sometimes move around. Incorporating that positional and usage information can add new opportunities for analytics and valuable services. This can also add additional features that have predictive value. Methods to leverage these techniques were covered in Chapter 9, *Applying Geospatial Analytics to IoT Data*.

Data science is a broad field with some exciting recent developments in the application of machine learning techniques. The key concepts of machine learning were covered in Chapter 10, *Data Science for IoT Analytics*, along with a couple of popular algorithms: random forest and gradient boosting machines.

Feature extraction, the bias - variance trade-off, and validation were discussed. Trend forecasting using ARIMA with R example code was also introduced. Deep learning was discussed as a potential method to wring extra value out of IoT data, if you have the right data.

In short, we covered the following recommendations:

- Use location to learn useful things from your IoT devices
- Build a rich set of features for machine learning
- Be careful when applying machine learning techniques but definitely explore their use
- Use deep learning when it makes sense and don't use it when it doesn't

Building revenue from IoT analytics

Considering costs versus benefits as a way to target the optimal ratio that maximizes profit is important in all industries. The following diagram shows how farmers consider cost and the amount of fertilizer versus the resulting yield and crop prices:

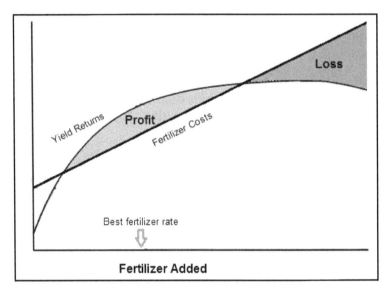

Fertilizer price and crop yields. Source: SMART! Fertilizer management

Data scientists spend most of their time arranging and cleaning data. Making their lives easier through the arrangement of data storage can accelerate your learning and the search for value. A method, which we have dubbed **Linked Analytic Datasets** (**LADs**), can help.

Designing a progression plan from experimentation to production for your analytics projects will help keep your environment manageable. Setting up a data retention strategy can allow you to hold on to valuable data while still keeping your costs low. All of this was covered in Chapter 11, *Strategies to Organize Data for Analytics*.

Maximizing profit means keeping costs low while searching for ways to increase revenue. The economics of cloud analytics was covered in Chapter 12, *The Economics of IoT Analytics*. Cloud environments are not always a panacea, as your costs can climb quickly if not designed appropriately. But keeping a close eye on your bill, while designing to scale up and down to take advantage of cloud economics, can keep your costs low.

Incorporating business case costs and benefits directly into your machine learning modeling will allow you to optimize the model's output. A method to create cost curves in order to visualize the impact of machine learning models was introduced. We also covered a deep dive into predictive maintenance economics with a hypothetical example.

In short, we covered the following recommendations:

- Organize data for your data scientists, not your database administrators
- Plan how an initial concept will grow into a production service
- Develop a data retention plan that retains potential data value
- Use the cloud appropriately to keep costs low
- Build costs and benefits into your machine learning process
- Predictive maintenance does not always make sense; incorporate costs and benefits to determine when it does

A sample project

If you are ready to challenge yourself, the following is a project that you can work out how to do on your own. There is no education like actually doing the work yourself, especially when you are not sure of the right answers:

The project steps are as follows:

1. **Set up the AWS environment**: Follow `Chapter 4`, *Creating an AWS Cloud Analytics Environment* to prepare a secure area for data storage and IoT analytics.
2. **Build a data feed to NOAA hourly weather data**: You could use Python code in an AWS Lambda function or a service such as Amazon Kinesis to process the feed.
3. **Import the dataset into a Hadoop environment** (store in HDFS): Practice querying data using Hive. Amazon EMR can be used for this or a Cloudera/Hortonworks distribution.
4. **Combine with another data set**: You choose; have fun.
5. **Analyze with Tableau to understand the data**: Connect to Hive and explore the combined data. Create a dashboard to communicate some metrics and alerts.
6. **Use R to create a machine learning prediction model**: Use random forest and gradient boosting machines to fit models. Judge which one is best using an ROC curve chart. Predict the weather; be your own weatherman!

Summary

This chapter reviewed the main themes of this book. We also added some short, boiled-down advice. Finally, we presented a challenge project - have fun with with it.

Good luck and happy hunting for IoT value through analytics!

Index

driver 140
DynamoDB 144

E

economic data, external datasets
  Federal Reserve Economic Data (FRED) 202
  Organization for Economic Cooperation and
    Development (OECD) 200, 201
edge analytics 28
edge nodes 132
elastic analytics
  building 66
  cloud infrastructure 66, 68
  concepts 68, 70
  designing 70
  designing, for scale 70
Elastic Compute (EC2) 85
Elastic Map Reduce (EMR) 87
Elasticsearch 260
EMR File System (EMRFS) 87
Enhanced Compression Wavelet (ECW) 252
environment
  cleaning up 119
  terminating 119
erosion 248
execution engine 140
Executor 146
external datasets
  adding 190
  demographic 198
  economic 200
  elevation 191
  geographical features 194
  geography 191
  National Elevation Dataset (NED) 192
  SRTM elevation 191
  weather 193, 194
external tables 140
Extract, Transform, and Load (ETL) 125

F

False Positive (FP) 279
false positive rate (FPR) 285
feature engineering
  centering 275, 276

missing values, dealing 270, 275
  scaling 275, 276
  time series, handling 276
  with IoT data 269, 270
Federal Information Processing Standards (FIPS)
  about 194
  URL 199
Federal Reserve Archival System for Economic
    Research (FRASER) 203
Federal Reserve Economic Data (FRED)
  about 202
  APIs 203
  URL 202
fiona 245

G

gateway 32
generalization 269
Generalized Search Tree (GiST) 256
Geographic Information System (GIS) 256
geographical features
  Google Maps API 196, 197
  Planet.osm 195, 196
  USGS national transportation datasets 197
GeoJSON 252
geospatial analysis
  concepts 239
  Coordinate Reference Systems (CRS) 240
  need for 237, 238
  of Null Island 239
geospatial data
  ArcGIS 256
  big data 260
  file formats 251, 252
  geospatial analysis software 256
  ogr2ogr 258
  PostGIS spatial functions 259
  processing 256
  QGIS 257
  R-tree 254, 256
  spatial extensions, for relational database 253
  spatial indexing 254
  storing 251
  storing, in HDFS 253
git flow 75

models
  Area Under the Curve (AUC) 289
  comparing, with R 284
  ROC curves 285, 289
Multi-resolution Seamless Image Database
    (MrSID) 252
MultiLineString 244
MultiPolygon 244
Multivariate Imputation by Chained Equations
    (MICE) 270
MySQL 253

N

NameNode 132
NAT gateway 107
National Aeronautics and Space Administration
    (NASA) 192
National Elevation Dataset (NED)
  about 192
  references 193
National Geospatial-Intelligence Agency (NGA)
    192
National Oceanic and Atmospheric Administration
    (NOAA) 159, 193
Natural Language Processing (NLP) 190
Near Field Communication (NFC)
  about 40
  card emulation 40
  peer-to-peer 40
  reader/writer 40
  use cases 41
Network Address Translation (NAT) 59, 79, 107
networking 30
nitrogen dioxide (NO2) 237
Nitrogen Dioxide Analyzer Module 238
Nitrogen Dioxide Sensor 238
node 132
NodeManager 132, 142

O

Object Management Group (OMG) 60
objective function 267
open source
  about 320, 323
  intellectual property, considerations 323

scaling 324
support 324
OpenGIS Simple Features Reference
    Implementation (OGR) 258
Operating Systems (OS) 131
Organization for Economic Cooperation and
    Development (OECD)
  about 200, 201
  URL 200
OSI model 30
overfitting 281, 283

P

pages 136
Parquet 135, 138
Personal Area Network (PAN) 38
piconet 33
pipeline 279
planet.osm file
  URL 195
pollution reporting problem
  solving 261, 262
positive predictive value (PPV) 280
PostGIS 253
PostgreSQL 253
precision 280
predictive maintenance example
  economics 328
  situation 328
  value decision, creating 329, 336
  value formula 329
probability of detection 281
public subnets
  versus private subnets 78
publisher 46, 72
Pyspark 145

Q

QGIS
  about 257
  URL 258
Quality of Service (QoS)
  about 48
  levels 51, 52
question tree 213

www.ingramcontent.com/pod-product-compliance
Lightning Source LLC
Chambersburg PA
CBHW060923060326
40690CB00041B/3019